tear here

The Complete Idiot's Refere

Waschka's Wealth Levels

Wealth Level 1

You are able to maintain your standard of living and at the same time, save enough money to achieve your Target Savings Goal (TSG), the annual amount you need to save to meet your needs at retirement.

Wealth Level 2

Your portfolio is large enough to produce, on its own, a total return each year equal to your TSG, as well as keep up with inflation.

Wealth Level 3

Your portfolio produces a total return large enough to cover your desired lifestyle and inflation.

Wealth Level 4

You have accumulated enough assets to produce a total return sufficient enough to substantially increase your current and future lifestyle while at the same time keeping up with inflation.

Wealth Level 5

You have accumulated enough assets to produce a total return well beyond what you would ever spend. You now have the option not to work, raise your standard of living, and bestow large charitable gifts.

The Habits of Very Wealthy People

- ✔ Save every month
- ✔ Avoid debt
- ✔ Shop before you buy
- ✔ Delay purchases of items you don't need
- ✔ Buy used when you can
- ✔ Take care of what you own
- ✔ Maintain a basic understanding of the stock and bond markets
- ✔ Take time to plan, research, and systematically measure your results

Characteristics of Wealthy People

- ✔ A passion for what you do
- ✔ The ability to make decisions
- ✔ Discipline
- ✔ Patience

alpha books

Wealth Builder Worksheet

Use these steps to plan to achieve Wealth Level 1. For more information about any step, see Chapter 4.

1. **Analyze your current income.**
2. **Analyze your current spending habits.**

   Estimate your total yearly expenses.

   __________ × 12 = (Monthly expenses)   __________ × 12 = (Yearly expenses)

   Project the growth of your monthly spending habits.

   __________ + __________ = __________

   (Yearly expenses) + (Estimated additions) = (Total yearly expenses)

3. **Estimate income needed to cover your expenses in before-tax dollars.**

   Calculate the inverse of your total average tax rate.

   1.00 – __________ = __________

   1.00 – (Total average federal, state, and local income tax rate) = (Inverse rate)

   Convert yearly expenses into a before-tax amount.

   __________ /__________ = __________

   (Total yearly expenses) / (Inverse rate) = (Pre-tax yearly expenses)

4. **Project the effect of inflation on expenses.**

   __________ × __________ = __________

   (Yearly expenses before tax) × (1.00 + inflation estimate) = Expenses

   Continue this calculation for the number of years until retirement.

5. **Estimate Your Target Portfolio Amount.**

   __________ /__________ = __________

   (Highest yearly expenses) / (Estimated net rate of return) = (Portfolio size needed)

6. **Estimate yearly and monthly TSGs.**

   Yearly TSG Calculation.

   __________ /__________ =__________

   Target Portfolio Goal/Future Value Factor = Yearly TSG

   (See Tables 4.2 and 4.3 in Chapter 4 to find the Future Value Factor.)

   Monthly TSG calculation.

   __________ / 12 = __________

   Yearly TSG / 12 = Monthly TSG

7. **Achieve your target savings goal.**
8. **Maintain your plan.**

The COMPLETE IDIOT'S GUIDE TO Getting Rich

by Larry Waschka

alpha books

A Division of Macmillan General Reference
A Simon & Schuster Macmillan Company
1633 Broadway, New York, NY 10019

International Standard Book Number: 0-02-861343-0
Library of Congress Catalog Card Number: 96-086455

98 97 96 8 7 6 5 4 3 2 1

Interpretation of the printing code: the rightmost number of the first series of numbers is the year of the book's printing; the rightmost number of the second series of numbers is the number of the book's printing. For example, a printing code of 96-1 shows that the first printing of the book occurred in 1996.

Printed in the United States of America

Publisher
Theresa Murtha

Editor
Lisa A. Bucki

Production Editor
Brian Robinson

Copy Editors
Phil Kitchel
Brian Robinson

Cover Designer
Michael Freeland

Illustrator
Judd Winick

Designer
Glenn Larsen

Indexer
Rebecca Hornyak

Production Team
Angela Calvert
Tricia Flodder
Linda Knose
Christopher Morris
Daniela Raderstorf
Megan Wade

Contents at a Glance

Contents

Foreword

When I was asked to write the foreword for *The Complete Idiot's Guide to Getting Rich*, I gladly agreed. As an author, financial contributor for NBC's *Today Show*, and financial advisor to corporate executives, I've experienced firsthand what it takes to be financially successful.

For those who have gone from rags to riches, getting rich was neither the journey nor the destination they intended. Rather, their wealth was the result of putting a plan into action and sticking to it. While there is clearly no certain path to financial success, you will see a common thread throughout this book as you read it. To achieve financial success, you must take charge of your finances and get involved. All too often people rely on others: an employer, the government, a broker, a financial planner, or family members, in hopes that someone else will take care of the financial planning. Things might work out, but if you want to be financially successful, you must become involved. For individuals who take charge, get involved, and follow their instincts, the results are much different.

This book is not a plan or a scheme for getting rich quick. Making true wealth is not easy to do. If it was, everyone who wants to be rich would be. However, the real-life stories you'll read in this book are the experiences of people like you and me, some with very modest beginnings. Some of the people who became rich possessed unsurpassed drive, dedication, and perseverance. Others had a plan, worked hard, and never gave up. But all followed the advice and techniques outlined in this book.

Read *The Complete Idiot's Guide to Getting Rich*. More importantly, experience it. Think about your situation and start to take control today. Remember, no one cares about your financial success more than you do. If you don't do your own financial planning, no one else will do it for you!

Ray Martin
Vice President, The Ayco Company L.P.
September 1996

Introduction

I first learned about wealth at the age of four when my mother persuaded me to go down the street to meet another child my age. Quickly, I noticed that the other family's house was much larger than mine and they had many wonderful things such as beautiful furniture, fancy cars, and above all else, an incredible selection of toys! Of course, what really excited me was their trampoline. They even had a tree-house in the backyard that a carpenter had built. Until this time, I had never seen a lifestyle like this.

My friend always had a nice new bicycle, and gosh did I want a bike like his. It was a Schwinn Orange Krate that had three gears. At that time I didn't even know what a gear was, but I sure didn't let him know that.

For nearly four years, I spent almost every afternoon with my best friend at this wonderful home. Don't think that I had a poor childhood, I lived in a comfortable home with the most wonderful family. My mother and father loved me and gave me everything I needed. Even my brother loved me in spite of all the noogies, wet willies, and other harassment I gave him. My childhood was wonderful and for that, I'm grateful. It was just obvious as I grew older that my friend's family was much wealthier than mine.

I knew my friend's father was a doctor, and back then, my other young friends told me that if you were a doctor, you were rich. Once I realized this, I certainly wanted to be a doctor. Then maybe I could live in a big house with wonderful things. This dream of wanting to be a doctor was only temporary. Occasionally, I would spend the night at my friend's house and almost every time, I would hear my friend's father take a call at 3:00 in the morning. I decided that being a doctor was just a little too difficult.

What I continued to dream about, however, was being rich. I wanted to live in the house of my dreams and have enough money to buy whatever I wanted, which at that time was a Schwinn Orange Krate bicycle with three gears!

It has taken me 25 years to realize just how much this friendship affected my life. It was one of the catalysts that helped drive my desire for wealth. However, my family was the backbone of this drive. I was (and still am) the luckiest child in the world. My parents and step-parents raised me in an environment of love and support. Whether I deserved it or not, they supported my adventures as a child (and now that I'm an adult, they do the same). I knew that one day I would have enough money to buy whatever I wanted for myself and family, but I also knew that this was going to take a lot of work.

But soon I learned that building wealth would require even more than sweat. One day while in college, I learned from some classmates that there was a company called HBO that sold software to hospitals. This company was growing fast and their stock was going up. After researching the company in the library for hours, I called my father and told him about it. He agreed to buy 200 shares.

At first, the stock went up. My immediate thought was "Wow! Here's a way to make money with my brain doing what I love to do." This meant that I didn't have to necessarily work hard, I just had to work smart. I could use my brain power to build wealth. All this stupid research my professors had me doing really could help me.

When the stock fell back below our purchase price, my heart sank. I was embarrassed that I had talked my dad into buying the stock. His money was lost and I felt horrible. However, I learned some very valuable lessons about the market and about making money with my brain. That brief time the stock was up was just enough to make me realize that wealth was not just born of hard work, but of smart work. I knew that my mind was the key here and not my hands. From that moment on, I dedicated part of my life to studying the stock market. That one single experience changed my entire concept of work and the vision I had of building wealth. Thanks Dad! I love ya, but please don't ask me to pay you back for the HBO loss!

After college, my ultimate professional dream was to start my own fee-based money management company. Fee-based means that the company's income would be derived from a fee charged to the client, which would be based upon a percentage of assets in the account (1 percent). After interviewing with several firms, I realized that I had nothing to offer except a desire to learn. They all told me that Merrill Lynch had the best training program on Wall Street. However, working at Merrill Lynch meant that I would have to sell securities for a commission, which is completely different from my dream of managing money for a fee. Nonetheless, it would be a great place to start. When I interviewed with Merrill Lynch, the interviewers said they primarily cared about my ability to sell. In fact, the manager told me to go get a year's worth of sales training with a national company and he would hire me. So I got a job with Warner Lambert selling consumer goods to retail and wholesale stores. Exactly one year later, I returned to Merrill Lynch.

My plan was to spend 10 years at Merrill Lynch learning the business, and then start my own firm. However, some clients encouraged me to leave just prior to my five-year anniversary. In 1990, at the age of 28, I started my company with 13 clients and $3 million under my company's management. By the middle of 1996, I had 350 clients and $73 million under management. My company, Waschka Capital Investments, is a fee-only money management firm that specializes in global diversification using no-load mutual funds. I've also hosted a state-wide radio show for three years called "Waschka's Moneytalk" and have written a monthly column for several publications in Arkansas. I'm truly living my dream and grateful for it all.

I recently spoke to 400 high school sophomores about building wealth. One student asked me, "Are you rich?" This was a fair question to ask. If I can't claim some degree of wealth, what gives me the authority to speak on the matter? So I explained that I'm 34 years old and, according to my research, the fair market value of a money management firm is equal to approximately two times gross revenues. My gross revenue currently annualizes over $900,000, which gives my company a net worth of about $1.8 million. Then I explained that, to some people, that makes me wealthy. Other people would say I'm far from it. So being wealthy also depends upon your definition of wealth.

It doesn't matter where your drive for wealth comes from. Having supportive parents like mine may increase your chances, but it's not necessary. I know of many wealthy people who were not quite as fortunate. Many of them used tough circumstances as a motivational factor. For some people I know, the desire to be wealthy came from being brought up in a terribly poor family. The simple challenge of making it completely on their own drove them forward. They wanted to prove that they could do it. Many never had a father around. The lesson is that *whatever* your circumstances are, *wealth is achievable.*

Through my experiences, I've learned that there is no real "get rich quick" method to achieve the wealth you want. My goal with this book is to teach you long-term techniques to build and maintain wealth. My hope is that this book does just that for you. With persistence, patience, and diligence, your work will pay off, enabling you to achieve the level of wealth that you want. Thank you for buying the book, and I hope you enjoy reading it.

How to Use This Book

This book is carefully organized to present the tools and techniques you can use to set and reach your goals for wealth. I've defined five levels of wealth, to make it easier for you to plan your journey to wealth, and the book leads you through each level.

Part 1, The Basics: Wealth Levels 1 and 2, is all about the basics of getting rich. It breaks down the definition of wealth into five measurable levels and shows you how to design a plan to achieve the first two levels. This part covers the habits and characteristics of wealthy people, as well as how to get rich as an employee.

Part 2, Achieving Wealth Level 3 by Taming the Portfolio Beast, shows you how to become financially independent. It focuses on the investment tools and strategies you'll need to beat the market.

Part 3, Achieving Wealth Levels 4 and 5 With Your Own Business, will explain the basic details of starting, growing, and selling your own business. It will show you how to achieve the top two levels of wealth using your own business.

Part 4, Rich People Have Rich Habits, lists all the basic tax strategies, mental paradigms, and planning secrets you'll need to build your wealth. It will also teach you why so many people fail to achieve wealth.

You also get an appendix of wealth-related terms and definitions that will help you better understand the words of the wealthy. These terms will also help you keep up a conversation with any wealthy person.

Extras

The text in each chapter provides full coverage of each topic. However, while I wrote each chapter, certain related topics would come to mind that were just too good not to include. I've placed these extras in four different types of informational boxes within each chapter:

That Reminds Me...

It seems that every significant lesson I've learned about building wealth has been the result of my own experience or the experiences of others. These boxes explain such lessons for you in the form of a story or observation so that you will get a better understanding of the concepts within this book.

Words of the Wealthy

These **terms and definitions** are part of the language of the wealthy. If you know and understand these words, you are well on your way to building wealth. These terms will also help you have more meaningful discussions with your financial advisors.

Wealth Warning

If you know what to avoid in your financial life, you can significantly reduce your chances of experiencing problems. These warning boxes will help you do just that. Consider these the caution signs on your journey toward wealth. They are common errors or just things to be aware of.

Treasure Tip

These are helpful little hints to make life easier. If you prefer the "path of least resistance," be sure to read them.

Acknowledgments

My clients have been the single most influential source of information for this book. I am grateful for all you've taught me over the last 10 years. Thanks for sharing your lessons in wealth with me. I dedicate this book to all of you.

Special thanks to my associate, Sharon Kolb. You made this three-month, 300-page adventure so much easier to do and I really appreciate your help. I would also like to thank my other associates Linda Giles, Angie Johnson, and Michael Love for all your hard work and dedication on this project. Thanks for making WCI what it is today.

I'd like to thank Christy Heady for referring me to Macmillan Publishing. This book would not have been possible for me if it weren't for you and your advice. You've been a huge source of inspiration.

Thank you, Debbie Englander at Macmillan Publishing, for giving me the opportunity to write this book. Special thanks to Lisa Bucki and Brian Robinson for your help in editing all my work.

I would also like to thank my parents Beverly & Tom Brewer, and Lawrence & Julie Waschka for all your love, advice, and tolerance. I owe a great deal of thanks to all my family, especially my Mamoo, for all your love and spiritual guidance. Thank you, Joe Paul, for being the big brother I never had.

Many of my friends have been very instrumental in helping me with ideas for this book, especially Mary Ann Campbell, Shannan Ormond, Greg Hatcher, Steve Tucker, Stewart Welch III, Ron Yolles, Mike Hengehold, Bob Markman, Mike Brorman, Hank Neely, Barry Jewell, Ted Grace, Pete Maris, George Worthen, Don Munro, Stuart Bowles, Brandon Rogers and his family, and Brian Tracey. Thank you. I sincerely appreciate everything you've done for me.

Special Thanks from the Publisher to the Technical Reviewer...

The Complete Idiot's Guide to Getting Rich was reviewed by an expert who checked the technical accuracy of what you'll learn and provided insights and guidance to help ensure that this book gives you everything that you need to understand about how to build wealth. We extend our special thanks to Dr. Jerald W. Mason, who, as President and CEO of Evergreen Enterprises, has over 20 years of experience as an internationally known lecturer and workshop leader on financial planning and financial counseling topics. He is a co-founder of the Association for Financial Counseling and Planning Education, and also developed and served as the first Director of the Accredited Financial Counselor certification program, among his other accomplishments. Dr. Mason has published extensively, including his books *The Easy Family Budget Book* and *Debt Addiction: You Can Break the Habit*. In addition to holding an MBA from Stanford and a Ph.D. from the University of Missouri, Dr. Mason is a Certified Financial Planner (CFP), a Chartered Life Underwriter (CLU), and a Chartered Financial Consultant (ChFC).

Part 1
The Basics: Wealth Levels 1 and 2

Wouldn't it be nice to win a million-dollar lottery? Just the thought of it might seem nice, but if you really examine how a lottery is paid, you'll probably be surprised. Lottery winners think that they're going to get all the money at one time. Not true. If you win a million-dollar lottery, in most states your payout will be sent to you in yearly increments, minus federal and state taxes, based on your life expectancy. Once you really examine the truth about winning the lottery, you'll find that it's not all that attractive anymore.

The opposite is true with building wealth. I have found that once you really examine the truth about building wealth, it's not only more attractive, it's also a lot easier to achieve than you may think. You just have to break it up into different levels and design a plan to achieve the first level first, then the second, and so on. That's exactly what I've done in this part of the book for you. All you have to do is read and implement the steps, habits, and characteristics needed and you will be on your way to building wealth.

Chapter 1

Who's Really Rich and Do You Have What It Takes to Be Rich?

In This Chapter

- Stories of self-made wealthy people who are under 30
- Rags-to-riches stories about real people who built their wealth from simple means
- A test to see if you have what it takes to be wealthy
- Why is it so difficult to get rich?
- Wealth is a journey, not a destination

It's easy to find stories of wealthy people. Occasionally you'll find them featured in magazines or on television. Robin Leach's "Lifestyles of the Rich and Famous" is a great example. However, the wealthy people that I'm the most proud to know are those who built their wealth with their own hands. This is self-made wealth. It's not inherited, acquired through marriage, or won in the lottery. It's built with hard work, determination, and passion.

What is difficult to understand is that this kind of wealth is often invisible. You don't see it or recognize it because it's owned by people who don't flaunt or talk about it. You can learn a lot from these people, but they aren't featured in magazines or television. They may live next door to you and have a incredible knowledge about building wealth, but you'd never know to ask.

This chapter is about these people. I'm going to discuss a few wealthy people featured in magazines, but most of this chapter is focused on the invisible wealthy people. I dedicate this book to them because they taught me the secrets of building wealth. The second part of this chapter will enable you to find out if you have what it takes to be wealthy.

Who's Really Rich?

Time Magazine (2/19/96, p. 42) featured five guys who really scored big in the technology industry. Software designer, Marc Andreessen, at the age of 24 was worth an estimated $131 million after his company Netscape went public. Netscape's Internet browser called the Navigator was a huge success.

At 40, Steve Jobs was worth an estimated $728 million after his company Pixar Animation Studios went public. The other three men were worth $22, $79 and $86 million, and all were under the age of 45.

A story in **Cosmopolitan** (5/96, p. 214) featured eight women who became millionaires before the age of thirty. Each one did it in a unique way in eight different industries—parking garages, clothing, marketing, stock trading, asbestos abatement, frozen yogurt, computers, and medical screening.

Words of the Wealthy

Wealth is defined by Webster's Dictionary as, "abundance of valuable material possessions or resources," and the word **wealthy** is defined as, "extremely affluent." But the definition of **affluent** sounds even better, "having a generously sufficient and typically increasing supply of material possessions."

Thirty-four year-old Lisa Renshaw of Baltimore, controls 51 parking garages in Maryland, Washington, D.C., and Virginia with $25 million in revenues. She started at 21 years old by renting a parking garage and leasing out spaces herself.

While in Italy studying printmaking and fashion, Jennifer Barclay missed the beginning of her college semester and decided to start a business tie-dying and block-printing cotton clothing and scarves. She went from her parents' garage to a company with $10 million in sales before she turned 29.

Former nurse and aerobics instructor, Karen Behnke, became a millionaire prior to her 30th birthday by starting a company called Execu-Fit. Her company offered medical screenings of executives and analyses of employee health. She built sales by calling on personnel departments and signing large companies like Pacific Gas & Electric. When bank loans were impossible, she used credit cards at 22 percent interest. Later she traded 10 percent of her company for additional capital. In 1993, Karen sold her company to PacifiCare HMO for nearly $5 million.

There are more examples in this article. They all started their own business. However, you don't have to start your own business to be wealthy. There are plenty of wealthy people who never had their own company. Sure, starting your own business definitely increases your chances, but it's not a requirement.

Invisible Rags-to-Riches Wealth

The stories that give us all hope are the stories of real people who built fortunes out of almost nothing. I'm talking about wealthy people who earned every dime they made. Most of them don't wear flashy clothes or drive fancy cars. They don't live in mansions or travel to Paris for a vacation. They live next door to you and you may not even know their name. Many of my clients fit this description. Some of these people drive old trucks with worn out tires. If I pointed them out to you on the street you would never believe they had any money. They earned every dime and they're darn proud of it.

Frank Lalli wrote an article about Anne Scheiver in **Money Magazine** ("How She Turned $5,000 into $22 million," by Frank Lalli, p. 64, January 1996, Money, copyright 1996 Time, Inc.) that I found to be priceless. It read, "In the depths of the depression, when she was already 38-years-old and earning only a little more than $3,000 a year, Anne invested a major portion of her life savings in stocks. She entrusted the money to the youngest of her four brothers, Bernard, who was getting started at 22 as a Wall Street broker. He did well picking issues for her as the market drifted upward in 1933 and '34; but his firm did not. It went bust suddenly, and Anne lost all her money. In 1944, 10 years after her big loss, she started fresh with a $5,000 account at Merrill Lynch Pierce Fenner & Bean and slowly built the nest egg up to $20 million by the time she died last January, loveless and alone at 101. It's now worth $22 million."

The article stated that her performance of 17.5 percent per year exceeded some of the best known investment professionals in the world, including John Neff and Ben Graham. In 51 years, this incredible lady built a fortune using simple strategies that anyone can follow. Those that knew her said she lived a terrible existence as a recluse who never enjoyed her money. My bet is that investing was her passion, her love, and her life. I'm also willing to bet that this woman enjoyed her money more than most people ever will. She enjoyed managing it, not spending it. As a result, she turned near-disaster into an almost unbelievable fortune with nothing more than patience, interest in the market, research and a little planning. So what if she didn't take vacations or eat out. This woman left a legacy behind that all of us can learn from. She was able to outperform trained professionals in their own field for over 50 years! The story of Anne's life is what I call an invisible rags-to-riches story.

Even the Postman Can Build Wealth

My favorite story is about a couple who attended my investment workshop back in 1993. This is a true story from which everyone can learn something—I know I did. This couple, let's call them Mr. and Mrs. Post, met with me after the workshop to discuss some specific questions they had regarding their no-load fund portfolio. As usual, I asked some questions and found that Mr. Post had worked all his life for the United States Postal Service and was considering retirement the next year. His wife raised their children and had never earned any additional income. Mr. Post told me that the most they had ever made in one year was $30,000. They were conservatively dressed, simple in their ways, and almost shy about talking to me.

Words of the Wealthy

No-load funds are mutual funds that can be purchased, sold, and owned without any commission charges (or loads). The only charges involved are yearly management fees. A commission-paid broker or salesperson would never offer to sell you a no-load fund because there is no commission available for them.

Wealth Warning

Two other common ways to become wealthy include inheritance and marriage. Most people who achieve wealth in that manner do not become good stewards of their money.

They wanted me to review their no-load mutual fund portfolio to see if I thought anything needed to be sold. As Mr. Post began to show me his portfolio, I put my pen down and got ready to take a look. I was prepared to see a small portfolio of funds.

Wrong! Their portfolio had over 35 different no-load mutual funds worth over $800,000! To say the least, I was dumbfounded. How could this couple have so much money? Well, of course, I made all kinds of assumptions. First, I asked if any of the money was inherited. They replied quickly and firmly, "No, not one dime." I asked if they owned any real estate other than their home. They replied, "No." I was impressed.

They quickly told me that they had also purchased homes for each of their two daughters as wedding presents. They, of course, paid cash. They had also pre-funded their four grandchildren's college education.

I gave up and asked how they did it. They came to me for advice and I turned the appointment around and asked for theirs. What I learned from them that day, I will never forget. I share their secrets of wealth in Chapter 5. Their story immediately made me want to write a book so I could share what I learned. By the way, you are holding that book in your hands, and I hope it helps you achieve the wealth you dream of. This couple told me later in the most humble tone, "If we can do it, anybody can." They too were invisibly wealthy.

That Reminds Me...

I've learned over the last 10 years that most of the really wealthy people do not own fancy cars, jet planes, or huge mansions. Most of the wealthy people I know are more like Sam Walton. They drive older cars or trucks, fly coach seats on commercial airlines, and wear very simple clothes. To my surprise, most of them live well within their means in simple homes. They tend to avoid anything flashy, and they avoid large mortgages and car payments by often paying cash. My point is that you would never think these people had any more money than the average citizen. As a matter of fact, they keep their wealth very confidential.

You Don't Need a College Education

What may surprise you is that many wealthy people never finished college. My second favorite story about wealthy people is about a man who built a $10 million net worth from the ground up without a college education. He decided to retire last year in his early 50s. He worked hard and earned his net wealth.

When he was 18, he decided to skip college and work in a soft drink distribution company. He was dedicated and worked harder than anyone in the company. If fact, he worked so hard that a truck driver at the company told him, "Don't work so hard. You'll make all of us look bad." This didn't even faze him. He soon became a truck driver, and then a supervisor for all the truck drivers. After four years, a national soft drink company saw what he had done for his employer and asked him to be a division manager. This position gave him the opportunity to help other soft drink distributors in several states. In only a few years, one of his distributors offered him 20 percent of the company to manage his distributorship. He agreed and soon they bought other distributorships and added other brands to their line. The original owner wanted to retire, so he offered the remaining stock to my client. The transaction involved a lot of money for my client at that time, so he took on a partner to make the transaction. Soon they bought other distributorships in five states, including Hawaii.

The business became larger than my client ever dreamed. I asked him to sum it all up in a few sentences how he built his wealth. He said, "Dedication, hard work, and going that extra mile." I asked him where he got his motivation to work so hard. He replied, "Believe it or not, it had a lot to do with the fact that I didn't have a college education. I felt like everyone else did, and I had this complex about not finishing college."

I really believe that a college education is a great idea, but it certainly is not a requirement for building wealth. My client proved that determination, hard work, and the willingness to go that extra mile are much more important than a college education. By the way, the truck driver that told him to not work so hard is still a truck driver! I bet my client's wealth isn't invisible to *him*.

You'd Never Think These People Had Any Money

One day, a retired couple in their 60s came to my office for some help. They were a tiny couple both about 5 feet tall and wore clothes that had to be ten years old. You couldn't ask for a nicer couple. They asked almost bashfully if I would take a look at their "little" portfolio and make some suggestions. They both apologized for the "small" size of their holdings. The husband said, "I know that you are accustomed to dealing with much larger amounts, but would you please just give us some advice?" I explained that size didn't matter and that I would be glad to help them in any way I could. I nearly fell out of my chair when I opened the portfolio to find over $1 million in stocks, bonds, and mutual funds. You would never think that these people had any money. It never ceases to amaze me how people like this can be so humble and simple, yet be completely sophisticated with their investment knowledge.

I asked them a little about their background. They said that the most they ever made in income in one year was $27,000 and they didn't inherit anything. I just love these people! They are another example of invisible wealth.

The Wealth Test

Just because someone makes a lot of money doesn't mean they're wealthy. If their expenses equal or exceed their income, they don't qualify as wealthy. Just because someone works hard, earns a great salary, and has nice things, it doesn't make him or her wealthy. The person may look like wealth and smell like wealth, but it's all a big show. In Texas, they call these people "Hodads." They're all hat and no cattle. They wear fancy hats and talk the talk, but they don't even have a pasture or a cow to put in it.

Words of the Wealthy

Hodad is word used to describe people who are generally a fake or phony. They may look like they're rich, they might smell like they're rich, but if you take a close look, you'll find they owe lots of money and lease everything they have.

Somewhere along the way, these seemingly wealthy people didn't learn the habits and characteristics necessary to build real wealth. No one taught them the concept of saving for a rainy day, much less retirement. They don't have what it takes to be wealthy.

That Reminds Me...

I knew a business owner once who didn't have any capital so he leased every single thing in his business. He leased his car, his condo, his office furniture, his office equipment, his office, and all his manufacturing equipment. Leases typically are ridiculously expensive, and therefore he didn't make enough money for his business to survive, so he gave it all back and moved out of that industry and went to another state. For a while there he looked like a rich young man. He looked rich, but after a closer look, you could tell he was a Hodad.

I know what you're saying, "So Larry, how do I become wealthy? Most everyone I know would like to be rich. They may not all be willing to admit it, but it's the truth. If this is the case, then why do so few people get rich? What do these people do to become so wealthy? Why can't I do that?" We are going to discuss the answers to all these questions throughout this book, but first we must ask the most important question:

Do you have what it takes to be rich?

Let's see if you do.

I have designed a test based solely on my own experience and the experiences of wealthy people I have met. There are certain habits and characteristics that almost all of them share. This test is not scientifically perfect, but the scoring levels measure your probability of achieving wealth.

The purpose of the wealth test is to get a picture of yourself today based upon what you have learned in the past and what you are doing now to achieve wealth. If you answer honestly, you will see what your chances would have been if you hadn't purchased this book and made the necessary adjustments. You don't have to show your results to anyone. Remember, your chances will increase once you've finished the book and implemented what you've learned. For now, let's focus on the "old you," and after the test, we'll focus on the "new you."

The Wealth Test

1. Do you enjoy your work? Yes No
2. Do you often visualize yourself achieving something bigger than what you are currently doing? Yes No
3. Do you save money almost every month? Yes No
4. Do you invest at least some of your money directly in the stock market now either through individual stocks or mutual funds? Yes No
5. Do you shop before you buy most of the time, especially for big ticket items? Yes No
6. Do you take care of your home or apartment, performing regular maintenance as well as repairs? Yes No
7. Do you perform regular maintenance on your car and other expensive items? Yes No
8. Do you pay off the full balance on your credit cards each month? Yes No
9. Are you comfortable buying used big ticket items such as cars and appliances? Yes No
10. Have you ever started your own business? (Even a lemonade stand counts.) Yes No
11. Have you ever estimated how much money you would need in a portfolio to produce enough income to cover your current living expenses? Yes No
12. Do you measure the performance results of your portfolio at least each quarter? Yes No
13. Do you maximize your personal contribution to your IRA or company's 401k plan? Yes No
14. Is your mortgage payment less than 20 percent of your total gross household income? (If you do not own a home, is your rent less than 20 percent of your total gross household income?) Yes No
15. Do you spend less than you make? Yes No
16. Have you ever read a book about building wealth or an autobiography about someone who was wealthy? Yes No
17. Do you have your own business now that produces a positive net income? Yes No
18. Have you ever worked all night or more than 24 hours on a project? Yes No

For each question that you answered "yes," give yourself one point.

Total these points then compare it to the scale below to check the probability of becoming wealthy.

Score	Probability of Becoming Rich
1-5	Low
6-10	Average
10-15	Very likely
16-18	You are on your way!

Even if you scored low on the test, don't worry about it. Regardless of your score, you can achieve wealth. Your score just identifies your weak points. Take a moment and look at the questions that you answered "No."

These are your areas of weakness. By identifying these areas now, you will recognize the solutions as you study this book.

Treasure Tip
No matter what your education or resources, the key to building financial wealth is to put together and follow a plan of action you design to meet your specific needs and goals. Your plan should identify and combat your weaknesses.

Why Do So Few Make it?

Why is it so difficult to get rich? It might be that most people don't have any of the characteristics noted in the text in the last section. These people don't have the discipline or patience it takes to keep trying. Brian Tracy, in his famous cassette tape series, "The Psychology of Achievement," mentioned a study that was done several years ago that involved a group of people who were worth over $1 million before the age of 30. They were all asked, "How many different businesses were you involved in before you became a millionaire?" The average answer was 18! Can you imagine? What does this tell you? It tells me that achieving wealth takes a heck of a lot of tenacity and patience. You have to be willing to stick to this goal and be willing to fail more than once. I speak from experience. When I don't enjoy what I'm doing, the chances are good that I'm going to give up after failing the first few times. My money management firm lost money during the first three years of business. But this didn't get me down. I had a passion for building my firm that would never let me quit. Now my profit margin exceeds 50 percent.

That Reminds Me...

It seems that so much motivation and accomplishment can come from adversity. This has certainly been true for me. My first job out of college was not what I expected. I was a southern boy traveling the Northeastern states, I was all alone, and my company was taking advantage of

continues

me. They were not paying me the bonuses that I had earned. It was a miserable nightmare. To make things worse, when I quit, my boss followed me out of the door yelling, "You're a quitter, a loser. You'll never get a job anywhere. You're finished. You'll never achieve anything." He had no idea how much this motivated me. All I could think about at that time was making enough money to buy the company one day and have him work for me! Thank goodness I quit. It enabled me to go into the investment industry, which is where I wanted to be in the first place.

Wealth Deception

Now that I've seen both sides of the story, I've learned that there are many misconceptions regarding wealth. People simply misunderstand what wealth is and how you get it. It may sound simple, but it's the truth. I've seen it all my life. I remember growing up as a child, hearing people make hundreds of comments about their concept of wealth. These misconceptions may hold these people back from wealth for the rest of their lives. If you hold any of these misconceptions, one of the things you should do immediately is stop using them as an excuse not to build your wealth. Here are a few of the most common misconceptions. I call them the fallacies of wealth:

- If I just had a little more money, I'd be happy.
- If I were wealthy I could buy anything I wanted.
- I wish I were wealthy so I wouldn't have to worry about money anymore.
- I'm young, I've got plenty of time to become wealthy. Why save money now?
- I'm too old to start saving money.
- I wish I would have saved more money when I was younger.
- There's no chance of me ever becoming wealthy. I only make $20,000 a year.
- The only way to get rich is by inheritance, winning the lottery, owning commercial real estate, or starting a business.
- If I were really wealthy, I wouldn't care how much I paid in taxes.

Wealth Warning

In spite of the fact that the chances of winning the lottery are usually worse than a million to one, it seems that most Americans use lottery tickets to plan for their retirement. The irony is that a large percentage of people who win the lottery end up in serious trouble, if not dead broke.

It's Not Impossible

I think most people aren't willing to make the decisions or sacrifices it takes to become wealthy. The whole process seems too overwhelming to them. Admittedly, if you are starting with very little or no money, this process of building wealth might seem overwhelming. *But it's not impossible!* If you think becoming wealthy is impossible, well, you can bet it will be. You'll never make it. Someone once said, "Argue your limitations…and they're yours."

This Is a Journey, Not a Destination

Occasionally you'll have set backs. You can plan for most of these in advance. However, if you do fall back, all you have to do is retrace your steps and continue your journey. Remember that wealth is a journey and not a destination. When you make the decision to seek wealth, you have taken the first step on a life long journey. Let's get started.

The Least You Need to Know

- ➤ Wealth can be built by anyone at any age who is willing to learn and develop the habits and characteristics necessary.
- ➤ The habits and characteristics are simple to understand, easy to implement, but grossly overlooked by so many people.
- ➤ Avoid becoming a "hodad" who is someone living in a fancy home or driving a fancy car but doesn't have a dime in the bank or investment account.
- ➤ Start identifying the common misconceptions of wealth and don't let them hold you back from achieving your fortune.
- ➤ Wealth is a journey that requires a high-level of tenacity and determination to overcome the occasional set backs.
- ➤ In order to build real wealth, you have to believe that it can be done.

Chapter 2

Ten Key Concepts of Building Wealth

In This Chapter

- The definition of liquid and illiquid wealth
- How time affects your portfolio
- How your standard of living affects your portfolio
- When the amount of money you save is more important than your portfolio performance
- Why compound growth is so powerful

Every industry has its own unique language which consists of the jargon and concepts that are used every day. Since almost everyone deals with at least some financial issues, most of the terms should already be familiar. Even so, it is important to make sure that we are all using the same language for our discussions. In this chapter, we'll review some of the basics.

How Do You Define Wealth?

Everyone's definition of financial wealth is different. So, to make things simple, I've defined **five** specific, measurable levels of wealth which will be discussed in the next chapter. These levels of wealth reduce the confusion surrounding the concept of wealth by breaking down the definition into easy-to-understand pieces.

Before discussing the five wealth levels, let's go over 10 concepts that are very important to understand. If you don't understand these concepts, you will have trouble understanding the logic of the five wealth levels.

- Portfolio
- Time
- Standard of Living Expenses
- Total Return
- Risk
- Inflation
- Taxes
- Compound Growth
- Actual Savings Amount
- Target Savings Goal (TSG)

Portfolio

For the purpose of this book, the term *portfolio* primarily refers to a collection of liquid assets (an asset being something you own) that are traded in a regulated market like the banking or stock markets. An asset is considered liquid if it can be easily sold for cash within an established financial market. This includes stocks, bonds, CDs (certificates of deposit), mutual funds, and foreign securities. The most common liquid assets are checking and money market accounts. You can sell or liquidate these assets and get your money within 24 hours.

Words of the Wealthy
An **asset** can be liquid or illiquid property that can be sold for cash. This can include stocks, bonds, and real estate.

A portfolio could also include illiquid assets such as privately held securities or commercial real estate. These assets are not easily sold for cash because you have to go out and find a buyer yourself. However, there is absolutely nothing wrong with illiquid assets. For example, the most commonly held illiquid asset is a home. It can be sold and converted to cash, but it can take some time. Another example of an illiquid asset would be privately held stock (not listed on an exchange like the New York Stock Exchange.)

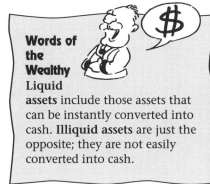

> **Words of the Wealthy**
> A **privately held company** is one in which its shares are not publicly traded. Privately held stock is issued to a small number of shareholders, and the value or price of the stock is usually determined by comparisons with other similar companies using factors such as company earnings and gross income.

What's the problem with owning illiquid assets? Establishing a price tag. Illiquid assets are not always easy to value. Therefore, they must be evaluated by an expert to establish a fair market value.

Many wealthy people have built their fortunes using illiquid assets such as land, commercial buildings, and privately held company stock. However, these people understood the characteristics and risks unique to each particular illiquid asset. Do not attempt to get involved with illiquid assets without doing some serious homework. If you understand what you own and the market you participate in, you can make money by investing in illiquid assets.

Time

Time is a very powerful tool. If you are in your 20s or 30s, you have an advantage over someone who is in their 40s or 50s. When I think of the time component, I think of an old expression, "Give me a lever long enough and I can move the world." Time works the same way with wealth. Give me enough time and I can build a fortune. The opposite is also true. The less time you have, the less likely it is that you will build any significant wealth. It's not impossible, though. Remember Anne Scheiver in the first chapter who began saving at the age of 50 and died with a $20 million portfolio. If she can do it, so can you. Let's take a closer look at how important time is in the accumulation of wealth using the following illustration of how a portfolio accumulates for an early saver versus someone who starts saving later.

> **Words of the Wealthy**
> **Liquid assets** include those assets that can be instantly converted into cash. **Illiquid assets** are just the opposite; they are not easily converted into cash.

The Early Saver versus The Late Saver

	Early start			Late start		
Age	Savings per Year	Total Annual Return 9%	Total Portfolio	Savings per Year	Total Annual Return 9%	Portfolio
22	$2,000	$180	$2,180	$0	$0	$0
23	$2,000	$376	$4,556	$0	$0	$0
24	$2,000	$590	$7,146	$0	$0	$0
25	$2,000	$823	$9,969	$0	$0	$0
26	$2,000	$1,077	$13,047	$0	$0	$0
27	$2,000	$1,354	$16,401	$0	$0	$0
28	$2,000	$1,656	$20,057	$0	$0	$0
29	$2,000	$1,985	$24,042	$0	$0	$0
30	$2,000	$2,344	$28,386	$0	$0	$0
31	$0	$2,555	$30,941	$2,000	$180	$2,180
32	$0	$2,785	$33,725	$2,000	$376	$4,556
33	$0	$3,035	$36,761	$2,000	$590	$7,146
34	$0	$3,308	$40,069	$2,000	$823	$9,969
35	$0	$3,606	$43,675	$2,000	$1,077	$13,047
36	$0	$3,931	$47,606	$2,000	$1,354	$16,401
37	$0	$4,285	$51,890	$2,000	$1,656	$20,057
38	$0	$4,670	$56,561	$2,000	$1,985	$24,042
39	$0	$5,090	$61,651	$2,000	$2,344	$28,386
40	$0	$5,549	$67,200	$2,000	$2,735	$33,121
41	$0	$6,048	$73,248	$2,000	$3,161	$38,281
42	$0	$6,592	$79,840	$2,000	$3,625	$43,907
43	$0	$7,186	$87,025	$2,000	$4,132	$50,038
44	$0	$7,832	$94,858	$2,000	$4,683	$56,722
45	$0	$8,537	$103,395	$2,000	$5,285	$64,007
46	$0	$9,306	$112,701	$2,000	$5,941	$71,947
47	$0	$10,143	$122,844	$2,000	$6,655	$80,603

	Early start			Late start		
Age	Savings per Year	Total Annual Return 9%	Total Portfolio	Savings per Year	Total Annual Return 9%	Portfolio
48	$0	$11,056	$133,900	$2,000	$7,434	$90,037
49	$0	$12,051	$145,950	$2,000	$8,283	$100,320
50	$0	$13,136	$159,086	$2,000	$9,209	$111,529
51	$0	$14,318	$173,404	$2,000	$10,218	$123,747
52	$0	$15,606	$189,010	$2,000	$11,317	$137,064
53	$0	$17,011	$206,021	$2,000	$12,516	$151,580
54	$0	$18,542	$224,563	$2,000	$13,822	$167,402
55	$0	$20,211	$244,774	$2,000	$15,246	$184,648
56	$0	$22,030	$266,803	$2,000	$16,798	$203,446
57	$0	$24,012	$290,815	$2,000	$18,490	$223,936
58	$0	$26,173	$316,989	$2,000	$20,334	$246,271
59	$0	$28,529	$345,518	$2,000	$22,344	$270,615
60	$0	$31,097	$376,614	$2,000	$24,535	$297,150
61	$0	$33,895	$410,510	$2,000	$26,924	$326,074
62	$0	$36,946	$447,456	$2,000	$29,527	$357,601
63	$0	$40,271	$487,727	$2,000	$32,364	$391,965
64	$0	$43,895	$531,622	$2,000	$35,457	$429,422
65	$0	$47,846	$579,468	$2,000	$38,828	$470,249
	$18,000			$70,000		

**Please note that this illustration is for comparison purposes only.*

**Taxes are not calculated into the equation.*

The first investor deposits $18,000 between the ages of 22 and 30 and ends up with a $579,468 account. The second investor gets a later start and deposits $70,000 between the ages of 31 and 65 which is almost four times as much money, but his account only grows to only $470,249. That's a difference of $109,219! How is this possible? The first investor simply had the advantage of more time to compound the growth. Notice that by the time the second investor began saving money, the first investor's gain exceeded the second investor's deposit. This is powerful stuff and ironically is often completely overlooked. Use the power of time.

Standard of Living Expenses

There are many different categories of expenses. There are variable expenses like entertainment, clothing, and travel. And there are fixed expenses such as rent or mortgage payments. This might seem like a relatively boring subject, but most people don't understand just how important the expense component can be in building wealth. When you are just beginning to build your portfolio, the amount of money you spend monthly for expenses directly affects the speed of your journey to wealth. If you are accustomed to a high standard of living with no willingness to be flexible, your chances of saving money in the early years are quite small.

> **Wealth Warning**
> The tool of time can also work in reverse. The longer you wait to start your portfolio, the harder it is to build any significant wealth.
>
> A good place to start your investment portfolio is a $2,000 IRA which can grow tax deferred until all the money is drawn out during retirement. This account allows you to combine the tools of time, compound growth, and tax deferral.

I truly believe that the main reason why people don't save money is that they are unwilling to limit their standard of living. I see this in young couples mostly, but also in older retired couples. In the later years, especially during retirement, if you spend more than your portfolio produces, you deplete your capital source or principal. I now have a client that started with a $100,000 retirement account. For the past two years, this client has lived beyond his means and the account is now worth only $33,000. His portfolio grew faster than the world stock market index, but didn't grow fast enough to keep up with his spending habits. This scenario is a nightmare that didn't have to happen. The client did not measure spending habits, ignored his resources, and now has a very big problem. Don't let this happen to you. It's important to understand that systematic measurement of your monthly expenses is vital to the wealth building process. I'll show you how to do this in Chapter 3.

> **Wealth Warning**
> You must be willing to make some sacrifices now to build wealth in the future.

Total Return

The next concept is the total return on your capital. Total return consists of dividends, interest, and capital gains. A capital gain is the price appreciation realized from the sale of an asset. If you invest in real estate, your portfolio might also produce rental income. Total return is also known as portfolio gains, portfolio performance, and portfolio growth.

> **Wealth Warning**
> Ignoring your spending habits relative to your income will get you into hot water fast.

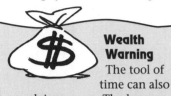

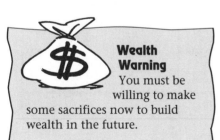

The most confusing thing about total return involves the concept of taking regular monthly income from your portfolio which is most commonly needed once retirement begins. When it comes time to take income from a liquid portfolio for living expenses, most investors only look at dividends and interest (cash flow). They pay little, if any, attention to capital gain because they claim it's not reliable. This is conventional thinking.

Words of the Wealthy

Harvesting is a term I came up with to describe a more unconventional method of deriving income from a portfolio that includes not only dividends and interest, but also the harvesting of capital gains. These capital gains can be easily obtained by occasionally selling (harvesting) pieces of a portfolio that have appreciated.

In the long-run, capital gains can be reliable given a properly diversified portfolio. Whether you are building wealth in the early years or maintaining wealth in the later years, you should not ignore capital gains. You should harvest them over time and consider them part of the "cash flow." This concept of harvesting might be new to you and therefore, a bit unconventional. That's okay. In order to build and maintain the levels of wealth this book discusses, you're going to have to think unconventionally.

Risk

There are many different types of risk, which I will discuss in more detail later. Risk, for now, can be defined as the volatility (potential to rise or fall quickly) of the total portfolio value. Some investors are willing to accept higher levels of volatility for higher rates of return. Return is your reward for your willingness to assume risk. In general, risk can increase your potential for return, but it can also lead to more potential for loss. Setting proper return goals involves determining your acceptable level of risk.

Wealth Warning

Risk tolerance is the degree to which an investor can withstand or live with the volatility of his/her portfolio. When asked, most investors tend to over estimate their tolerance for risk. However, only when confronted with significantly poor performance or losses from an investment do they fully understand their true tolerance.

Inflation

I'll spare you the economics lesson that explains what causes inflation. Think of it simply as an increase in the price of goods and services. The most important thing to remember about inflation is that it will affect your future living expenses. What costs a dollar today may cost five dollars in the future. You must take this into account when making projections about the future. The easy way to measure and project inflation is by using the Consumer Price

Index (CPI) growth rate. This is the yearly growth rate of the total price of a basket of consumer goods. All financial publications show this rate as the CPI. You will need to know the growth rate of this index in Chapter 3 when I show you how to project your future living expenses.

> **That Reminds Me...**
>
> The Consumer Price Index (CPI) is a price index tabulated by the U.S. Government's Bureau of Labor Statistics that measures the cost of a representative basket of consumer goods. The price of the basket is not that important. The most important aspect of CPI is the rate of change from one month to another. The amount of change from month to month in the cost of this basket of goods is stated as a percentage of the CPI for the previous month. This percentage is known as the rate of inflation and is usually quoted as an annualized percentage. This measurement can be found in the Wall Street Journal every month in Section A at approximately the middle of the month.

Taxes

When I mention taxes, I am referring to all income taxes that include federal, state, and local. Specifically, in the next chapter, you will need to know your average over-all percentage income tax rate. An easy way to calculate this is to add up the total of all federal, state, and local taxes you paid last year and divide that amount by your gross income. This will give you your average income tax rate. If you need help calculating this, ask your CPA.

(Federal + State + Local Taxes) ÷ Gross Annual Income = your average income tax rate

For example, if you had a gross income of $30,000 with federal taxes of $3,540 and state taxes of $1,344, your average income tax rate would equal 16.28%

Taxes can be avoided or deferred using certain investment vehicles. However, the most important goal of an investor should be to make money, not avoid taxes. If you focus primarily on avoiding taxes, you might accomplish your goal, but I can promise you that you will not make much money in the process. Later in this book, I will discuss some ways you can defer taxes without sacrificing total return.

Compound Growth

Compound growth is different from compound interest. It is achieved when you invest in stocks (or anything that appreciates in value) over a long period of time while allowing the capital gains and dividends to reinvest into the original investment.

Dr. Albert Einstein left Germany to come to the United States to escape potential conflict with Hitler. It's been said that a young reporter met Einstein when he arrived at the Port of New York and asked him what he believed was the eighth wonder of the world. Einstein replied, "I believe it is compound growth."

Treasure Tip
Compound growth over time allows even moderate rates of return to produce great wealth.

Over the past seven years, I have spoken to over two thousand investors—both successful and unsuccessful. What seems to be common among those who are successful is really very simple: Successful investors understand that compound growth is the most powerful investment tool—second only to research.

What makes compound growth so attractive is the added effect of price appreciation with reinvested interest or dividends.

That Reminds Me...

The rule of 72 is a way to estimate how fast money can compound over time. You can divide the number 72 by the rate of return you expect to receive. The result is the number of years it will take for your money to double. If you were getting 6 percent, your money would double in 12 years. If you were getting 8 percent, your money would double in 9 years, if 10 percent, 7.2 years, if 12 percent, 6 years. As you can see, it also works in reverse. You can divide the number 72 by the number of years you have to invest. The result will be the percentage of total return you'll need to double the portfolio. I cannot explain how this phenomenon works, but it does work. This equation measures pure compound growth without the effect of any taxes. Therefore, it works best in measuring the growth of tax deferred accounts such as 401(k)s and qualified plans.

Actual Savings Amount

Your actual savings amount is just what it says, it's the difference between your total household income and expenses. This surplus is what goes into your investment account. If there is money available for savings, you are living within your means and that's great. If you have a negative actual savings amount, you are living beyond your means, and that's not good at all.

This amount is very important in the early stages of your life. Therefore, your focus should be on saving and investing as much as you can when you are young. During the first years of saving when your portfolio is small, total return is relatively less important than the amount of money you save (deposits you make). The deposits you make at first will dwarf the amount of money you make on your investments (dividends and gains). Therefore, this is a great time to learn about investing. When you are new to the game of investing, you tend to make a lot of mistakes. If you can make those mistakes early, when the returns have relatively less effect on your overall portfolio, you will save your portfolio from harm later when your return really counts.

Target Savings Goal (TSG)

A very important concept for building wealth is your Target Savings Goal (TSG). This is the amount of money you need to save every year in order to build a portfolio large enough to produce a total return by a certain date (usually retirement) that will sustain your standard of living plus keep up with inflation. I realize that this might be a mouthful, but, don't worry. We'll take this step-by-step in the next chapter and make it easy for you.

The Least You Need to Know

- To understand the definition of wealth, you must first understand the concepts that make up that definition.
- The more time you allow your portfolio to compound its growth, the more potential you have to build significant wealth.
- If you are accustomed to a high standard of living with no willingness to be flexible, your chances of saving money in the early years are quite small.

Chapter 3

The Five Levels of Wealth

In This Chapter

- Defining the five levels of wealth
- Building wealth in stages
- Shortcuts to the higher levels
- When saving money becomes less important

The first thing you must realize in your search for a personal definition of wealth is that your definition will always be a relative term. Relative to what? A poor immigrant family might say that being rich would mean having an apartment with running water and a roof over-head. You might like to be wealthy relative to your neighbor or friend. I was guilty of this when I was a young man in my 20s. I found myself constantly in a battle to beat other people, which was silly and futile. I constantly met new people who were more wealthy than the last. The benchmark kept moving and it always seemed out of reach. Your definition of wealth should be defined relative to your desired standard of living—not your neighbor's or your friend's, but your own. Be realistic about this and focus on what income level makes you happy. Your life will be a lot easier and you will feel more fulfilled in the process.

To learn more about wealth, you must associate yourself with wealthy people. You can do this through clubs, non-profit organizations, church, and through friends who can introduce you. An alternative would be to read books about wealthy people. You need to learn how they think, how they got there, and what is important to them—their values.

The most common way to define your current level of wealth is by measuring your net worth. When you go to a bank and apply for a loan, one of the first things they want is a "Net-Worth Statement." This statement lists both liquid and ill-liquid assets, subtracts your liabilities (debts you owe, such as your mortgage) and results in a bottom line net worth amount. Ask your local bank for a blank net-worth statement.

Now that you understand the 10 key wealth concepts from Chapter 2, let's discuss the five levels of wealth. Please understand these are my definitions. Each person has his/her own definition of wealth, which might or might not involve anything financial. Wealth to one person might be extensive wisdom. Wealth to another might be artistic ability. This book focuses on financial wealth.

For this book I have defined five stages of financial wealth; each level is defined relative to your current or desired standard of living.

Wealth Level 1

At this level of wealth, you are able to maintain your standard of living and save enough money to achieve your Target Savings Goal. When you live within your means and your actual savings amount equals or exceeds your TSG, you've made it to Wealth Level 1. It's the easiest level to achieve and can be your wealth safeguard if you fail at other levels.

Words of the Wealthy

Your **Target Savings Goal** or TSG refers to the amount of money required each year to build a portfolio large enough to support your preferred standard of living at retirement, as calculated in Chapter 4.

Focus

To make it to Wealth Level 1, the most important thing to focus on is your actual savings amount. This will affect the portfolio much more than the total return on your portfolio. For now, total return is of secondary importance. The most common mistake made by neophyte investors is that they focus too much on total return. To achieve and maintain this level, you should focus on maximizing your actual savings amount as much as you possibly can.

During your journey toward Wealth Level 1, you should also focus on learning as much as you can about investment management, and learn from your mistakes now. These mistakes, if made now, will not have nearly the effect they will later, when your account is much larger and the mistakes are much harder to recover from. For example, a common mistake made by neophyte investors is the use of futures and options contracts. This is not a wise way to start out investing. I know because I did it and lost a lot of money! However, I'm glad I did this in the early part of my life. It taught me early on to stick with stocks, bonds, and mutual funds.

Wealth Warning

The attitude today in the U.S. seems to be "spend now, save later." While the Southeast Asians save over 30 percent of their income, we only save about 4 percent. If this keeps up, we are going to have a serious problem.

Stages

If this all seems too overwhelming, it may be easier to conquer this level in stages. For example, you could set your first target savings goal at 5 percent of your net monthly income. The second goal could be 10 percent, third, 15 percent, and so on. The last stage would be to save your true total TSG. If you save in slowly increasing amounts over time and continue this habit through life as your income increases, you will dramatically increase your chances of reaching Wealth Levels 2 through 5.

Setting and sticking to a savings goal may sound easy, but I know so few people following through to meet savings goals. Either they are unwilling to cut back their standard of living in order to save the 10 percent or they are unwilling to try harder for more income. They procrastinate saving money, have too much pride to cut back their spending, borrow too much to keep up with the neighbors, or just never think about the future. Whatever the reason, they will never achieve the level of wealth they desire.

Treasure Tip

You don't need a college education to earn a high income, but it does help. According to Census Bureau surveys in 1993, less than 6 percent of U.S. households earn more than $100,000 per year, 68 percent of which are headed by college graduates. The median household income of college graduates is $55,000, which is 76 percent higher than the median income for all households.

Shortcuts

You can skip this level completely if you are starting a business that you believe could substantially increase your income and net worth. This might get you to Level 3 or 4 faster. If you take this route, get ready for an exciting ride. There's much more risk of failure, and recovery time might be very slow depending upon the damage done if the business fails. Therefore, you must be willing to accept failure and keep on going. Before skipping this level and starting your own business, you must be willing to accept the worst thing that can happen. I was willing to accept the risk years ago when I started my own business. I'm glad I did. Would I do it again? You bet I would—even if I couldn't manage money. As long as I had a vision and was excited about it, I would do it. Later in Part 3, I will discuss how you can develop your own vision and improve your chances of success in your own business.

Wealth Level 2

At the beginning of this wealth level, your portfolio is large enough to produce, on its own, a total return each year equal to your TSG. That means you have now, in essence, doubled your TSG: One part comes from your monthly TSG deposit, and the other part from portfolio gains. Now you've really harnessed the power of compound growth. The combined effect of your TSG deposit and total return produce enormous portfolio growth power for you.

> **Wealth Warning**
>
> **Total return,** also known as portfolio performance, refers to the percentage return of an investment or portfolio that includes dividends, interest, and capital gains. By the way, when the total return is reinvested into the investment or portfolio, the result is compound growth.

Focus

Because at this level your actual savings amount and total return are equal, they become equally important. You must focus on both of these components. This is also the stage of wealth where knowledge of risk becomes vital to the remainder of the wealth-building process. Unfortunately, most people wait until this stage to begin learning about risks. Bad investment decisions made now in Wealth Level 2 are much more costly than they would have been in Level 1.

Stages

You haven't completed Wealth Level 2 when your portfolio's annual return equals your TSG. There are actually three stages to this level. Stage 2 continues as your portfolio produces a total return equal to two times your TSG. Therefore, your portfolio is growing by three times your TSG. One part is your actual TSG deposit, and the other two parts come from portfolio performance. The most important component now becomes total return. Your actual savings amount still helps speed the process, but total return now is much more important and powerful. If total return is twice the size of your actual savings amount, then your downside risk is also twice as big. This makes mistakes much more difficult to recover from. Making the right investment decisions becomes paramount and risk management becomes vital.

You've reached the third stage of Wealth Level 2 when your portfolio produces a total return equal to three times your TSG. The compounding effect is expanding your portfolio geometrically. Now the relative effect of an additional deposit equal to your TSG has very little influence on the growth of the portfolio. Total return is vital and investment management has never before been so important.

Shortcuts

This level can also be skipped if you start a business that substantially increases your income and net worth. But, you must be willing to accept and manage the risks involved.

Wealth Level 3

If your portfolio produces a total return large enough to cover your desired lifestyle and inflation, then congratulations! You've made it to Wealth Level 3. Now employment is optional and your money is working hard for you. According to my research, only about 5 percent of the population achieve this level of wealth by retirement age. Most of my clients have made it to this level. They enjoy life by doing what they love to do. Once they make the decision to retire, or at least slow down, their living expenses usually decrease. Maybe they take more vacations and spend more money, but they still live within their means. The habit is so ingrained that they actually feel uncomfortable spending more than normal, even if they can afford it.

> **Wealth Warning**
> Our Social Security system has produced a population of citizens who believe in their right to a subsidized comfortable retirement. After seeing thousands of workers realize their benefits are much less than they expected, I came to the conclusion that my comfortable retirement depends on myself and my efforts.

Focus

If you are not relying upon your portfolio for income, the most important component is total return. The amount of money you're saving now is probably dwarfed by the effect of total return. Likewise, your potential downside is also significant, which reduces your ability to recover from a loss using additional deposits. This is especially true if you are no longer earning a salary. Therefore, if you're not comfortable managing your own portfolio when it's this large, you'd better get some help.

If you are relying upon your portfolio for income (such as to pay your living expenses after you retire), you have to focus on two components: total return and standard of living expenses. If you spend more than your portfolio produces, over the long run, you'll erode your income-generating capital and drop back into level 1 or 2 with no source of income to replace what you lost. The wealthy people I know in this level prevent this from happening by simply making it a habit to live well within their means. They always spend less than their total income.

Wealth Level 4

You have accumulated enough assets to produce a total return sufficient enough to substantially increase your desired lifestyle, while at the same time keeping up with inflation. If you've made it beyond Level 3 and you've built your portfolio big enough to support your dream lifestyle, you've made it to Wealth Level 4. You now have the option not to work and, at the same time, raise your standard of living. You might buy a bigger home, travel more, or just spend more money. You not only have enough total return to cover your desired lifestyle, you also have a little extra to build your portfolio further.

That Reminds Me...

According to official Social Security projections, in 1990, only 4 percent of Americans were over 65. By 2040, the figure will be approximately 25 percent. That means that the number of Social Security beneficiaries will more than double by the year 2040. In 1960, there were 5.1 taxpaying workers to support each Social Security beneficiary. Today there are 3.3 and by 2040 there will be no more than 2 or perhaps as few as 1.6. One of four things must happen: We must raise taxes, raise the official Social Security retirement age, radically change the existing Social Security system, or radically change our own personal retirement savings program. The only option we have complete control over is the last one.

Only about 1 percent of the population make it to Wealth Level 4. Most people aren't willing to take the time to plan, make the sacrifices, or take the risk. That's right: This level involves planning, sacrifices, and risk! Oh no! There's that word RISK, again! After reading this book you will understand more about risk and how to manage it properly.

Most of the individuals who make it to this level are business owners. Their wealth was built from net income, the sale of the business, or both.

Focus

Your two master components are total return and risk management. The portfolio now is very large and you want to reduce volatility. You can do this yourself, but it must be a hobby you enjoy. Most Wealth Level 4 people hire help in the investment management process.

Wealth Level 5

You have accumulated enough assets to produce a total return well beyond what you would ever spend. You now have the option not to work, raise your standard of living, and bestow large charitable gifts. Once you reach this level, you will need some serious estate planning help.

If you want to make it to this level, you could become a famous movie star or corporate executive with lots of stock options. However, the most common way people make it to this level is through the sale of a large cash generating asset like a business or commercial real estate. You can also get there by building and selling a company. It happens all the time. Just look back at the stories in Chapter 1.

Focus

What do you think Wealth Level 5 people focus on in regard to their money? I can tell you from experience that the answer to this question is risk. The master component is risk and more specifically the management of risk. When you make it to this level, you tend to focus on protection of principal. It doesn't matter whether you make 5 percent or 15 percent on your portfolio. Your needs are covered either way. Therefore, you tend to focus on maintenance instead of total return. First, you want to reduce the possibility of a substantial loss. Second, you want to maintain an adequate rate of return.

Certainly it would be great to achieve this level of wealth, but most people would be content with level 3 or 4. Therefore, this book will focus primarily on the first four levels.

The Least You Need to Know

- Your definition of wealth should be relative to your own desired standard of living and not your neighbor's.
- In your early years of building wealth, the actual amount you save is much more important than the performance of your portfolio.

- In your attempt to reach Wealth Level 1, learn the basics, go with your gut instinct, and don't worry so much about your investment mistakes.
- You can take a shortcut to the higher levels of wealth by starting your own business, but the risks can be greater.

Chapter 4

The Eight Steps Toward Achieving Wealth Level 1

In This Chapter

- Analyzing your income and spending habits
- Estimating your future income needs
- Estimating your target portfolio goal
- Estimating yearly and monthly target savings goal
- Maintaining your wealth plan

Most people never achieve any significant wealth because they have no idea how to build wealth or even how to get started. There's not a class or television show that really shows you how to do it. You might find a few books on the subject, but rarely do you find an actual formula that works. If you do find a formula, it is probably either too complicated or too ambiguous. Therefore, I sat down and designed an easy step-by-step plan that would help others get to Wealth Level 1. It's simple to complete and it should be your first step in your journey toward wealth. You'll learn about the plan in this chapter.

Getting Ready for the Journey

I've learned that wealth, when achieved over a long period of time, tends to be appreciated more and wealth acquired suddenly tends to be squandered. This is especially evident among lottery winners. An article in the *New York Times* (April 23, 1995) titled "Ticket To Trouble" stated, "There are no statistics on what happens to jackpot winners. But a growing body of evidence suggests that winning big often brings big, if not ruinous trouble." For example, William Post of Oil City, PA., won a $16.2 million jackpot in 1988. Five years later, he was completely broke and his brother was in jail charged with hiring a hit man to murder William and his wife for the lottery money.

Treasure Tip

The great wealth hunter Waschka says, "If you always hunt elephants, you may die of starvation. But if you focus on the easier little game like rabbits and birds, you'll be better prepared when the elephant comes along."

Why do these lottery winners end up in so much trouble? Just think about it a minute. They win the lottery, suddenly they feel like they're rich, they begin spending money like never before, and they pay little attention to planning for the future. Who cares about the future when you're rich and have all this money coming in? Well, that's the problem. These winners see wealth as a destination, and they feel like they have definitely arrived. What they don't understand is that wealth is a journey, not a destination. You can't just get to Wealth Level 3 and go nuts. You have to continue to be a good steward of your money, which requires some responsibility.

Treasure Tip

Looking back at all the wealthy people I've met in my life, it seems that the ones who built their own wealth slowly over time seem to appreciate and maintain it better than those who inherited or married it.

If you want to achieve and maintain wealth throughout your lifetime, you must see wealth as a journey. As you saw in Chapter 3, this journey has many levels and transitions, and most people don't understand them. If you take the time to plan and prepare for each step or transition, you improve your chances of becoming and staying wealthy. It also helps to be patient along the way, especially at the beginning of your journey.

Let's begin your journey by focusing on accomplishing the first level of wealth. Here are the steps to follow:

1. Analyze your current income—and focus on maximizing it.
2. Analyze your current spending habits—and focus on minimizing spending.
3. Estimate how much you need to cover your future expenses (such as your living expenses after retirement) in before-tax dollars.

4. Project the effect of inflation on expenses.
5. Estimate your target portfolio amount (the amount of money you'll need in your portfolio to retire).
6. Estimate your yearly and monthly target savings goal.
7. Achieve your target savings goal.
8. Maintain your plan.

What you are about to embark on is a simple process of estimating income and expenses designed to give you an approximate target savings goal. You could get really serious here with this exercise and build a complex model of expense analysis and wealth projections. That's great if you want to take the time. I suggest using computer spreadsheets or personal finance software that will do all this for you. But, to make things easy for now, let's establish some approximate goals so you can at least get started. The overall tool you'll use is the Wealth Builder Worksheet, shown next. The subsequent sections in this chapter walk you, in detail, through each of the steps in the Wealth Builder Worksheet, particularly those steps that require calculations. Read the chapter before using the worksheet, then make numerous copies of it so you can update it from year to year to review your progress toward your goals.

Wealth Builder Worksheet

1. Analyze your current yearly income._______________

2. Analyze your current spending habits.

Estimate your total yearly expenses:

_______________ × 12 = _______________

(Monthly expenses) _______________ = × 12 (Yearly expenses)_______________

Project the growth of your monthly spending habits.

_______________ + _______________ = _______________

(Yearly expenses) + (Estimated additions) = (Total yearly expenses)

3. Estimate income needed to cover your expenses in before-tax dollars.

Calculate the inverse of your total average tax rate:

1.00 – = _______________

1.00 – (Total average federal, state, and local income tax rate) = (Inverse rate)

continues

continued

Convert yearly expenses into a before-tax amount.

_______________ /_______________ = _______________

(Total yearly expenses)/(Inverse rate) = (Pre-tax yearly expenses)

4. Project the effect of inflation on expenses.

_______________ × _______________ = _______________

(Yearly expenses before tax) × (1.00 + inflation estimate) = Expenses

Continue this calculation for the number of years until retirement.

5. Estimate Your Target Portfolio Amount.

_______________ / _______________ = _______________

(Highest yearly expenses)/(Estimated net rate of return) = (Portfolio size needed)

6. Estimate yearly and monthly TSG'S.

Yearly TSG Calculation:

_______________ / _______________ = _______________

Target Portfolio Goal/Future Value Factor= Yearly TSG

Monthly TSG calculation:

_______________ /12 = _______________

Yearly TSG /12 = Monthly TSG

7. Achieve your target savings goal.

Step 1: Analyze Your Current Income

Write down on a piece of paper your current yearly salary or income before tax. Under that amount, write this question: "What can I do to increase my income now and in the future?" Find a peaceful place of solitude and complete 20 answers to this question. If you can't come up with 20 answers, ask a friend to help you. Here are a few ideas to get you started:

Ask the boss for a raise.

Offer to take on more responsibility for more pay.

Start a small income generating business on the side.

Come up with an idea at work that will make the company more profitable.

Find another job that will pay you what you're worth.

Afterwards, select the best answers and make an effort to implement them. If building wealth is really important to you, you'll take the time to complete this step. As I've mentioned in Chapter 1, your journey toward wealth doesn't require a huge salary. However, if you'll at least attempt to maximize your income, you might shorten the distance you have to travel. There are so many different ways to do this. If you're creative and proactive by nature, you'll have no problem doing this. In Chapter 6, I will discuss several techniques you can use to maximize your salary if you work for others. In Part 3, I'll discuss ways to maximize your net income if you're self-employed.

The ultimate goal in this step is to calculate the amount of yearly income you would like to make before taxes and 401(k) contributions. What amount of income would you need to be happy? Before you answer this question, you might want to complete step two regarding expenses.

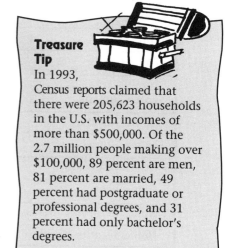

Treasure Tip

In 1993, Census reports claimed that there were 205,623 households in the U.S. with incomes of more than $500,000. Of the 2.7 million people making over $100,000, 89 percent are men, 81 percent are married, 49 percent had postgraduate or professional degrees, and 31 percent had only bachelor's degrees.

Step 2: Analyze Your Current Spending Habits

What are your current yearly expenses? How much money do you spend each month? The best way to keep track of this is by keeping pen and paper with you for a month. This sounds like a lot of trouble, but remember, we're talking about building your wealth here. I always find that whatever is measured seems to improve. If you take the time to do this, you will learn a lot about yourself and quickly see where your money is going. Do this for one month and calculate your actual monthly expenditures. Then multiply this by 12. This should give you an approximate idea of your yearly expenses.

If you prefer a more structured approach, the Weekly Expense Worksheet in this chapter is designed for you to copy four times, one for each week of the month. (Make five copies if the current month spans five weeks.) You may want to enlarge it to fit a full page. Take a sheet with you and begin recording now. Record every penny you spend for one month. This includes all cash, credit, and checkbook expenditures.

Weekly Expense Worksheet

Expense Items	Mon	Tues	Wed	Thurs	Fri	Sat	Sun	Total
Auto: Gas								
Auto: Maintenance								
Children: Tuition/Child Care								
Food: Dining Out/Credit Card								
Food: Grocery								
Fun:								
Fun:								
Fun: Vacation/ Entertainment								
Home: Furniture								
Home: Housekeeper								
Home: Pest Control								
Home: Rent								
Home: Repair/Maintenance								
Home: Security Monitoring								
Home: Yard Maintenance								
Insurance: Auto & Liability								
Insurance:								
Insurance: Disability								
Insurance: Health								
Insurance: Life								
Loan:								
Loan: Home Mortgage								
Membership: Athletic Club								
Membership:								
Membership Dues:								
Misc:								
Misc:								
Misc: Clothing								

Expense Items	Mon	Tues	Wed	Thurs	Fri	Sat	Sun	Total
Misc: Contributions/Gifts								
Misc: Laundry/Dry Cleaning								
Misc: Medical/Dental								
Misc: Parking								
Misc: Personal Care								
Misc: Transportation								
Taxes: Property								
Taxes: Income (out of paycheck)								
Taxes: Quarterly Federal								
Taxes: Tax Account to Pay April								
Utility: Electric								
Utility: Gas								
Utility: Phone								
Utility: Water								
Retirement Account (SEP, 401k)								
Other								
Other								
Other								
Other								

At the end of each week, total each row. Once you have all four sheets, total the corresponding row entries. For example, total your four week's worth of expense for Misc: Personal Care. Make copies of the Monthly Expense Worksheet, shown next in this book, and record the sum of the four weekly totals for each expense item. If you don't want to complete the Weekly Expense Worksheet now, you may want to just estimate your monthly expenses for each category so that you can get started. That's okay, but don't disregard the Weekly Expense Worksheet. If you do, you may be basing your entire financial future on incorrect data.

Monthly Expense Worksheet

Expense Items	This Month	Actual	Next Month's Budget
Auto: Gas			
Auto: Maintenance			
Children: Tuition/Child Care			
Food: Dining Out/Credit Card			
Food: Grocery			
Fun:			
Fun:			
Fun: Vacation/Entertainment			
Home: Furniture			
Home: Housekeeper			
Home: Pest Control			
Home: Rent			
Home: Repair/Maintenance			
Home: Security Monitoring			
Home: Yard Maintenance			
Insurance: Auto & Liability			
Insurance:			
Insurance: Disability			
Insurance: Health			
Insurance: Life			
Loan:			
Loan: Home Mortgage			
Membership: Athletic Club			
Membership:			
Membership:			
Misc:			
Misc:			
Misc: Clothing			

Expense Items	This Month	Actual	Next Month's Budget
Misc: Contributions/Gifts			
Misc: Laundry/Dry Cleaning			
Misc: Medical/Dental			
Misc: Parking			
Misc: Personal Care			
Misc: Transportation			
Taxes: Property			
Taxes: Income (out of paycheck)			
Taxes: Quarterly Federal			
Taxes: Tax Account to pay April			
Utility: Electric			
Utility: Gas			
Utility: Phone			
Utility: Water			
Retirement Account (SEP, 401k)			
Other			
Other			
Other			
Total			

Once you enter each monthly total, take a look at where you're spending money. Find the expenses that are unnecessary. What could you do without? In the second column of the Monthly Expense Worksheet, "Next Month's Budget," record what you think your expenses should be. This will be your budget. If you want, do the same exercise again next month, record your actual expenses in the third column, and see how close you came. I have found that by simply measuring expenses I tend to be more in control of my spending habits. The goal is to find additional money that you can save.

Using your monthly expense total, calculate a yearly total by multiplying by 12. You will need this yearly total for the next step. If you want more exact numbers, look back over the past year's expenses using your checkbook register and credit card statements. Set these up on a computer spreadsheet and see what your actual yearly expenses have been. The most effective way to do this is by using one of the personal financial software packages that are now available, such as Quicken. This program will help you do an expense analysis in great detail. For those who are computer illiterate, good old fashioned notebook paper works just as well; it just takes longer.

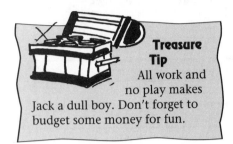

Treasure Tip

All work and no play makes Jack a dull boy. Don't forget to budget some money for fun.

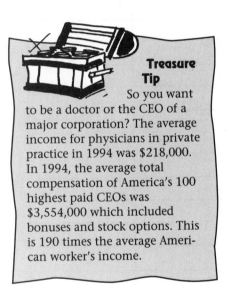

But you're not finished yet. Do you foresee any change in these spending habits? Here are some common spending habit changes: marriage, buying a home, having a child, or sending a child to college. Ask yourself what changes you expect to make in the next five years. Estimate the costs and project how much your monthly spending will increase or decrease. Multiply this by 12 to get a yearly figure. The result should be the amount of money you will need per year for the added expense, and you should add it into the expense total you've just calculated. Make sure that this is a conservative figure with some room for error. Pad the amount some if you want, just to be sure you've covered all your expenses. Your goal should be to establish the lowest amount of expenses you'd be happy to live with now. If you are not satisfied with your current standard of living and you feel you would need additional money, then add it. Just remember that if you do so, your Target Savings Goal will be higher and more difficult to achieve.

Treasure Tip

So you want to be a doctor or the CEO of a major corporation? The average income for physicians in private practice in 1994 was $218,000. In 1994, the average total compensation of America's 100 highest paid CEOs was $3,554,000 which included bonuses and stock options. This is 190 times the average American worker's income.

Step 3: Estimate Income Needed to Cover Your Expenses in Before-Tax Dollars

This step is easy. Estimate your total federal, state, and local income tax rate. You may want to use your Average Income Tax Rate which we calculated earlier in Chapter 2. You may want to call your CPA if you have one or get a federal and state tax table from the Internal Revenue Service and your state tax agency. Once you have your estimated tax rate, subtract the percentage from 1 to calculate the inverse of your tax rate. For example, if your Average Income Tax Rate is 35 percent, then the equation would look like this:

$1 - .35 = .65$ .65 is the inverse of your tax rate.

Then take your projected yearly expenses that you calculated in the preceding section and divide your expenses by this number. For example, if your estimated yearly expenses added up to be $40,000 the equation would look like this:

$40,000 / .65 = $61,538

Therefore, you are going to need $61,538 in income per year before tax in order to maintain your spending habits.

Words of the Wealthy
The **inverse** of a percentage number is easily calculated by subtracting the percentage number from 1.

Step 4: Project the Effect of Inflation on Expenses

The next step is to calculate the effect of *inflation* on your expenses in later years. If we continue the example you saw in the last section, we know you'll need $61,538 each year in today's dollars to cover your expenses, but what about when you retire? What will inflation do to prices by that time?

The only way to answer that question is to make an estimate of future inflation and calculate its effect on your yearly expense needs. This process involves a simple calculation. To calculate the one-year effect of inflation, just take the yearly expense total and multiply it by 1 plus your estimate of inflation.

(yearly expenses before tax) × (1 + estimate of inflation) = next year's expense estimate

If we use a 3 percent estimate of the annual inflation rate, here is what the calculation would look like:

$61,538 × (1 + .03) = $63,384

This calculation shows you that you will need $63,384 in income next year to cover the same amount of expenses if the inflation rate is 3 percent.

Now that you understand the calculation, you can project out further into the future. First you have to decide how many years you are willing to wait to achieve Level 3 wealth when your portfolio is producing enough income for you to retire. Let's say you're willing to wait 25 years. Just continue the calculation 24 more times. Using the same example, Table 4.1 shows what the result should look like:

Words of the Wealthy
Most people think that **inflation** is the simple rise in prices. The technical definition is an increase the volume of money and credit relative to available goods, which results in a substantial and continuing rise in the general price level. The rate of inflation is measured by the month to month percentage change of the Consumer Price Index (CPI).

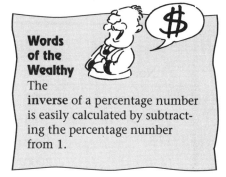

Table 4.1 Estimating Future Income Needs Based on Inflation

No. of Years	Year	Pre-Tax Income Needed for Expenses (base of $61,538)	Estimated Inflation
1	1997	$63,384	3%
2	1998	$65,286	3%
3	1999	$67,244	3%
4	2000	$69,262	3%
5	2001	$71,339	3%
6	2002	$73,480	3%
7	2003	$75,684	3%
8	2004	$77,954	3%
9	2005	$80,293	3%
10	2006	$82,702	3%
11	2007	$85,183	3%
12	2008	$87,738	3%
13	2009	$90,371	3%
14	2010	$93,082	3%
15	2011	$95,874	3%
16	2012	$98,750	3%
17	2013	$101,713	3%
18	2014	$104,764	3%
19	2015	$107,907	3%
20	2016	$111,144	3%
21	2017	$114,479	3%
22	2018	$117,913	3%
23	2019	$121,451	3%
24	2020	$125,094	3%
25	2021	$128,847	3%

As you can see from Table 4.1, in 25 years, you will need approximately $128,847 in income to cover your yearly expense needs. Isn't it scary what inflation of only 3 percent can do to your standard of living?

> **Wealth Warning**
>
> Social Security was never intended to fully fund retirement. It's a U.S. government program established in 1935 for old-age, survivor, and unemployment insurance. It was meant to supplement income, not replace it.

Step 5: Estimate Your Target Portfolio Amount

You have to assume several variables before you can estimate how much money you'll need. You have to estimate your rate of return. Depending upon who you ask, estimates of rate of return can vary widely. If you ask a very conservative investor, the answer could be as low as 5 percent. On the other hand, a very aggressive investor might say 15 percent. Your return obviously depends upon the level of risk you take and how your investments perform. For now, let's continue to assume a 10 percent rate of return, which is a little below the average return on the S & P 500 (the major New York Stock Exchange performance index) over the last 40 years.

> **That Reminds Me...**
>
> To achieve real wealth, you must be open-minded enough to recognize and break down the self-imposed barriers that keep you in your present financial condition. These barriers are usually mental paradigms or mind-sets that need a little adjustment. Normally the adjustment requires a catalyst or disruption to get it started. The most common catalysts and disruptions come from reading and discussing ideas with others. First, take some time to understand your own paradigm barriers about building wealth. Then discuss them with others who have achieved the level of wealth you desire. How do these people think? How did they overcome the same barriers? Did they have similar barriers or different ones? This meeting might be just the catalyst you need.

Now divide your yearly before-tax income, adjusted for inflation, by your estimated net rate of return.

Yearly before-tax income adjusted for inflation / Estimated net rate of return = Target Portfolio Goal

For example, here is the calculation using the assumptions above:

$128,847 / .10 = $1,288,470

Therefore, in order to retire comfortably and begin living off the return from your portfolio, you'll need a portfolio of assets totaling $1,288,470 producing a rate of return of 10 percent per year.

Isn't this great? Now you can measure exactly what you will need in assets to achieve Wealth Level 3! Don't be overwhelmed by the result. You're about to learn how to build this pool of assets.

Step 6: Estimate Yearly and Monthly TSGs

Using Table 4.2, Future Value Of Annuity Due, you can find what your yearly target savings goal should be. Let's review the assumptions before we calculate:

Target portfolio goal	$1,288,470
Yearly before-tax income needed at retirement	$128,847
Estimated rate of return	10%
Number of years until retirement	25

In Tables 4.2 through 4.4, find the future value of annuity due factor that corresponds to your assumptions. Look at the top row and find your estimated Rate of Return of 10 percent. (If you want to use a different Rate of Return, select it from the table, instead.) Look down the column until you find the factor for the number of years until you retire—in this case, 25 years.

Table 4.2 Future Value of Annuity Factors (Annuity Due), Part 1

Rate of Return							
Years til You Retire	1%	2%	3%	4%	5%	6%	7%
5	5.1520	5.3081	5.4684	5.6330	5.8019	5.9753	6.1533
6	6.2135	6.4343	6.6625	6.8983	7.1420	7.3938	7.6540
7	7.2857	7.5830	7.8923	8.2142	8.5491	8.8975	9.2598
8	8.3685	8.7546	9.1591	9.5828	10.0266	10.4913	10.9780
9	9.4622	9.9497	10.4639	11.0061	11.5779	12.1808	12.8164
10	10.5668	11.1687	11.8078	12.4864	13.2068	13.9716	14.7836
11	11.6825	12.4121	13.1920	14.0258	14.9171	15.8699	16.8885
12	12.8093	13.6803	14.6178	15.6268	16.7130	17.8821	19.1406
13	13.9474	14.9739	16.0863	17.2919	18.5986	20.0151	21.5505
14	15.0969	16.2934	17.5989	19.0236	20.5786	22.2760	24.1290
15	16.2579	17.6393	19.1569	20.8245	22.6575	24.6725	26.8881
16	17.4304	19.0121	20.7616	22.6975	24.8404	27.2129	29.8402
17	18.6147	20.4123	22.4144	24.6454	27.1324	29.9057	32.9990
18	19.8109	21.8406	24.1169	26.6712	29.5390	32.7600	36.3790
19	21.0190	23.2974	25.8704	28.7781	32.0660	35.7856	39.9955
20	22.2392	24.7833	27.6765	30.9692	34.7193	38.9927	43.8652
21	23.4716	26.2990	29.5368	33.2480	37.5052	42.3923	48.0057
22	24.7163	27.8450	31.4529	35.6179	40.4305	45.9958	52.4361
23	25.9735	29.4219	33.4265	38.0826	43.5020	49.8156	57.1767
24	27.2432	31.0303	35.4593	40.6459	46.7271	53.8645	62.2490
25	28.5256	32.6709	37.5530	43.3117	50.1135	58.1564	67.6765
26	29.8209	34.3443	39.7096	46.0842	53.6691	62.7058	73.4838
27	31.1291	36.0512	41.9309	48.9676	57.4026	67.5281	79.6977
28	32.4504	37.7922	44.2189	51.9663	61.3227	72.6398	86.3465
29	33.7849	39.5681	46.5754	55.0849	65.4388	78.0582	93.4608
30	35.1327	41.3794	49.0027	58.3283	69.7608	83.8017	101.0730
35	42.0769	50.9944	62.2759	76.5983	94.8363	118.1209	147.9135
40	49.3752	61.6100	77.6633	98.8265	126.8398	164.0477	213.6096
45	57.0459	73.3306	95.5015	125.8706	167.6852	225.5081	305.7518
50	65.1078	86.2710	116.1808	158.7738	219.8154	307.7561	434.9860

Table 4.3 Future Value of Annuity Factors (Annuity Due), Part 2

Rate of Return							
Years til You Retire	8%	9%	10%	11%	12%	13%	14%
5	6.3359	6.5233	6.7156	6.9129	7.1152	7.3227	7.5355
6	7.9228	8.2004	8.4872	8.7833	9.0890	9.4047	9.7305
7	9.6366	10.0285	10.4359	10.8594	11.2997	11.7573	12.2328
8	11.4876	12.0210	12.5795	13.1640	13.7757	14.4157	15.0853
9	13.4866	14.1929	14.3974	15.7220	16.5487	17.4197	18.3373
10	15.6455	16.5603	17.5312	18.5614	19.6546	20.8143	22.0445
11	17.9771	19.1407	20.3843	21.7132	23.1331	24.6502	26.2707
12	20.4953	21.9534	23.5227	25.2116	27.0291	28.9847	31.0887
13	23.2149	25.0192	26.9750	29.0949	31.3926	33.8827	36.5811
14	26.1521	28.3609	30.7725	33.4054	36.2797	39.4175	42.8424
15	29.3243	32.0034	34.9497	38.1899	41.7533	45.6717	49.9804
16	32.7502	35.9737	39.5447	43.5008	47.8837	52.7391	58.1176
17	36.4502	40.3013	44.5992	49.3959	54.7497	60.7251	67.3941
18	40.4463	45.0185	50.1591	55.9395	62.4397	69.7494	77.9692
19	44.7620	50.1601	56.2750	63.2028	71.0524	79.9468	90.0249
20	49.4229	55.7645	63.0025	71.2651	80.6987	91.4699	103.7684
21	54.4568	61.8733	70.4027	80.2143	91.5026	104.4910	119.4360
22	59.8933	68.5319	78.5430	90.1479	103.6029	119.2048	137.2970
23	65.7648	75.7898	87.4973	101.1741	117.1552	135.8315	157.6586
24	72.1059	83.7009	97.3471	113.4133	132.3339	154.6196	180.8708
25	78.9544	92.3240	108.1818	126.9988	149.3339	175.8501	207.3327
26	86.3508	101.7231	120.0999	142.0786	168.3740	199.8406	237.4993
27	94.3388	111.9682	133.2099	158.8173	189.6989	226.9499	271.8892
28	102.9659	123.1354	147.6309	177.3972	213.5828	257.5834	311.0937
29	112.2832	135.3075	163.4940	198.0209	240.3327	292.1992	355.7868
30	122.3459	148.5752	180.9434	220.9132	270.2926	331.3151	406.7370
35	186.1021	235.1247	298.1268	379.1644	483.4631	617.7493	790.6729
40	279.7810	368.2919	486.8518	645.8269	859.1424	1145.4858	1529.9086
45	417.4261	573.1860	790.7953	1095.1688	1521.2176	2117.8060	2953.2439
50	619.6718	888.4411	1280.2994	1852.3359	2688.0204	3909.2430	5693.7543

Table 4.4 Future Value of Annuity Factors (Annuity Due), Part 3

Rate of Return					
Years til You Retire	5%	16%	17%	18%	19%
5	7.7537	7.9775	8.2068	8.4420	8.6830
6	10.0668	10.4139	10.7720	11.1415	11.5227
7	12.7268	13.2401	13.7733	14.3270	14.9020
8	15.7858	16.5185	17.2847	18.0859	18.9234
9	19.3037	20.3215	21.3931	22.5213	23.7089
10	23.3493	24.7329	26.1999	27.7551	29.4035
11	28.0017	29.8502	31.8239	33.9311	36.1802
12	33.3519	35.7862	38.4040	41.2187	44.2445
13	39.5047	42.6720	46.1027	49.8180	53.8409
14	46.5804	50.6595	55.1101	59.9653	65.2607
15	54.7175	59.9250	65.6488	71.9390	78.8502
16	64.0751	70.6730	77.9792	86.0680	95.0218
17	74.8364	83.1407	92.4056	102.7403	114.2659
18	87.2118	97.6032	109.2846	122.4135	137.1664
19	101.4436	114.3739	129.0329	145.6280	164.4180
20	117.8101	133.8405	152.1385	173.0210	196.8474
21	136.6316	156.4150	179.1721	205.3448	235.4385
22	158.2764	182.6014	210.8013	243.4868	281.3618
23	183.1678	212.9776	247.8076	288.4945	336.0105
24	211.7930	248.2140	291.1049	341.6035	401.0425
25	244.7120	289.0883	341.7627	404.2721	478.4306
26	282.5688	336.5024	401.0323	478.2211	570.5224
27	326.1041	391.5028	470.3778	565.4809	680.1116
28	376.1697	455.3032	551.5121	668.4475	810.5228
29	433.7451	529.3117	646.4391	789.9480	965.7122
30	499.9569	615.1616	757.5038	933.3186	1150.3875
35	1013.3757	1300.0270	1668.9945	2143.6489	2753.9143
40	2045.9539	2738.4784	3667.3906	4912.5914	6580.4965
45	4122.8977	5759.7178	8048.7701	11247.2610	15712.0750
50	8300.3737	1210.5353	17654.7170	25739.4510	37503.2500

Your factor for this example should be 108.1818, which we'll call the future value factor. Thus, the calculation to find your yearly TSG looks like this:

Target Portfolio Goal / Future Value Factor = Yearly TSG

Here are the actual numbers for example:

$1,288,470 / 108.1818 = $11,910

Now to calculate your monthly TSG, just divide this number by 12.

$11,910 / 12 = $992.50

Please understand that this simple calculation does not take into consideration the effect of taxes on the total return of your investments. If this amount of money were saved in a tax deferred qualified retirement plan like a 401(k) or SEP, the math is almost perfect. However, if you are saving in a taxable account (like a savings account, certificate of deposit, or taxable mutual fund) or the combination of a taxable account and a tax deferred qualified plan, then you must consider the effect of taxes each year on your total return accumulation. Here are a few things to consider.

Let's assume your net tax liability on dividends, interest, and capital gains is 30 percent. If you make an average total return of 10 percent, then you could subtract 30 percent of the 10 percent return to get a net total return of 7 percent. This 7 percent can then be used to estimate your target portfolio return. (That is, you should choose a 7 percent Rate of Return factor from Table 4.2 rather than the 10 percent Rate of Return factor from Table 4.3 before making your calculation.) However, remember this is an estimate. Your capital gains may not all accrue each year, which means that there will be irregular capital gains taxes to pay each year depending upon when your investment transactions result in a capital gain.

> **Wealth Warning**
> This process is not difficult to complete, but it is easy to make a mistake. Once you complete all the necessary steps and calculations, be sure to go back and check your math.

Step 7: Achieve Your Target Savings Goal

If you are overwhelmed by your target portfolio size, don't be concerned. Don't forget that this amount is based upon some assumptions you made that can be adjusted. First, you could decrease the assumed inflation rate used to project your future living expenses. Second, you could accept some more risk and increase your estimated total return assumption. Third, you could extend the number of years you are willing to wait before you reach Wealth Level 3.

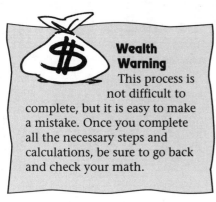

If you want to achieve your target savings goal, you have to ask yourself what factors you have the most control over. You have the least control over things like inflation and total return. You have the most control over expenses. You have some control over income, but reducing your expenses is usually easier than increasing income. It may not be as glamorous, but it is very effective in achieving a larger savings goal. The less you spend, the more you have available for savings. The following list of ideas is designed to reduce your expenses. This is a very small list (the rest of the book presents more tips and ideas, but it's a start).

- **Lower expenses.** Find expenses you can do without. Don't eat out as much. Turn down your heat at night or when you're gone. Use the phone book instead of information when you can. Stop smoking and you'll not only save the money you spend on cigarettes, you'll also save on your health insurance, not to mention medical bills later.
- **Avoid buying lottery tickets.** If you understand the odds of winning the lottery, you would never buy a ticket.
- **Home and auto maintenance actually lower expenses.** I just replaced my 15–year-old air-conditioning system with a new one. My electric bills are less and my home is much cooler when it's hot outside.
- **Don't use life insurance for investment purposes.** This is one of the most common mistakes investors make. The cost of the insurance and commissions drain your investment, which decreases the total return you get. A friend who is an insurance agent says, "But the investment grows tax deferred." And, my reply is, 'I don't care! It costs too much and the policy holder is limited to only a handful of investment choices that usually are mediocre at best." My suggestion is to separate your investment money from your life insurance. Consider going to a less expensive term policy and depositing the savings in a no-load mutual fund. WARNING: Do not drop your existing life insurance first. If you plan to change to the term policy, do it first. Once it is set up, then cancel your past insurance. You don't want to be uncovered. If you can't get a term policy because of a pre-existing condition, you will have your existing policy to fall back on.
- **Shop by phone for life insurance.** Now you can get quality life insurance by phone. Here are three companies that will shop the term life insurance market for you and show you the best deal:

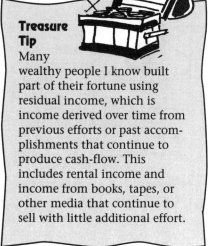

Treasure Tip

Many wealthy people I know built part of their fortune using residual income, which is income derived over time from previous efforts or past accomplishments that continue to produce cash-flow. This includes rental income and income from books, tapes, or other media that continue to sell with little additional effort.

Select Quote	800-343-1985
Quotesmith	800-431-1147
Master Quote	800-337-5433

These companies will contract with a medical technician who will come to your office to draw blood and fill out medical forms.

- **Save money when you travel.** Smart travelers know that airlines want to charge business travelers more money than vacationers. They assume that business travelers can write off the travel and therefore are more willing to pay higher prices. By simply staying at your destination over a Saturday night, you can sometimes save 75 percent off your airline ticket.

  You can also book hotel rooms cheaper in large cities by using services that offer more inexpensive lodging by purchasing rooms in bulk. Here are a few companies that offer this service:

Hotel Reservations	800-964-6835
Express Reservations	800-356-1123
Quickbook	800-789-9887

Step 8: Maintain Your Plan

The last step is to maintain your plan. Redo all the calculations for the Wealth Builder Worksheet and the other two worksheets in this chapter at least once a year. Your monthly expenses should be measured each month; if not quarterly. If you continue to measure your expenses, you will be better able to meet your goal. I guarantee that your plan will change over time. Some of these changes will be small and some large. Your success in maintaining your plan depends a great deal upon several things:

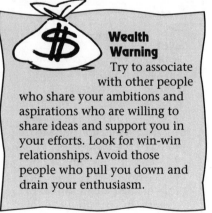

- **Your flexibility and creativity.** You must be willing to respond to the inevitable changes that life brings.
- **Your organizational skills.** You must keep current with all of the elements of your plan.
- **Your willingness to work on your plan.** Your journey toward wealth will take some time but the payoff will be worth it!

Wealth Warning

Try to associate with other people who share your ambitions and aspirations who are willing to share ideas and support you in your efforts. Look for win-win relationships. Avoid those people who pull you down and drain your enthusiasm.

The Least You Need to Know

- In order to save enough money to retire, you have to regularly measure your expenses, compare them to your income, and maximize your savings.
- The effect of taxes and inflation are staggering and always need to be part of your wealth-building equation.
- If you calculate your Target Savings Goal every year, you will always know what you need to save each month.
- If you can let your assets grow tax deferred in a qualified plan and then roll them over to an IRA when you retire, your portfolio will grow faster and the end result will be more money when you need it.

Chapter 5

The Habits and Characteristics Needed to Reach Wealth Level 2

In This Chapter

- Saving money systematically each month
- Avoid debt and pay cash for items
- Make it a habit to shop around
- Wealth and passion can work together

Remember the couple I mentioned in Chapter 1, Mr. and Mrs. Post, who never made over $30,000 per year, yet their portfolio was worth over $800,000? How could this couple have so much money? Well, that is exactly what I asked, and they said, "We saved it and invested it in no-load funds." I said, "Please tell me your story. There's got to be more to this, right?" They sat back and shared some simple truths that every investor should follow. I call them the seven habits of very wealthy people, and I detail them in this chapter.

The seven habits for building wealth include saving every month, staying out of debt, shopping before you buy, buying used when you can, taking care of your stuff, investing in stocks, and taking time to plan your future.

1. Save Every Month

The Posts said that each month, no matter what they made in salary, they put money in savings and invested in no-load mutual funds. They said, "No matter what happens, pay yourself first and make it a habit." The combination of systematic savings and compound growth is incredible. Here are several ways you can start saving money now:

- **Maximize your 401(k) or SEP-IRA contributions.** If your company or employer offers one of these plans, take advantage of it now and try to maximize your contributions. Millionaires are made of these plans. The assets grow tax deferred, and you get the benefit of using Uncle Sam's money in the compounding process.
- **If you are self-employed, consider starting your own SEP-IRA (an IRA plan for self-employed people).** You'll be able to shelter up to 15 percent of your income until you retire. This is powerful stuff and simple to implement. All you have to do is fill out an application, make a deposit, and you're on your way.
- **Maximize your IRA contribution.** An IRA is an Individual Retirement Account into which a maximum of $2,000 of earned income can be deposited each year. The true benefit of the IRA is that all interest, dividends, and capital gains are tax deferred until they are withdrawn. The second benefit is the flexibility of investment alternatives that are available. You can invest in CDs, stocks, bonds, and mutual funds. Since there are over 5,000 different mutual funds, your alternatives are almost endless. The third benefit is convenience. An IRA is very simple to start. All you have to do is fill out an application and make a deposit.

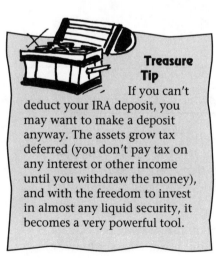

  The tax deductibility of your deposit depends upon your income and involvement in a qualified plan. If you are not enrolled in a qualified retirement plan, you may be able to deduct your deposit from your total taxable income. Be sure to check with the IRS, your CPA, or a financial planner to find out more about your situation.

> **Treasure Tip**
>
> If you can't deduct your IRA deposit, you may want to make a deposit anyway. The assets grow tax deferred (you don't pay tax on any interest or other income until you withdraw the money), and with the freedom to invest in almost any liquid security, it becomes a very powerful tool.

- **Write yourself a check.** Before you start paying your bills each week or each payday, write yourself a check and deposit the checks in a separate account. The whole idea is to pay yourself before anyone else. Your goal should be to save your target savings goal. Then use the remainder to budget your spending. Act like the target savings goal amount doesn't even exist and budget accordingly.

- **Let a mutual fund direct-debit your account.** Most mutual funds offer a direct-debit feature that automatically withdraws a pre-determined amount from your checking account each month. This is one of the easiest ways to save money. Each month at bill-paying time, just record the withdrawal in your check register. Don't be afraid of this feature. Try it for a year and cancel if you don't like it.
- **Save your pennies, nickels, dimes, and quarters.** I spend only whole dollar bills and save my change every day in a bowl. When the bowl is full, I deposit it in my investment account.
- **Save your raises.** Another trick is to ignore any raises in income when budgeting for expenses. When you get a raise, save the entire raise. Instead of increasing your spending habits, increase your saving habits. Let the raise boost your saving percentage.

2. Avoid Debt

Many rich individuals pay cash for everything and avoid debt (except for their home mortgage). Instead of borrowing money to purchase an item, they wait until they save enough money to buy the item with cash. Save money for the things you want and pay cash.

Here are four ideas that will help you eliminate debt faster and reduce the total cost of debt interest:

- **Refinance your mortgage.** Shop around when mortgage rates drop to see if you can get a better fixed rate. If you plan to stay in your home for more than two years, and you can improve your mortgage rate by as much as 1 percent, you should consider refinancing. This may reduce your mortgage payments and reduce the amount of money you spend each year on interest payments. Try to reduce or avoid points and origination fees. These are often negotiable. Offer to refinance if the mortgage company will reduce their fees.
- **Use only low interest credit cards.** Do some research to find the credit card with the lowest possible rate. I personally have a Wachovia Visa Card (800-842-3262). The rate on this card is 8.25% now, which is one of the lowest, if not the lowest, in the country. Also, you may want to consider getting a debit card. These cards look like a standard credit card but directly debit your checking account for purchases.

Treasure Tip

Debt used to build a business or increase cash flow is acceptable. Consumer and credit card debt used to build your image in society is not acceptable in your quest to be wealthy, and will reverse the wealth-building process.

Since you are not financing your purchase, there is no finance charge. Check your local bank for this option.

- ➤ **Home equity loans can help.** If you have a great deal of credit-card debt and own your own home, you might consider going to your bank or mortgage company to apply for a home-equity loan, and use the loan money to pay off your credit-card debt. Be sure to avoid origination fees and points, which tend to counteract your overall interest savings. Check with your tax preparer to see if this interest is deductible. This is one way to convert a non tax-deductible expense to a tax–deductible one.

- ➤ **Pay more each month on your mortgage.** If you can afford to add additional money to your mortgage payment each month, you will reduce the overall interest costs on your mortgage and speed up the time it takes to retire your mortgage. If you can double your payments, your home will be paid off much faster.

Treasure Tip

Don't be seduced by the low introductory rates on credit cards. If you read the fine print on most of these cards, you'll see that much higher rates kick in after the first year.

3. Shop Before You Buy

The Posts also said that they shopped extensively before they bought anything. This is a very simple concept, but few people take the time. It is my belief that women by nature are shoppers and men are not. My personal habit is to get into the store, buy exactly what I need, and get out of there. Take a moment and think about your own habits. Do you take the time to shop around? Are you an impulsive buyer?

- ➤ **Shop at warehouse clubs.** I learned many years ago that I could save a lot of money by shopping at discount warehouse clubs. It was difficult to store the large quantities when I lived in my tiny, 500-square-foot apartment, but it is much easier now in my house.

- ➤ **Buy seasonal items out of season.** If you want to buy a boat, start shopping towards the end of the summer. Owners will accept a lower price knowing the expense of keeping it another winter in storage. Most people buy their boat in the early spring. Avoid the buying pressure, and get it cheap later in the summer. You can say the same thing about lawn mowers, convertible automobiles, and landscaping materials. If snow is a problem in the winter, buy a snow blower in the late spring. If you time your purchases right and negotiate properly, you might only pay a fraction of the normal in-season price.

- **Learn to haggle.** The United States is the only country I know of where people accept paying the full price on merchandise without negotiation. I'm guilty of this, too. However, I've learned to always ask, "Is there any way I can get a better price on this?" And, it works. A few months ago, I offered to purchase $8,000 worth of antiques from a large antique warehouse. I asked if they would give me a discount for the amount of money I wanted to spend. They gave me over 10 percent off, which added up to over $800. What a great reward for asking such an easy question! The next time you buy a big ticket item, try to negotiate.

- **Delay purchases of items you don't need.** Before you rush out to the store or pick up the telephone to buy that widget you just have to have, write it down, and think about it for a week. Then ask yourself if you still want it as much. How many things do you have in your closet, storage room, or drawers that you only used a few times? I've practiced this over the past five years, and even built a file of things I've wanted to buy. Would you believe that I've bought maybe 10 percent of them? This habit really cuts down on the amount of stuff you'll be selling in your next garage sale.

Words of the Wealthy

The word **haggle** came from the Old English term "heawan," which meant to beat or cut. Haggling is the process of negotiating the lowest price possible in a purchase transaction. The U.S. is one of the few countries where haggling is not a normal part of everyday shopping.

4. Buy Used When You Can

The Posts often bought used merchandise, especially if they could find good quality at lower prices. They spent a lot of time shopping for used items in the local want ads. They said they saved a lot of money over the years focusing on used instead of new cars. They bought quality used cars from previous owners and eliminated the commission paid to the salesperson, along with the heavy depreciation incurred in the first year. Don't be a fanatic about buying everything new. Consider a used car before you purchase a new one. Consider antique furniture instead of new. Check the want ads before you buy.

Used cars seem more attractive than ever before. New car prices have risen approximately 29 percent since 1990 and consequently, buyers are not as eager to buy any more. We have also seen a huge supply of "program cars" or previously leased cars hit the market. This large supply of two-and-three-year old cars has resulted in more competitive prices.

If you have to buy a new car, call eight of the surrounding dealers within four hours driving distance and ask them for their best price on the automobile of your choice. Be sure to be specific with your model and desired options.

I tried to buy a used Chevy Suburban two years ago but could not find one available at a reasonable price. They were in such high demand that the used prices actually exceeded the new prices! Therefore, I had to look at new models. I did some homework and found a company in California called IntelliChoice (800-227-2665) that offers a service called "Just The Facts," which gives you dealer's cost and discounts available on most cars available here in the U.S. The service is $14.95 by mail and $17.99 by fax. I called Intellichoice to find the dealer's cost on the model I wanted. I then called eight dealers around the state and actually negotiated a price $200 above the dealer's cost. If you have to buy new, IntelliChoice can help you.

Treasure Tip

If possible, sell you own car instead of trading it in. You have a better chance of getting a higher price than a dealer will offer you on trade in.

That Reminds Me...

If at all possible, don't lease a car. The commission and financing charges are all disguised in the payment, which makes it very difficult to make an intelligent decision. Most of the time, the lease is much more expensive in the long-run. If you purchase a used vehicle, take care of it with regular maintenance, and sell it later. Your total out of pocket expense should be much less than a lease agreement.

When you buy a used automobile, focus on quality and resale value. In the mid 1980's, I purchased a used, year-old Jeep Cherokee with no frills or extras. I paid $7,000 for it, drove it 20,000 miles, and sold it 18 months later for $6,800.

If you want to know approximately what an automobile is worth, call your bank and ask for "Blue Book" values. There are three prices to pay attention to. First is the loan value, which is the amount of money a bank is willing to loan a customer to buy the car. Second is the trade in value or wholesale price, which is what a car dealer might be willing to pay for the car on a trade in. Third is the retail price, which you might pay if you were buying it from a used car dealer. Your goal as a buyer is to buy the car at or below the loan value. Your goal as a seller is to sell it at or above retail. Either way, if you don't get the price you want, you have to be willing to walk away.

If you do have to get a loan to buy a car, be sure to shop several banks for the best rate. If you do this before you look for a car, you'll be better prepared to negotiate.

Consider antique furniture. A few years ago, a very dear friend taught me an invaluable lesson. I was looking for furniture for my office and he said, "Larry, don't waste your money on new furniture. Buy functional antiques." He explained that, "You can depreciate them on your balance sheet as they appreciate in value." This man is a genius. My office is full of these antiques. Not only are they beautiful, but they have also appreciated since I bought them.

Wealth Warning
Before you buy a used car, take it to an independent car repair service for a check-up. If you unknowingly buy a poor-quality, unreliable car, you may end up with big problems later. There's nothing worse than sinking your hard-earned money into something that's not reliable. If there is, it's having to sell it later.

Buy quality. If you do buy used, you must focus on quality and resale value. Always research the big-ticket items in the classified ads before you buy, and look at how they fall in price relative to their original retail price. How do they fall in price each year? Are there any consumer reports out on the product? Go to the library and look in the periodical index for the particular item you want to buy. See if there are any studies done. *Consumer Reports* is a magazine that can save you a lot of money. They do studies on different products regarding quality, maintenance, and resale value. Why not subscribe?

5. Take Care of What You Own

Another little pearl of wisdom the Posts shared with me involved simple maintenance. They said they took care of what they owned. They said that it is amazing how long things will last if you take good care of them.

Keep up automobile maintenance. This couple had both of their automobiles serviced every 4,000 miles, which included an oil and filter change. They also waxed their cars every six months. These simple steps helped keep their cars running better and helped maintain the resale value.

Home maintenance is also important. Have your heating and air-conditioning system checked once a year to prolong the life of your equipment. Pay for a good pest control service now, so you don't have to pay later for termite damage. Prevent exterior damage of your home by regularly cleaning out your gutters and replacing the old ones.

6. Maintain a Basic Understanding of the Stock and Bond Markets

The next habit this couple taught me was to develop a basic understanding of the stock and bond markets. They studied the basics, knew the benefit of owning stocks, invested in stocks through no-load funds, and learned on their own the hard way. They learned a great deal from the mistakes they made, and understood that investing money in the stock market involves making occasional mistakes. In spite of all that, they kept learning more each day and stayed the course.

> **Words of the Wealthy**
>
> When you buy shares of **stock** directly or though a mutual fund, you become part owner of a company. These shares can build your wealth by paying you dividends and by rising in price.

If you feel uncomfortable with your investment knowledge, get proactive and do something about it now. There is no excuse for ignorance. There are books and classes available that can teach you everything you need to know. Do yourself a favor and learn all you can now.

> **That Reminds Me...**
>
> When you purchase a bond or bond mutual fund, you are essentially buying IOUs of companies or the government. The total interest paid each year is your reward for loaning the money. Additional reward comes when interest rates fall and the price of the bond increases. The reverse is also true. If rates go up, the price of the bond will fall. A bond is simply a source of future cash-flow that can be bought and sold at different prices until maturity. However, at maturity, the bondholder is paid only the face amount or maturity value of the bond along with the appropriate interest amount.

The best way to learn is to start investing. You'll want to learn more because your money is at stake. The next best way to learn is to join an organization dedicated to educating investors. One of the best organizations I've found is the American Association of Individual Investors (800-428-2244). Call and ask for an information packet. You might also read some books on investing. Here are some of my favorites:

- *Beating the Street*, Peter Lynch, retired manager of Fidelity Magellan.
- *One Up on Wall Street*, Peter Lynch, retired manager of Fidelity Magellan.

- *Value Investing*, Ben Graham, father of value investing.
- *Bogle on Funds*, John Bogle, past chairman of Vanguard Funds.

7. Take Time to Plan, Research, and Systematically Measure Your Results

Finally, Mr. and Mrs. Post also did their homework. They took time to research their options before they made an investment, and they understood that quick decisions get you hurt in the market. Rumors get started and before you know it, a "hot tip" turns out to be a cold nightmare. They recognized and avoided the traps.

Don't forget to measure the results of your portfolio. This is one of the most common mistakes made by individual investors. They invest for years, never actually knowing their true performance on a monthly or yearly basis. They might estimate it, but they rarely do it accurately and they almost never compare it to the proper benchmark indexes. We'll talk more about this in Part 2.

> **Treasure Tip**
> Time is money and therefore requires just as much management as your money. If you don't have a day planner, get one. If you do have one, shop around and make sure yours is the best for your needs. I've used a day planner since I was 13 years old! They just make my life so much easier.

Characteristics of Wealthy People

If you want to improve your odds of achieving your desired level of wealth, you have to think like a wealthy person. Over the last 10 years in the investment business, I have spoken to thousands of wealthy individuals like Mr. and Mrs. Post. I've learned a great deal from these people. Mr. and Mrs. Post taught me the seven habits just listed, but they and other wealthy individuals also taught me things that went unspoken. These unspoken lessons were characteristics they portrayed. All these people were happy and enthusiastic about life, and I have a lot of admiration for them. In fact, I had so much admiration, I began to make notes about them. It was fascinating because they all seem to have several mental characteristics in common. The rest of this section presents the four most common. If you incorporate them into your life, you will have little difficulty getting to Wealth Level 2.

> **Treasure Tip**
> According to the Census Bureau, the number of poor people making less than the poverty threshold of $15,000 per year in the U.S. fell by more than 1 million in 1993—the first decline in five years.

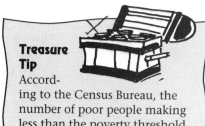

A Passion for What You Do

The world is so competitive now that markets around the world have opened up their doors to outside consumers. To compete in any business today, you have to work harder and be smarter than your competition. In the long run, the winners in any industry will be those companies and individuals who were passionate enough about their work to spend the time and effort it takes to produce outstanding products and services. Without this passion, a company or individual will be less likely to make the effort or spend all night to meet a deadline. During the first four years of building my company, I spent at least one full night a month in my office working. Sometimes I would work 32 hours straight! I've fallen asleep right in the middle of a conversation with a client!

It's not that I'm an advocate of working this many hours. It's very unhealthy. My point is that I was excited enough about my company to want to! The question I'm asking here is this: In your present position, are you willing to work all night on a project if you have to? If the answer is no, then you need to seriously consider making a job change or starting your own business doing what you enjoy.

The happiest wealthy people I know have a passion for what they do, which seems to naturally create a certain level of tenacity and perseverance toward achieving their goals. They have a vision and they are very enthusiastic about life. Their enthusiasm is sincere and it comes from deep inside. They don't necessarily have a passion for building wealth. Wealth, for them, is a result of their passion and effort for the work they do.

A student asked me recently, "If you could change anything in the business world, what would it be?" I told her that if everyone loved what they were doing in their life today, or if everyone at least had a plan to achieve this, the world would be a better place. There would be less frustration, anger, and unhappiness. People would feel more gratification.

When you love what you do, your chances of great achievement improve dramatically. If you are unsure about where your passion lies, here are three questions that will give you some ideas to consider. There are no right or wrong answers, so relax and enjoy yourself. Write down exactly what comes to mind. *Do not judge any answer!* Let your mind go and list anything that comes to mind, no matter how impossible it might seem. Write each question at the top of a separate page. Go to a quiet place where you will not be interrupted.

1. Your doctor calls and tells you that in exactly six months, you will die a peaceful death due to a weird, unknown virus. What would you do during this six-month period? Who would you spend time with? What activities would you spend time doing? What would be important to you? (List at least 20 answers.)

2. An unknown relative dies and leaves you a portfolio of cash totaling $2,000,000. What would you do? Who would you spend time with? What activities would you spend time doing? What would be important to you? Would you quit work? How would you spend your money? (List at least 20 answers.)
3. What three great endeavors would you dare to attempt if you were guaranteed you could not fail?

The answers to these questions simply give you insight into your most important values in life. If you really took the time to list 20 or more answers, you might have found some things you enjoy doing that you haven't participated in for a long time. One of your answers could be something you're passionate about that you can use as a business idea. It might be another position within a company or your own company.

If you can't figure it out now, put the three pages away and try this exercise again in a week. Be sure to change your surroundings next time. Sit in a comfortable spot with no interruptions. Try it a third time if you have to.

Wealth Warning

Remember that no matter what you do in life, you will always reap what you sow. Therefore, in your journey towards wealth, make sure your work helps others or improves the world in some way. If not, your efforts will eventually backfire and reverse the wealth-building process.

Take the Time to Make Good, Educated Decisions

The wealthiest people I know are good decision makers. They don't procrastinate or live in denial. They take the time to identify all the issues, research the alternatives, and select the best answer. They also look carefully at all the possible consequences of each decision. They list the pros and cons, take time to think about all the options, and finally ask themselves, "What is the worst thing that can happen?" If they can accept the worst possible outcome, they press forward. If not, they hold back. They understand *zero-based thinking,* which I will cover later in more detail. These are the keys to making educated decisions.

Discipline

The clients I have who built their wealth from the ground up have a certain discipline that helps them adhere to the simple habits necessary to build wealth. Climbing the social ladder is unimportant to them. They focus instead on what they are passionate about.

Discipline is simply a subconscious habit that is established by repetition. It's difficult to start a habit, but I'm told that after 21 days, it becomes part of your life. Here's an idea. For 21 days, take 15 minutes in the afternoon to plan tomorrow. This will give your brain time to think about what you have to do, which will help you get closer to your vision.

Patience

Wealthy people are patient and maintain a long-term outlook. They plan for the future, do what it takes to build wealth, and over time, they naturally know they will succeed. When they're faced with failure, they get right back on track again and go for it. They understand that wealth building is a journey, not a destination. It's a practice of patient habits that naturally produces riches.

The Least You Need to Know

- The best thing you can do to build your wealth is to save systematically every month and avoid debt.
- Delay those purchases you don't need by writing them down, filing them away, and not thinking about them for a week or month.
- Used cars and antique furniture can save you a fortune in commission and depreciation expense.
- To be really wealthy in life, you must have enough passion for what you do that you lose yourself in your work.
- Building wealth requires certain habits that are easy to implement and maintain.

Chapter 6

Building Wealth as an Employee

In This Chapter

- Getting the job you've always wanted
- Finding out what you really enjoy doing
- Developing a job proposal
- Maximizing income while working for others
- Buying your company's stock

If you have a high-level of excitement about what you do, you will be the best at it and people will want to hire you. Every employer in your field will want to have you around, and they might be willing to pay you a lot of money to get you on their team. Enthusiasm is contagious and employers look for it. They know that's the one thing they can't teach. If they can find sincere enthusiasm, they can teach everything else. Some people are naturally enthusiastic and that's great.

However, if you put a naturally enthusiastic person in a job they hate, you kill the enthusiasm. Therefore, to maintain your enthusiasm and get paid what you're worth, you must enjoy your work. It may take some time to figure it out, but in order to maximize your salary, you have to be good at what you do. As I said in the last chapter, to be good—I mean really good—at what you do, you have to be passionate about it. To be passionate, you have to love what you're doing.

How to Get Your Dream Job

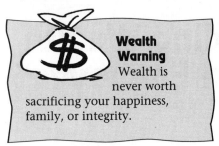

> **Wealth Warning**
> Wealth is never worth sacrificing your happiness, family, or integrity.

Many people live their lives in frustration and unhappiness working at jobs they despise and for people they don't respect. They stay in this self-imposed prison, locked in by their own fear of change, their inflexible standard of living, or procrastination. Often it takes something dramatic or life threatening to break them out. What they don't realize is that this eats away at their self-confidence and self-worth. Don't let this happen to you.

Three Questions Revisited

If you don't know what you like to do, or you lack the vision or ability to see yourself advancing from your current position, don't get discouraged. That's a common problem that you can solve, and here's how to solve it. Go back again to the three questions in Chapter 5 in the section titled, "A Passion for What You Do." Follow the instructions and list your answers. If you have already done this, try it again. Your answers will give you insight into what you are the most passionate about. Find something you can focus on that will make you money.

If you think you can't make money doing what you love, you might be right. If nothing else, you could write a book about it. As I said, if you are passionate enough about your work, you will be the best at it and people will want to be a part of your world. If you are passionate about painting, then focus your time and energy on being the best painter you can be. A high school student asked me recently if I thought he should get a real job or continue pursuing his real love, which was painting in oils. I said both, but I also said that he should focus most of his attention on painting. People love art and are often willing to pay big money for it. Several friends of mine are now professional artists. They took the hobby they were the most passionate about and made it into a business. One of them travels the world and sells his paintings to people in many different countries. One of his paintings recently sold in an auction for over $2,500! His wife manages his business affairs and schedules his appearances. What a great idea. No matter what your passion is, find a way to make money doing it.

Do You Enjoy What You Do Now?

Take some time to answer the question, "Do you enjoy what you do now?" Here are a few more that might help you decide:

- Do you find yourself stressed out on Sunday night before work on Monday?
- Do you have a vision of what you want in life?
- Is your current job part of that vision?
- Do you see yourself working at your present job for a long time?
- Does your employer treat you with respect?
- Is your job a stepping stone for what you really want to do?
- Do you have a plan for the next step?

Treasure Tip
One of the most common characteristics of happy wealthy people is their attitude every Sunday night before work. Most of them enjoy their work so much that they don't know the difference between a weekday or weekend night.

Your answers should tell you whether or not you are in the right job now. If you're not, why waste your time, your life, or the money you could be making? Develop a plan and move on.

The Perfect Day at Work

Next, find an hour of peace and quiet where you can think clearly. Take a piece of paper and write a vision of you at work doing what you love to do. Title it, "The Perfect Day At Work." Make sure you have no interruptions and let your imagination run. Don't worry about grammar, spelling, or order. Just write whatever comes to your mind. Get as specific as you can. Imagine yourself in your dream job doing exactly what you love to do. Where are you? Describe your surroundings, the people you work with, your boss, and the company. Fill at least one page if not several.

Once you complete this exercise, take some more time to brainstorm how you can make this dream a reality. Don't accept defeat immediately by saying, "This is only a dream. I can't really do this." This is a self-imposed limiting thought. If you can think it and believe in it, it's possible. But if you don't believe in your vision, you'll never get there. Brainstorm for a minute on how you can make this dream a reality.

Once you finish brainstorming, design a plan to get there. If the dream is really worthwhile, it will take some time to accomplish it. But if it's what you really want, you won't mind the effort it takes to get there.

Looking at Your Options

Now that you have a better idea of what's important to you, think about all your options. They are unlimited. I can think of four basic directions you can go:

1. Stay with your present employer and design a job proposal to move into the position you want or a new position that might not even exist.
2. Look into other companies or employers within your industry who might appreciate your work and give you more opportunity. Find the best firm in the industry and submit a job proposal.
3. Study other fields of interest. Find the best companies or employers in that industry and submit a job proposal.
4. Start your own company. We'll discuss this in Part 3.

Each option involves some homework on your part. For now, focus on role models and job proposals.

Go Find a Role Model

Spend some time identifying the people who do what you want to do. Then find the very best in the business. Ask everyone you know in that field, "Who's the best at this?" Find at least three people who are successful at what you want to do. If you can, find out in advance what makes them different or special. Call these people or write them a letter. First, compliment them by saying, "I've been told that you are one of the best (whatever) in the country." Compliment them further by mentioning what you think makes them so special and unique. They will be impressed with what you know. Second, tell them that you are very enthusiastic about learning more about their industry and business. Third, ask them if you can talk with them about their success for a few minutes. Just say, "I'd like to hear your story. Would you have a minute to meet with me now or next week (over the phone or in person) for a few minutes?" If you compliment these people (without overdoing it) and ask them about their story, most of them will meet with you.

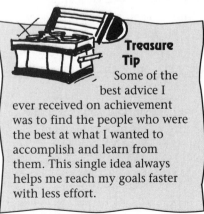

> **Treasure Tip**
> Some of the best advice I ever received on achievement was to find the people who were the best at what I wanted to accomplish and learn from them. This single idea always helps me reach my goals faster with less effort.

When you do meet with them, ask them specific questions and let them talk. Here are some questions to choose from. Don't forget to take notes.

- ➤ What do you love about your work?
- ➤ What do you dislike about your work?

- What are your biggest concerns each day?
- What do you focus most of your time on?
- Describe a typical day.
- If you had to do it all over again, what path would you take?
- Where would you start?
- Would you share with me your five- or ten-year vision?

Now take some time and review their answers. Did you find what you expected? Are you still as excited as you were? After the appointment, be sure to write them a thank-you note. You might even mention in the letter the one thing that excited you the most. They will appreciate your attention to detail and welcome another contact from you, which could prove to be valuable later.

The Job Proposal

This is an idea I came up with years ago to help my brother get the job he wanted. It's a simple idea that can get you the job you want. The first step in building the job proposal is to know what you really want to do. The job for which you are making the proposal must be your dream job, or a stepping stone toward your dream job.

Second, your vision must match the vision of the company or the duties of the position you want. To ensure this, go interview the company or supervisor for that position. Study everything you can and make sure this is where you want to be.

Third, describe the position you want on paper and be as specific as you can. What are you willing to do? What are you willing to be responsible for? What are you willing to accept in salary and benefits?

Fourth, design the employment (job) proposal. I have included a copy of the proposal I helped my brother design. He is an electrical engineer who wanted to work for a small software company. He interviewed for the job first and was told they were going to hire someone else. He was discouraged, but still wanted the job. We sat down and came up with a job proposal that he submitted later that week. A week later, he got the job.

There are no rules here and your proposal will be completely different from his, but I thought that an example might help you design yours.

Wealth Warning

The job proposal is a very unique and powerful tool. If you use this just to get a job, with no attention to your values or interests, you may get a job you eventually dislike. Before using this technique, make sure you have an idea as to what you enjoy doing.

Employment Proposal For XYZ Company

I. Why I want to work for XYZ Company.

A. I want to work for a small, growing company.

B. More opportunity for growth and experience.

C. Opportunity to work in a team-oriented atmosphere.

D. I admire the management's philosophy and vision.

II. What am I able to offer XYZ Company?

A. Sales assistance in the marketing department as you acquire new clients.

B. Project assistance.

C. Hardware design, development, and installation.

D. Programming assistance in producing the best software available.

E. Troubleshooting and maintaining the highest-quality service in the industry.

III. What I expect to be paid initially.

A. Hourly pay of $X per hour.

B. $X per hour after forty hours in a one week period.

IV. Available working hours.

A. Regular working hours (8:00 A.M. to 5:00 P.M.).

B. After hours.

C. Weekends.

D. Moment's notice.

V. Future compensation expected.

A. To be negotiated in two months.

B. Subject to the value you think I can add to your business. (You could be more specific here if you want.)

C. Bonuses based upon a percentage of net profits.

D. Full benefits including health insurance and retirement plan.

VI. Trial period.

A. Two months.

B. If things do not work out, I will walk away with no questions asked.

VII. Vision for the future: My goal is to be the chief engineer for XYZ Company and, if possible, stockholder/partner in the firm. I would like to develop new product services that compliment existing ones and participate in strategic planning and development for XYZ.

Conclusion: The best thing that can happen is that you get a good engineer with education and experience that adds more value to your company than you pay him. The worst thing that can happen is that you get a good electrical engineer at an annualized salary of $XX,000 ($X per hour) for two months.

The proposal should be done on a word processor and printed on bond paper. It doesn't have to be fancy. It just has to look good and use correct grammar and spelling. Be sure to present this proposal in person and go over it if you can. If you cannot get a face-to-face meeting, then send it registered mail. Then call within two days of receipt. Don't ask what your contact thinks of your proposal. Instead say, "I'd like to stop by next week on Wednesday. Would 10 in the morning be good, or would 2 in the afternoon be better for you?"

If there's no interest, go to the company's competitor and offer the same proposal. Don't waste your efforts on someone who doesn't appreciate your enthusiasm and talent.

How to Maximize Your Income while Working for Others

The one thing I learned while working for others is that salary is always negotiable. The second thing I learned was that if I was good at what I did, there was always another company out there willing to pay me what I was worth. At least I had to convince my current employer of this fact. If I was successful, I would be paid what I was worth. If I was unsuccessful, I moved on to an employer who recognized my talent and the value I could add to the company. Therefore, you should always make it a habit to do some research into the salary range of your current job. What are other people in your field getting paid? How do these salaries compare to yours? Be sure to take into account the living expenses of the cities these people live in. For example, everything else being equal, someone in New York City will naturally be paid a higher salary than someone in Little Rock, Arkansas.

If you think you are worth more than what you are currently paid, but you think that getting a raise is impossible, I have got an idea for you. Don't ask for a raise. Raises are the traditional means to higher pay, but they are limiting and often obscure in nature. Most companies don't even have a written policy on how raises are given. Many employers don't realize that this can lead to a lot of disenchantment among the employees.

The better alternative is a what I call performance-based bonuses, which are bonuses usually based upon a percentage of a company's net income. The benchmark that measures the bonus must be a net result of income and expenses. If they are based solely on gross income, employees pay little attention to expenses. But, if they are based on net income after expenses, something magical happens. Employees begin to consider the cost of everything. Your employer may not understand this concept.

I know this from experience. Until recently, I did bonus my employees on gross income. The day I changed the benchmark to net income, the entire atmosphere changed. My employees began to act like shareholders and started paying much more attention to the costs of everything. We'll get into more detail about performance-based bonus programs in Part 3, but my point is that if your company does not have a performance-based bonus program, ask for it. Convince your boss that if you and the other employees were paid a bonus based upon net profits of the company, you would all pay more attention to reducing expenses and increasing gross income. This means that the company would make more money that would more than pay for the bonuses. If your company does not start one, put together a proposal. Include in that proposal all the benefits, which include:

- More productivity because employees will be more motivated to produce.
- Employees will pay more attention to the cost of everything.
- Employees will be more efficient.
- The company's capacity for work will increase.
- Employees will be willing to do more.
- Decreased expenses.
- Increased income.

Note, however, that this might be difficult to do if you work for a large company with policies already in place.

How to Maximize Savings while Working for Others

Can you get to Level 3 or 4 without starting your own company? Absolutely! I've met hundreds of people who've done it. If you want to build serious wealth, whether you work for yourself or someone else, the key is to live well within your means so you can save money systematically each month. At each pay period, a certain percentage of your income must go to your investment account, retirement plan, and savings account. It's even better if this takes place automatically at the time you get your pay check.

If you are not doing this now, or haven't made the decision to do this, then stop right now and make the decision. Read this out loud: "I am a saver and a good steward of my money and financial future. I save a significant percentage of my income each month, which I invest for my future." If you don't make this a habit now, you may never reach Wealth Level 3 or 4. You might have an excuse now to wait, but you may always have an excuse.

Maximize Your Contributions to a 401(k) or SEP— The Last Tax Shelters

A 401(k) or Simplified Employee Pension (SEP or SEP-IRA) plans are great ways to save money systematically. They are both accounts into which you can deposit a percentage of your salary before tax. Your money can then be invested in stocks and mutual funds within the accounts. The taxes you would normally pay on the income are deferred until you withdraw the money after you retire. Plus, the capital gains taxes you would normally pay on the growth are deferred until you start making withdrawals. The combined effect of compound growth and tax deferral can be very powerful in building your portfolio.

Words of the Wealthy

401(k)s and SEPs are some of the types of qualified plans that will allow employees to deposit part of their own salary into the plan. The deposit is made pre-tax and the account grows tax deferred. Each employee has his/her own individual account in which he/she can select from a number of different investment alternatives.

A qualified plan like a profit-sharing plan, 401(k) or SEP-IRA is one of the last true tax shelters. The term qualified means that they meet the IRS rules for tax deferral both on the deposits as well as the earnings. These are retirement plans or investment accounts which are qualified under IRS law to be sheltered from any taxes until withdrawal at retirement age, which begins 59 1/2. They could have chosen 60 or even 59, but for some unknown reason, 59 1/2 is the established age after which you can begin withdrawing money from a qualified plan. The plan grows tax deferred until the money is withdrawn, which means that all capital gains, interest, and dividends can be reinvested. There is a 10 percent penalty for early withdrawal of funds, which is levied on top of the taxes that also have to be paid. Therefore, it is usually smarter to borrow money rather than make an early withdrawal. Almost all qualified plans will allow you to roll-over your account tax-free into an IRA once you retire or terminate your employment. This will allow your money to continue growing tax deferred until withdrawal. Partial withdraws become mandatory once you become 70 1/2 and are based upon life expectancy tables. Examples of qualified plans include SEP, 401(k), profit sharing, money purchase, and defined benefit plans.

Treasure Tip

Most of my clients have a net worth that exceeds $1 million. How did they do it? Did they sell a business? Did they inherit money? No! The most common characteristic among all these clients is that they all systematically contributed to a 401(k), SEP, or similar type plan.

If you do have a 401(k) or SEP, make sure it offers a large number of investment alternatives. For example, the most common missing alternative in a

401(k) plan is a foreign investment fund. If you want additional alternatives like this added to your plan, ask for them. If you are put off, do your own homework and find out what it would take to get the alternative added.

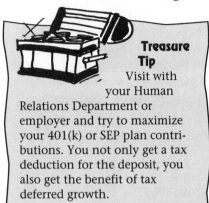

> **Treasure Tip**
> Visit with your Human Relations Department or employer and try to maximize your 401(k) or SEP plan contributions. You not only get a tax deduction for the deposit, you also get the benefit of tax deferred growth.

If your employer doesn't offer either an SEP or 401(k), encourage the employer to start one. Most employers think that a retirement plan costs too much money or that it involves putting extra money in for everyone. The 401(k) and SEP are different. The SEP costs almost nothing to start. Just go to a discount brokerage firm and get the paperwork you need.

Another wonderful feature of 401(k)s and SEPs is that they can be set up to take money out of your paycheck before you receive it. This means that saving money becomes systematic and requires no extra effort. It's the perfect portfolio builder.

Get into Another Qualified Defined Contribution Plan

There are other types of retirement plans that are different from the 401(k) type where the employer can put an extra contribution into a tax-deferred account on your behalf. These plans are known as defined-contribution and defined-benefit plans. These can be somewhat complicated but they are a great company benefit. If your company doesn't offer these, you might want to suggest it.

Maximize Savings in Your Investment Account

Even though you might have maximized your 401(k) or SEP contributions, you should continue to maintain your own investment account deposits. Look back at Chapter 5, where I discussed several different ways to save money so you can invest it. You should always continue saving in as many ways as you can.

> **Wealth Warning**
> The real risk in maximizing 401(k) or SEP plan deposits is higher tax rates at the time of withdrawal. If your heart believes that tax rates will be higher tomorrow, then investing after tax dollars outside of the plan may be the best alternative.

Now you need a place to put that money you save. Where should it be invested? If you work for someone else and you want to get to Wealth Level 3 or 4, you have to invest in stocks (also known as equities). This includes the money in your retirement plans and investment accounts. It may also include privately held stock of your own company or your employer's company. The stock market is one of the most powerful tools you can use to truly grow your portfolio and beat inflation. Don't overlook ownership of your employer's stock as an investment alternative. My research has convinced me that in the last century, more fortunes have been built with stocks, both private and publicly traded, than with real estate or any other asset.

In the next chapter, I will cover more on the benefits of owning equities of publicly traded companies. For now take a look at the company you work for currently. Would you ever want to be a shareholder?

Treasure Tip

If you want to build wealth, you must consider investing in something that can produce a double-digit return. The most common investment with this potential is stock in a fast growing company. There is risk, but your exposure can be reduced by spreading your investment among many different companies.

Buying Stock in the Company You Work For

First, before you even consider doing this, look back at the answers to the questions in the earlier section titled "Do You Enjoy What You Do Now?" If you answered favorably and you plan on staying with this company for a long time, then buying their stock might not be a bad idea. You also need to consider your employer's earnings growth potential. Is your company making any money? If the company's earnings aren't growing, you may want to avoid their stock.

Second, you have to consider the size of the company and the availability of the stock itself. If the company is small and owned by a few people (that is, if it's owned privately rather than traded on a stock exchange), then it may be difficult if not impossible to become a shareholder. You might have to convince the owners to let you buy shares or take shares instead of salary or bonus. Your employer might say "no" but it won't hurt to ask. Remember, if your company is small and experiencing normal cash-flow problems, your employer might welcome the idea. They may prefer to pay part of your salary or bonus in stock.

If you work for a large company that has stock publicly traded on an exchange, this concept becomes much easier to do. Whether your company is small or large, or has closely held or publicly traded stock, it might be available through an employee stock ownership plan or ESOP. ESOP's are becoming very popular now as employers begin to see the benefits of employees being shareholders. The plan issues shares to its employees each month or year based upon their salary or profits of the company. ESOP's can also be part of a retirement plan, which means the gains and dividends can be tax deferred until retirement. It's a great idea if you want to own your company's stock. If not, don't participate. One of the most successful ESOP plans ever was Wal-Mart's employee stock-purchasing plan. This plan made hundreds of their employees millionaires who might otherwise have retired with a little pension and a small Social Security check.

The Least You Need to Know

- In order to be happy and get paid what you are worth, you have to have passion and enthusiasm for what you do.
- Consider all your employment options, which include staying where you are, looking at other similar companies, looking at other industries, or starting your own business.
- Decide what you want to do, find role models, and build a job proposal that can help you get there.
- Maximize your income at work, save as much money as you can in tax-deferred qualified plans, and buy stocks.

Part 2
Achieving Wealth Level 3 by Taming the Portfolio Beast

If you know how to get to Wealth Levels 1 and 2, then Wealth Level 3 is easy to accomplish. All you really need to know is how to properly manage an investment portfolio. Your portfolio can be like a wild animal. Occasionally it will seem like it's turning against you, especially when the market takes a dive. However, if you know how to tame this beast, you'll sleep better and build wealth faster.

First, you need to be able to recognize the investment tools that should be avoided. Second, you need to understand the investment tools that will help you achieve your objectives. Third, you should learn how to hire professional help. Fourth, when you're ready to take your first step into the investment world, you need to know what to look for. Fifth, in order to be your own successful portfolio manager, you must have six key fundamentals. Sixth, you need to know how the investment cycle works. Seventh, there are ten investment tactics you should know. Eighth, you must know how to keep your investment-related expenses and mistakes to a minimum. Ninth, there are certain laws of investing that might come in handy. Tenth, it might also be helpful to know the most common mistakes made by investors. I discuss all of these in this part.

Chapter 7

The Portfolio Tools You Need To Avoid

In This Chapter

- Why most investors continue to use bad tools
- What happens if you use the wrong tools
- Identify the three killers of wealth
- The worst investment tools
- What your broker doesn't want you to know

Have you ever noticed in every nice neighborhood, there's always one house that just doesn't fit? Maybe the builder used poor quality materials, wrong tools, or just did a poor job altogether. Whatever the case, you know the end result is a money pit, and every home owner's nightmare is to own one of these. I look at portfolios the same way. I meet these wonderful people who have built their portfolios from scratch. Many of them have been built correctly and only need an adjustment or two. But, a good number of them are just waiting to cave in. I call these "investment pits." The investor usually doesn't have a clue as to the risks and costs they're incurring.

Before you can build anything, you need to know the proper tools to use. Whether it's a house, building, or investment portfolio, if you use the wrong tools and materials, eventually you're going to have problems. Unfortunately, you may not know you've made a mistake until it's too late. The tools I'll be discussing in this chapter are all financial tools, most of which are investment vehicles used to maximize a portfolio's total return. I've met thousands of investors over the last 11 years, and a great many of them were using the wrong tools to accomplish their goal. These tools were either too expensive, mediocre in quality, unsuitable, or all of the above. Why is this the case? I explain the answer in this chapter and show you how to not make the same mistake.

> **Words of the Wealthy**
> A secondary market is any market where previously issued securities are traded. The New York Stock Exchange (NYSE) is the best known example. Here investors can buy and sell stocks from each other through the designated traders on the floor of the exchange.

> **Wealth Warning**
> The biggest investment nightmares I've observed in the last 10 years seem to be the result of complicated tax shelters, limited partnerships, bad stock tips, life insurance products, or futures contracts. As long as there are unsuspecting investors and commission-based sales people, the nightmares will continue. The best defense is knowledge.

Reasons Why People Use the Wrong Tools

One of the first keys to building wealth is knowing the correct investment tools, which means you also need to know the tools to avoid. It might be appropriate to start with what you should avoid. Improper tools are the most common killers of wealth. If that's true, then why don't people do something about it? Well, as I said before, most of them have no idea there's a problem. Here are some of the reasons people get themselves into the wrong investment tool.

They Don't Do Their Homework

The first reason is that most investors simply do not do enough homework before they invest their money. I've met hundreds of investors who spend more time planning a vacation each year than they do planning or researching their own investment portfolio. This is scary. Maybe they know the basics, but they justify quick investment decisions with their limited knowledge.

They Take Advice from Commission-Based Salespeople

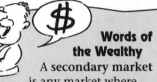

The second most common reason investors use the wrong investment tools is that they buy their investments from commission-based sales people. Not all commission-based brokers are bad, but there is a conflict of interest here. If you are an experienced investor, understand the details of the market, and how brokers charge for their services, then you probably know how to work with a broker. You use their research, you both come up with ideas, and then make a decision. You also know how these folks are paid and you know commissions are negotiable. However, if you do not fully understand the details of the market, why would you buy from someone who gets paid a commission every time you buy or sell an investment? Since their paycheck depends upon you making transactions, their natural motivation is to promote transactions and not performance. If they are paid a commission on each trade, can you really count on the investment to be in your best interest most of the time? You have to ask yourself this question: What motivates the commission-based broker?

Toward the end of each month, brokers all across the country have to make their commission quota. What do you think is going through their minds during the last week of every month? I've been there. I was a broker for almost five years. If you deal with a commission-based broker, take a look at all your trades for the last year. Are most of them made during the last half of the month? Before you make another investment decision with a commission-based broker, read the next chapter on how to select an investment advisor. One thing I can almost guarantee is that a commission-based salesperson will ignore non-commission-based alternatives that may benefit you.

That Reminds Me...

The biggest problem I see with commission-based brokers are the hidden fees they charge. These are fees you might never find or know about. Before you buy any investment from a commission-based broker, have them describe in detail every expense that is involved in the investment. Then read the prospectus. If the broker left anything out, stay away from the investment. If the broker says there is no commission or the commission is built in, ask exactly how much it is. Demand an answer. If you can't understand all the fees and commissions, leave it alone.

They Don't Check for Bias and Conflicts of Interest

Many people use the wrong investment tool because they don't check for bias before they make a decision. They mistake marketing information for good advice. I believe that approximately 95 percent of what you read and hear about investing in your lifetime is marketing related. Most of the investment information available today is biased and does not portray the whole story. Your job as an investor is to uncover the truth to help your portfolio. If you can't find substantial unbiased evidence to support your investment choice, I suggest you keep looking, be patient, or move on to something else.

Why is bias so important? If the person is paid by a company to promote its investment products, they may have a one-track mind and focus only on the product. The end result is that bias tends to ignore the alternatives and drive investors into decisions based on limited thinking. Unfortunately, most investment decisions are made this way and knowledge of the mistake may go unrecognized for years. Often, the undoing of the mistake involves a penalty or exit commission, which in itself tends to further prolong the mistake. Investors don't like paying penalties. They would rather wait and keep the mistake alive until there's no penalty. It seems ironic, but I've seen this happen hundreds of times. If it's not a penalty, it's the absence of a secondary market that keeps the mistake alive. A secondary market enables you to sell the investment at a later date. If there is no secondary market and you have no buyers, you end up with a worthless investment, which is an even worse mistake. Therefore, recognizing the bias before taking advice can reduce your chances of making a mistake.

Words of the Wealthy

All mutual funds have a **prospectus**, which is the fund's disclosure document. This multi-page document explains in great detail all the aspects of the mutual fund, such as fees, commission charges, fund manager restrictions, and the objective of the fund. Newly issued stocks and bonds also have prospectuses.

Wealth Warning

I hosted a radio show titled, "Arkansas' Moneytalk" for three years and was never paid a penny by any fund or investment product I suggested on the show, but not all investment shows are the same. Beware of the TV and radio talk shows on investing with hosts who get paid to promote mutual funds, insurance products, or any investment. Most listeners don't understand the conflict of interest inherent in these programs.

The End Results of Using the Wrong Investment Tools

The end result of these bad tools is an investor with an unsuitable, expensive, or mediocre investment. The first seems like the most common.

Unsuitability of the Investment

Investors sit in front of me everyday with portfolios filled with unsuitable investments. Usually it is one stock that represents a huge chunk of their net worth. In Arkansas, it's Wal-Mart. In Michigan, it's Ford or GM. I can't call these people investors. I call them speculators or gamblers. If something went wrong with that one company, their net worth would take a big hit. If they really understood the risks, they would sell at least most of it immediately.

Even after I explain the risks, do you know how they justify hanging on? They say, "Well, I'll wait until the price comes back up to my original purchase price." Or they'll say, "The capital gains tax is too large." This is crazy. My next question is always, "If you had the value of this investment today in cash, would you buy this investment?" Their answer is almost always, "No", or "No way." I then tell them they ought to consider selling the investment because their subconscious is telling them something. This is referred to later in the book as "zero-based thinking." The reality of the risk, unfortunately, sets in too late. People may say they can handle risk, but they don't know the truth until the market takes a big fall.

Unknown Expenses

The second end result is a portfolio filled with unknown expenses that eat away at the profits, if any are even made. This is what I call slow portfolio death. I personally believe that over 50 percent of the individual portfolios in the U.S. are experiencing slow death. This percentage is beginning to decrease because investors are finally beginning to learn more about all the charges investment companies levy on their clients and shareholders. Publications like *The Wall Street Journal* and *Barrons* do teach investors most of the traps out there, but most novice investors don't read these publications.

Mediocrity

The third end result of using the wrong investment tool is mediocrity. Again, most investors don't know their portfolio performance is mediocre. Often, they don't even know how their own portfolio is actually performing. They get a monthly statement showing the dollar amount of change from last month, but that's it. Brokerage firms normally do not illustrate portfolio performance for their clients. I've always wondered why. It would be so easy to do. If my company can do it, why can't theirs? Instead of waiting for your brokerage firm to measure your percentage performance, learn how to do it yourself or get someone to do it for you. Your CPA might help.

The Tools You Need to Stay Away from

Some investment tools are good, and some are bad. If you know what tools to avoid, you can save yourself from expensive, unsuitable investments and significantly reduce the chances of mediocrity in your portfolio.

Proprietary Investment Products

Proprietary investment products are "packaged" securities that are sold by brokerage firms, usually in the form of unit investment trusts, limited partnerships, and mutual funds. They are underwritten or managed by the brokerage firm that offers them, and they are your portfolio's primary enemy. They will slowly squeeze your portfolio to death through unnecessary fees or bad investment performance. There are so many different possible conflicts of interest involved with these securities. For example, the manager might feed all his trades to one firm. If this is true, there are two big possible conflicts of interest. First, the manager might not be getting you the best commission rate available on the securities he's buying for you. Second, the brokerage firm could be filling the orders for the manager and adding on additional points to the spread that makes the stocks purchased more expensive. This is especially true with over-the-counter stocks. Run away from these blood sucking investments.

Heavily Loaded Mutual Funds

A mutual fund is an investment company that raises money by offering shares of the company to investors. The money is then invested into a diversified portfolio of securities for the benefit of the shareholder. Shares can be purchased directly from the mutual fund or through brokerage firms. The money from the purchase or redemption goes directly in or out of the portfolio. If a full-service brokerage firm offers a mutual fund to its clients, there is a *load* or commission involved. It may be hard to find without a prospectus, but it's there. This commission, or load, pays the salesperson and brokerage firm offering the fund. You can always find the commission charges of a fund listed in the first few pages of the prospectus. This is how mutual funds can be categorized according to the commission they charge to purchase or own the fund:

- Heavily loaded mutual funds—over 6 percent.
- Medium loaded funds—4 to 6 percent.
- Low load funds—2 to 4 percent.
- No-load funds—0 percent.

All mutual funds have a management fee that is paid to the manager of the fund. However, not all funds have commission charges. Legally, a mutual fund can charge up to 8.5 percent in commissions at the date of purchase. If you paid an 8.5 percent commission on a $1,000 mutual fund purchase, the end result would be an investment worth $915 ($1,000 × .085 = $85). In order to just break even with your original investment, you will first have to make a 9.29 percent return. I can't think of any investment worth that much commission.

Words of the Wealthy

A **full-service brokerage** firm is a firm that offers its clients securities as well as advice. The firm is compensated by commissions that are paid at the time transactions are made. A discount brokerage firm offers the same selection of securities, but because they do not offer advice, their commissions are usually lower than the full service firm's rates.

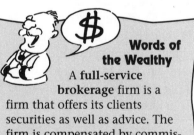

Killer B Funds

Often the load or commission is hidden from the investor, and unless he carefully reads the prospectus and understands it, he may never know how much he's really paying to own the fund each year. This practice of hiding the load has now become the newest and biggest investment trap in the investment industry. Back in the 1980s when no-load funds began to get popular, brokerage firms around the country came up with a defense mechanism using part of the investment company regulation code called 12b1. This regulation allows mutual funds to charge a fee in addition to the management fee for such things as "marketing expenses, distribution expenses, or sales expenses." In reality, these expenses disguise the commission, which is either paid in advance to the salesperson, each quarter, or a combination of both. Table 7.1 provides an example of fees for a municipal bond fund I found. Here's how it works.

Table 7.1 The Killer B Fund Expense Chart

Back Load	12b1 Fee	Management Fee
6%	1%	.35%
5%	1%	.35%
4%	1%	.35%
3%	1%	.35%
2%	1%	.35%
1%	1%	.35%
0%	1%	.35%

As you can see in Table 7.1, the original 12b1 funds had a declining back load that disappeared after a six-year period. If the investor sold the shares during the first year, there would be a six percent commission or back-end load due at the time of sale. If the investor sold the shares during the second year, there would be a five percent commission, and so on. After six years, there was no commission to sell the shares. It seemed that after six years, the fund became somewhat of a no-load fund. The only expense to pay seemed to be the management fee, which in this case is .35 percent. However, each year there is an additional 12b1 charge of 1 percent. This 12b1 fee can be higher or lower, but the average is 1 percent. Therefore, it didn't matter when you sold the fund, you were going to pay a six percent commission whether you waited six years or two months. If you waited six years, you still pay six years of 12b1 expenses. The fund becomes a killer since the 12b1 fees continue after the sixth year. This concept is only offered by brokerage firms and mutual funds that have little empathy for their clients and shareholders.

It's bad enough to disguise the commission in the 12b1 fee, but it should be a crime to charge it beyond a six-year period.

UITs

Unit Investment Trusts, or UITs, include municipal (bond) investment trusts, equity (stock) investment trusts, and corporate (bond) investment trusts. They are sold in $1,000 units just like a bond. These investments are similar to traditional mutual funds in that money is raised initially by selling units to investors and is then invested according to the prospectus of the UIT for the benefit of the unit holder. What makes UITs different from traditional mutual funds is the method of investment management used. UITs are passively managed, as opposed to traditional mutual funds which are actively managed. Passive management means that once the securities are purchased, they are not traded or sold until the maturing or ending date of the trust. At the time of the ending date of the trusts, all the securities are sold and the proceeds are dispersed to the unit holders.

If you examine them carefully, UITs don't offer a lot of advantages to the unit holder. They might offer diversification for small amounts of money and enable the unit holder to buy securities that might be difficult to buy, but that's about it. Since they are passively managed, the portfolio remains static and cannot be maneuvered to take advantage of changing market trends. The fees are usually extensive and are not talked about except in the prospectus. Normally there is an up-front commission to pay, plus a management fee. Why would you pay a management fee for a passive (unmanaged) portfolio?

Limited Partnerships

These are the real killers of wealth. They're not as popular as they were in the 70s, but they are still around. I personally have met hundreds of investors who have lost their entire fortunes in limited partnerships. The chain of events usually unfolds like this. The investor buys a limited partnership from a broker or advisor. The first problem that's encountered is a commission charge of unknown proportion. Unfortunately, the commission is not indicated on the confirmation slip you get in the mail and it may not be clearly stated in the disclosure document either. You can't see it, but believe me, it's ugly.

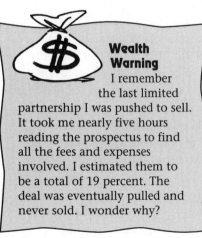

> **Wealth Warning**
> I remember the last limited partnership I was pushed to sell. It took me nearly five hours reading the prospectus to find all the fees and expenses involved. I estimated them to be a total of 19 percent. The deal was eventually pulled and never sold. I wonder why?

The second problem encountered is the pricing of the limited partnership on the brokerage statement each month or quarter. This price is usually held at the original purchase price, which is total garbage. After you purchase the partnership, you never know what your units are actually worth because there is no secondary market available. You might not ever know the true value of your units. If you did, it would make you sick.

The third problem occurs when you decide to sell the limited partnership. That's when you find there is no place to sell it and no one to sell to. The only way you can sell is to accept the price a "scrap yard" will offer you. A *scrap yard* is a company that researches limited partnerships around the country. They make their living by offering limited partners 20 – 50 cents on the dollar for their units. They are scavengers. They will buy the units and attempt to sell them at a higher price later or dismantle the whole partnership and sell off the partnership's individual securities, land, and so on. There are certainly exceptions to this rule. Not all limited partnerships are bad. The most common exception would be a private venture that just so happens to be beneficial to all parties. If you are considering a limited partnership and are well aware of all aspects of the venture, then by all means explore this as an investment. However, if you are approached by someone offering you a limited partnership in a venture you do not understand, chances are you'll be better off by running away immediately.

Initial Public Offerings of Closed-End Funds

A closed-end fund is a unique type of investment company or mutual fund that issues a set number of shares, after which no additional shares can be sold. The fund theoretically "closes" the door and manages the money. If you purchase closed-end shares when they are initially offered to the public, your money goes directly into the fund to be managed. If you want to sell your shares later, you must do this in a secondary market. Most closed-end funds can be sold on the New York Stock Exchange (NYSE).

Closed-end funds by their nature and function can be very attractive with one big exception; when they are offered initially to the public. Just like a stock, closed-end funds are underwritten by a brokerage firm. That firm is paid by marking up the shares of the fund above their net asset value. This mark-up is normally about 8.5 percent and is not felt until a few weeks after the underwriting is completed. Why a few weeks? Well, the firm underwriting the issue holds back some shares for it's own account and attempts to keep the price of the issue at least as high as the initial public offering price. Since the firm only buys so many shares, they can only keep this up so long. After the initial public offering, the shares become available on the secondary market and their price usually falls back to approximately what the shares are actually

Words of the Wealthy

The **net asset value** of a fund is the actual true value of each share of a mutual fund. This is calculated by dividing the total value of the fund by the number of shares outstanding.

worth, which is the net asset value. Therefore, there is usually little reason to buy a closed-end fund until it hits the secondary market.

> **That Reminds Me...**
>
> An initial public offering or stock underwriting is the process by which a brokerage firm or investment banker promises a company a certain amount of money for the securities they issue. The brokerage firm hires people to sell the securities and takes the risk of not being able to raise all the money promised. The brokerage firm is paid by marking up the shares before selling them. This is important to understand because many brokers explain this by saying, "The shares are offered net commission," which implies no commission. You better believe that if a broker is selling it, you're paying a commission.

Options

Options are marketable securities that give their owners the right but not the obligation to buy or sell a stated number of shares (usually 100) of a particular security, at a fixed price, within a predetermined time period. There are many different books published on this subject that go into great detail. Fortunately for both of us, this is not one of them! The one thing you need to understand is that they are complicated, involve a lot of risk, and are not worth any attention. What kind of risk am I talking about? You can lose 100 percent of your investment very quickly. I can tell you that I don't know anyone who made any significant money in the long-run using options. One of my first investment experiences involved a $1,500 option on gold. I lost every penny of it, but I learned two great lessons: Avoid options and don't always listen to investment advice from friends. No matter what your friends tell you, the risk in options is not worth the reward. The only possible exception is a strategy called selling covered calls. If you want to learn more, there are many other books available that can teach you about this technique.

Futures

A futures contract is a legal agreement in which a buyer promises to pay a seller some fixed price for a specified quantity of a particular good at some future date. The goods can be commodities or financial instruments such as treasury bills, or market indexes. These contracts are negotiable financial instruments that are bought and sold like stocks in a secondary market called commodity exchanges. Futures contracts are usually referred to as "futures" or "contracts." Just like options, the risk in futures is not worth the reward. You can lose more than 100 percent of your investment. Avoid futures like the plague.

Penny Stocks

Penny stocks are stocks that are initially offered to the public at a price of $1 or less and are traded primarily in the over-the-counter markets of Vancouver, Denver, and Salt Lake City. I've seen a few penny stocks trade as much as $10 or more, which seems very attractive, but this is the exception and not the rule. Penny stocks are the bastards of the investment industry. The brokerage houses that specialize in penny stocks are notorious for using fraudulent sales pitches. It is estimated that penny stock fraud costs U.S. investors $2 billion each year. The Securities and Exchange Commission came up with three primary warning signs of penny stock fraud.

- Unsolicited phone calls from brokers offering penny stocks.
- High-pressure sales tactics.
- The inability to sell the penny stock and receive cash.

Rumors and Hot Tips

It seems like every investor in the world has fallen victim to a rumor or hot tip. I certainly have. I get one almost every day. Rumors and hot tips are normally intended to show others at parties and meetings the brilliance of the person sharing them. The person might mean well by sharing the information hoping that others can profit too. However, what people don't realize is that these rumors and hot tips usually result in exactly the opposite of what they were intended to do. First, they can show the ignorance of the person sharing them. Second, if the information is garbage, the person receiving it may act on it and lose money. Avoid these in your wealth building program.

Insurance Products as Investments

Insurance products are not bad for what they are intended to be, but they are horrible if used for investment purposes alone. They became very popular in the 1980s when tax laws tightened and limited partnerships in real estate lost their tax savings appeal. Brokerage firms lost one of their most profitable sources of income. They could no longer make the big commissions they were paid by selling

Words of the Wealthy

An over-the-counter market is a secondary market where securities are traded by phone and computer. The NASDAQ market is the largest and most popular over-the-counter market.

the partnerships. Therefore, they had to find alternatives. They decided to focus on insurance products. Every major full-service brokerage firm bought or established an insurance company or at least an agreement with one. Soon brokers all over the country added insurance products to their quiver of investment arrows. Since the tax laws tightened, brokers and commission-based financial planners began selling insurance products such as fixed and variable annuities, as well as variable life insurance policies.

A variable life insurance policy can be a whole life or universal life insurance policy with a cash value and death benefit that varies in value according to the performance of a portfolio of mutual funds from which the policy holder can select. Typically these policies offer a stock fund, a bond fund, and a money-market fund.

> **Words of the Wealthy**
>
> A **fixed annuity** is a contract with a life insurance company whereby you give them a sum of money, and based on your age, life expectancy, and current interest rates, they calculate how much they'll send you each month for as long as you live. You decide when you want to receive payments, and until then, the money grows tax deferred.

They are described as mutual funds covered by a tax umbrella that allows them to grow tax deferred. The variable life insurance policy even allows the withdrawals to be completely tax free as long as the withdrawal is considered a loan against the policy. However, there are three primary problems with these investment products.

First, they are extremely expensive. You have to pay both the money management fees as well as the costs of the insurance. Second, the selection of mutual funds within these policies are usually very limited and usually mediocre. Third, these investments can become a ball and chain later in life. If you want your money back, you might have to pay an early withdrawal penalty to the insurance company. You might also have to pay the IRS a ten percent penalty if you withdraw money from an annuity before you become 59 1/2. Plus, you have to pay taxes on all your capital gains since the beginning if you terminate the policy. The variable life policy might offer tax free loans, but you have to keep the policy in tact for the rest of your life to keep them tax deferred.

> **Words of the Wealthy**
>
> A **variable annuity** works the same way a fixed annuity does, except its value and pay-out amount varies according to the performance of a portfolio of mutual funds from which the contract holder can select. Typically these policies offer a stock fund, a bond fund, and a money market fund.

If you really like the variable annuity idea, Fidelity, Vanguard, and Charles Schwab all have no-load variable annuities with the total average annual expenses of approximately 1.10 percent, which is much lower than the traditional loaded policies.

Variable life policies might be an excellent vehicle for estate planning, but not for investment purposes alone. We'll talk more about that later in Part 4.

Wrap Accounts

During the first five years in the investment business, I learned something very important. Out of all the wealthy people I had met, the best stewards of money were those who understood the importance of using other people's talents to manage their money. Most of them hired several individual money managers, which seemed very logical. Hiring several money managers provides more diversification than one single manager can provide. However, the problem with directly hiring several managers is that they can be expensive and time-consuming to fire.

Soon I saw that almost every full-service brokerage firm was coming out with a concept called the "wrap account." The wrap account concept works like this: A client fills out a questionnaire that measures risk tolerance, experience, and performance expectations. According to this measurement, the client is then shown two or three managers that match the client's measurement of risk tolerance, and so on. Most firms in the industry were using a list of approximately 17 money management firms. The minimum investment was $100,000 and once the client chose from the three managers in his corresponding risk level, the money was allocated among individual stocks and bonds within the client's own account. Each month, the client received a statement showing the securities the management firm had purchased as well as all the transactions. The annual fee for all this was 3 percent per year, which was based upon the value of the assets in the portfolio. What I couldn't help but notice in these accounts was the high level of trading volume. These accounts typically would have 10 – 30 individual trades per month. My experience and intuition told me that something was wrong. Why did these guys trade so much?

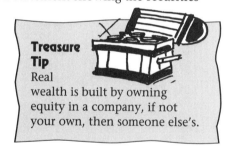

Treasure Tip
Real wealth is built by owning equity in a company, if not your own, then someone else's.

I studied further and found out why. The full-service brokerage firm makes money trading. The money management firm makes money by charging a management fee. If a brokerage firm hires a money manager and feeds him millions of dollars of new accounts, what do you think the brokerage firm hopes to get in return? That's right—trades. Trades equal commissions. Commission equals profit. But they also equal conflict of interest and slow death for the client. The media had a field day with this and found even further conflicts of interest.

Without the conflicts of interest, the concept was great, but the limitations on investment alternatives were horrible. How could you select from only 17 firms and expect to maintain a portfolio of the best minds in the world? I wanted more variety and convenience. That's when I began researching mutual funds, more specifically, no-load funds. At that time there were over 1,500 no-load funds available. Not only did I find variety, I also found a way to switch from one manager to another quickly and cost efficiently.

In the following chapters, I will show you how to combine these concepts to build and maintain a superior portfolio of no-load mutual funds.

The Least You Need to Know

- Before you make any investment decision, do some homework and make sure you fully understand the investment.
- Always be aware of the three biggest killers of wealth: biased investment advice, unknown risks, and excessive commissions.
- Avoid proprietary investment products, heavily loaded mutual funds, UITs, limited partnerships, initial public offerings of closed-end funds, options, futures, penny stocks, rumors, and hot tips.
- Never use insurance products, including annuities, for investment purposes only.

Chapter 8

Portfolio Tools That Work

In This Chapter

- The questions you need to ask before you buy an investment
- Hidden costs and conflicts of interest that most often destroy a portfolio
- When to use fixed income tools and when not to
- Why stocks are so powerful in the wealth building process
- Why mutual funds aren't just for small investors anymore

The tools presented in this chapter are the ones most often used by the wealthiest people I know. I have presented them in reverse order of importance and power. The first is the least important and powerful tool, while the last is the most important and powerful.

You can certainly buy non-liquid securities, but like I said in Chapter 2, you better understand what you're getting into. This chapter deals with liquid securities—ones you can sell and convert to cash quickly.

Five Questions to Ask Before You Buy Any Investment

Before you buy any investment, you need to fully understand what you are buying. There are many hidden traps you could fall into. Here are five questions that will help you make better investment decisions:

1. **In one sentence, what exactly am I investing in?** If you or the person selling you the investment can't explain, in one sentence, what you are investing in, then the investment might be too complicated. If so, don't buy it.

2. **Does this investment fit into my plan?** Make sure the investment meets your own personal goals. If you want no risk of fluctuation, you'll need to focus on money-market funds, short-term CDs, and treasury bills. If you have a long-term horizon and can withstand higher levels of fluctuation, then stocks may be what you need. Just make sure the investment accomplishes your mission, and fits into your portfolio goals. Don't worry, you may not know the details of your portfolio goals now. The next several chapters will help you narrow them down.

3. **What are the risks involved in owning this security?** Risk is always a confusing subject and will be discussed in a later chapter. For now you just need to remember to ask this question before buying an investment.

4. **Is there a secondary market for this investment?** This is very important and yet so few investors ask this question. You must have a secondary market that will allow you to sell the security later. If the security is a stock listed on the NYSE, then you know there is a real secondary market. If it is a packaged product like the ones mentioned in the previous chapter, then you need to stay away. Markets do change and you need to know if you can sell the investment later. If there is no established secondary market, the security becomes illiquid, and you need to avoid it.

   Another problem is monthly pricing data. Without actual known transactions involving the security, there is no way to get an accurate price each month. Therefore, the price on your statement each month becomes an estimate. If you have owned limited partnerships before, you understand what this is like. Full-service brokerage firms that sell limited partnerships usually list the original purchase price on the monthly statement. This practice should be illegal.

5. **What will this investment cost me?** Investment costs are so easy to hide. If you buy a stock from a brokerage firm, you will be charged a commission on top of the purchase price of the stock. What can be hidden from you is an additional commission, which is part of the spread. The spread is the difference between the price the brokerage firm paid for the security and the price at which they sold it to you. This is true for stocks and bonds.

> There are more ways commissions are hidden from the investor than I even know after almost 11 years in the business. You can always look in a prospectus when buying a mutual fund. But if there's nothing like that available, just ask this question: "If I sell this investment tomorrow and the price of the security remains unchanged from today, what will it cost me?" If your proceeds are significantly lower than your original purchase price, don't buy the security. It's probably a commission trap.

The tools listed in this chapter were selected based upon certain attributes that correspond to the questions just listed. Almost all of them can be easily researched and understood. They all have certain types of risk that are somewhat measurable, and each has a secondary market that is easily accessible. These securities will cost you less relative to most other types of securities. However, each one of them is still used today to indirectly hide commissions and fees. If you are aware of this possible practice and learn more about how to prevent it, you shouldn't have many problems.

The Fixed-Income Tools

Fixed-income securities are basically IOUs issued by companies and the government that pay a certain amount of interest each year and the full principal amount at a certain known date in the future. By their very nature, fixed income securities pay a fixed rate of interest that today, depending upon maturity and quality, is only a few points above the inflation rate. Since your goal of building wealth involves beating the rate of inflation by a significant amount, fixed income securities are not very powerful tools. However, if your goal were to reduce risk and maintain your principal instead of maximizing its growth, then fixed income securities may be just the thing for you.

Many investors think that the price of a bond stays constant while it pays its interest. This is not the case. In fact, bond prices fluctuate more than people know. Most bond holders only get a chance once a month (on their brokerage statement) to see their bond's price as opposed to stocks and mutual funds that are priced daily in the paper. What makes a bond fluctuate? Interest rates. When interest rates go up, bond prices fall, and when interest rates fall, bond prices go up. Therefore, when is the best time to own a bond? When interest rates go down. I'll discuss this in more detail later in the book, but for now you just need to understand that in order to get an above average return from bonds, interest rates must fall. Otherwise, they are not very powerful wealth building tools.

That Reminds Me...

Bonds represent the debt of a company while stocks represent equity ownership. Therefore, if a company files for bankruptcy, a bondholder will be paid off first, then the stockholder. The equity holder's claim to the company's assets is said to be subordinated to the bondholder's claim.

Words of the Wealthy

An **automated account** at a brokerage firm offers an automatic money sweep feature that deposits all deposits, interest payments, dividends, and proceeds of sales into a money-market account. When purchases are made within the account, or when checks are written against the account, money is automatically withdrawn from the account. Most full-service brokerage firms charge a custodial fee, but almost all discount brokerage firms waive their fee.

There is one prevalent conventional theory today that you need to understand. If you haven't heard it yet or read it somewhere, you will. It is the belief that an investor should have a certain percentage of his portfolio, equal to his age, invested in bonds. If the investor is 20-years-old, then 20 percent of the portfolio should be in bonds. If the investor is 80, then 80 percent of the portfolio should be in bonds. What a bunch of garbage! The percentage of bonds in a portfolio shouldn't have anything to do with the age of the investor.

Everyone has their own individual goals and risk tolerances. If my 80-year-old clients had 80 percent of their portfolio in bonds in 1994 when the bond market fell 15 plus percent, they would have all called me on the phone and said, "Uh, have you lost your mind? You manage every penny of our retirement money and we just lost 15 percent of it. What happened? We're extremely concerned." A portfolio's bond allocation should be based upon an individual's risk tolerance and interest rate forecast, not the age of the investor.

Money-Market Funds

A money-market fund is actually a mutual fund of short-term, fixed income securities that all have maturities of less than one year. Most investment accounts are automated now, which means that all deposits, dividends, interest, and proceeds from sales are automatically deposited into a money-market account. These funds are primarily used as parking places for cash. When the market seems overvalued, money-market funds come in handy. Parking a small percentage of your portfolio in a money-market fund might be a smart thing to do when you feel nervous about the market being too high. The perfect scenario would be to use the funds later when the market falls.

Money-market funds offer certain advantages no other security can offer. The biggest advantage is the price, which is designed not to fluctuate. It stays constant at $1 per share, which means that there is very little risk of loss. These funds have a next day settlement that means they can be sold one day and the proceeds will be available the next day. You can also write checks on most money-market funds. The only real disadvantage is that they don't pay a whole lot of interest.

Certificates of Deposit

Certificates of deposit, or CDs, are useful when you have short-term goals. If you have a sum of money that you know you'll need within three years, CDs might be a perfect idea. The advantages include the fact that they are insured up to $100,000 and pay higher rates than money-market funds.

The main disadvantage with CDs is the penalty for early withdrawal. This can be eliminated if you purchase marketable CDs from a brokerage firm. Many brokerage firms offer CDs from banks all over the U.S. If you want to sell before maturity, the brokerage firm will offer you a price based upon current interest rates. Just like a bond, if interest rates go up, the CD's price will fall. If rates have fallen, then you might get a capital gain on your CD when you sell. However, if you plan to hold the CD until maturity, it really doesn't matter if the price fluctuates because you are guaranteed to receive the face value of the CD at maturity.

The primary benchmark to use when comparing your CD's yield is the yield on a money-market account. If a money-market account offers higher interest, you might want to reconsider the CD.

Words of the Wealthy

Treasury bills are issued with 13, 26, and 52 week maturities. They are normally sold at a discount to the face value, which is $1,000 per bond. The difference between their face value and their discounted value is the interest you will receive at maturity. Until maturity, their price fluctuates daily according to short-term interest rates.

Words of the Wealthy

A **treasury note** is also an IOU offered by the U.S. Government, but they have maturities of 1 to 10 years. They are issued at face value and pay fixed interest payments every six months. Their price also fluctuates with interest rates and the fluctuation is a great deal more than that of treasury bills.

Treasury Bonds, Bills, and Notes

Treasury securities are IOUs offered by the U.S. Government. They have maturities extending from one day to 30 years and their interest payments are semi-annual and exempt from state taxes. Traditionally, the longer-term maturities pay higher interest rates than the shorter term. But because they all pay so little in interest, don't waste much time here looking for big gains in the long-run. Treasury bonds can be purchased in increments of $1,000. Bills can be purchased in increments of $10,000 in face value while notes come in increments of $5,000.

Investors use short-term treasury securities for temporary parking places. The longer maturing notes and bonds can be used strategically to take advantage of falling interest rates. Treasury securities offer one great advantage: They are guaranteed by the U.S. Government. The disadvantage is that they don't pay a lot of interest, but they are definitely safe investments if you hold them until maturity.

Words of the Wealthy

Treasury bonds are similar to notes, but their maturities extend from 10 to 30 years. Their prices fluctuate the most because of the longer maturities. This will be explained further in later chapters.

The one possible exception is the long-term zero coupon treasury bond. This can be an outstanding tool for exploiting falling interest rates. A zero coupon bond is a bond that pays no coupon interest, but is instead issued at a discount from its face or maturity value to yield income from capital appreciation. They are wildly volatile, but tend to do extremely well when interest rates fall.

Since treasury securities are used so much as benchmarks, it's hard to compare them to other securities. Before I've purchased any for clients, which is quite seldom, I check current CD rates. If CDs are paying more than the treasury security, I'll buy the CD. If I'm investing more than the $100,000 insured amount, I'll stick with the treasury.

Municipal Bonds

Municipal bonds are IOUs issued by state and local municipalities and the interest they pay is exempt from federal taxes, as well as state taxes within the state that issues the bond. They are rated according to their estimated ability to pay their interest and principal payments on a timely basis. Municipal bonds are only useful when they produce a tax equivalent yield that exceeds what you can get from high-quality corporate or treasury issues. To calculate the tax equivalent yield, simply divide the interest rate of the bond by the inverse of your tax rate:

(the interest rate paid by the bond) / 1 – (your tax rate)

Most people buy municipal bonds just because they are tax free. They focus on this first before they focus on total return. This is a big mistake. The total return should always be the first priority.

The primary advantage of owning municipal bonds is the tax free income feature they provide the bond holder. This feature is especially attractive to investors who are in the highest tax brackets. The disadvantage is that currently they pay relatively low interest rates, and the only way an investor can achieve a better return after purchasing the bond is if interest rates fall. This would cause the bond price to rise and therefore increase total return.

The *Wall Street Journal* prints several municipal bond indexes on a daily basis that are listed on the front page of the third section.

> **Words of the Wealthy**
> A **junk bond** is any corporate bond that is rated below the Standard & Poor's BBB rating or Moody's Baa rating. They are also known as **non-investment grade bonds** or **high-yield bonds.**

Corporate Bonds

Corporate bonds do offer higher yields than treasury bonds, but they involve a little more risk. They are also rated according to the issuing company's estimated ability to pay their interest and principal payments on a timely basis. High-quality corporate bonds are designed to give a portfolio stability. They are not designed to produce double-digit total returns.

> **Words of the Wealthy**
> The **risk/reward** ratio is a term used to describe a security's return relative to its risk. If a security has the potential for a 10 percent return on the upside, you should only be willing to accept an equal or lesser degree of risk on the downside. For example, why risk a 20 percent loss for a possible 10 percent return?

The real advantage in corporate bonds is in the lower non-investment grade issues called "junk bonds." A junk bond represents an IOU issued by a company whose ability to repay its interest and principal in a timely manner depends upon the economy and its ability to sell its products or services.

If you consider buying these bonds individually, you are asking for trouble. But if you purchase a fund, you get a manager who knows the junk market better than you ever will because this is all he works with on a daily basis.

Hybrid Fixed Income Securities

You can also use convertible bonds and preferred stocks, which I call hybrid fixed income securities. I call them hybrids because they act both like a stock and a bond. Like a bond, they do well when interest rates go down, and like a stock, they go up when the underlying company's earnings grow substantially. Occasionally these types of investments become attractive, but not very often. When you need to stabilize the value of your portfolio, these types of securities can help. They can be defined as a cross between a bond and a stock. They pay higher income than traditional stocks, but don't fluctuate as much in price.

The Equity Tools: Stocks and Such

Where do you invest your money? You can invest your money in a conventional savings account or CDs, but your net return after inflation and taxes will not be strong enough (at least at today's rates) to compound the portfolio growth at a sufficient pace. However, equities, or stocks, will. Whether they are publicly traded or privately held, they can compound much faster because their value or price is directly related to the earnings growth of the company. That's what makes them the wealth tool of choice. They are the key to building wealth because they represent equity ownership in a company and their value will grow relative to the growth in net earnings. If a company is expected to have continued earnings growth of 30 percent or more, then its stock price may have the same growth potential. There are very few opportunities in the investment world that offer this much growth potential. This is the single biggest and most popular wealth builder in the world, but ironically, most people don't take the time to understand the concept or its power.

Words of the Wealthy

The **P/E ratio** is a stock's price per share divided by its earnings per share. It is used to estimate the true value of a stock and is often used in comparison with other stocks. If Wal-Mart's market price closed at $25 per share today and its current quarterly earnings equaled $.25 (or $1 on an annualized basis), its P/E ratio would be 25.

Words of the Wealthy

A **value investor** is someone who looks for good value in the market. A stock selling at an unusually low P/E ratio is a great example. Occasionally stocks drop in price well below what they should. Value investors search for opportunities like this and try to take advantage of the stock's price returning to more normal (higher) levels.

The market value of a stock is based upon what people perceive the value to be. This perception of value is normally based upon the amount of net cash the company produces (or is perceived to produce) on a per share level after expenses. This cash is referred to as earnings or earnings per share. The majority of these earnings are usually retained by the company and are used to finance further growth with the remainder being distributed as dividends to shareholders. Small or fast growing companies usually do not distribute any earnings as dividends because they need the money to continue their fast paced growth. On the other hand, larger or slower growing companies usually distribute a great deal of their earnings as dividends. If you want to maximize the growth of your portfolio, your goal should be to focus on the smaller companies whose growth is compounding with the reinvestment of dividends.

The relative comparison of a company's stock price to its earnings is commonly referred to as the price/earnings ratio (or P/E). For example, according to *Investor's Business Daily* the stocks on the New York Stock Exchange (NYSE) are trading now at an average P/E ratio of 19. This means little unless you can look back over time and see what it has been. Looking back over the past five years, the lowest average P/E of the NYSE was 11 and the highest level was 40. If you know historical P/E averages, you can maintain a better idea of how under- or over-priced the market is on a daily basis. *Barron's*, another investment publication, prints the average P/E ratio on the Dow Jones Industrial Averages, as well as the S&P 500 index. When a stock's P/E ratio is much higher than comparable companies in the same industry, the stock might be considered over-priced. What I focus on is the opposite situation. I look for stocks that have P/E ratios below the industry average. That makes me a "value investor."

Domestic Stocks

Domestic stocks are stocks of companies that are headquartered here in the U.S. They should make up a good bit of your investment portfolio, but not the whole thing. This is a common mistake made by investors here in the U.S. I'll talk more about this later.

Domestic stocks can be purchased individually through a broker or through a mutual fund. One advantage stocks offer is protection from the risk of inflation, which bonds don't seem to do so well. The only real disadvantage is the performance risk that stocks carry. If the underlying company goes bankrupt, the stock could become worthless. You are also tied to the overall U.S. market, which can correct unexpectedly. Therefore, domestic stock prices can be very volatile.

Successful investors use certain stock indexes as relative benchmarks for their own portfolios. Therefore, it is important to understand the most common indexes and what makes them unique. The Dow Jones Industrial Average is the most popular benchmark used here in the U.S., but it only represents a basket of 30 different stocks. A better index to use is the S&P 500 index, which represents 500 different stocks. There are many other narrowly gauged indexes, but it's difficult to list them all. These indexes all act as broad-based windows into the stock market. If you were really interested in healthcare-related stocks, there are several healthcare-related indexes of stocks and mutual funds available. If you knew the healthcare-related stock index took a dramatic dive over the past year, you might consider this to be an over-reaction by the market and decide to buy a mutual fund specializing in this area.

If investing is your hobby and passion, it's okay to build a portfolio of individual domestic stocks. If it's not your hobby, and you're picking your own stocks, you may be setting yourself up for future losses. If you don't enjoy investing, you will not do a very good job. Consider mutual funds or hiring a fee-only investment advisor.

Foreign Stocks

Only in the last few years have investors understood the value of foreign stocks. If your portfolio is invested only in U.S. companies, you are actually taking more risk than someone with a portfolio diversified all over the world. Allocating approximately 35 percent of your portfolio into a diversified mix of foreign stocks will actually reduce your risk and, at the same time, increase your performance potential. I firmly believe that all stock portfolios should have a certain percentage allocated into foreign stocks.

The most popular benchmark that represents a portfolio invested all over the world is the *Morgan Stanley World Market Index*, which can be found daily in the *Wall Street Journal*.

The Mutual Fund Tools

A mutual fund, also known as an investment company, is a corporation, trust, or partnership into which investors combine their money in order to benefit primarily from professional management, diversification, and liquidity. Each fund has a manager or management team responsible for making the investment decisions of the fund and for purchasing securities with the money invested by the shareholders. The securities can include stocks, bonds, options, CDs, and real estate depending upon the fund's stated objective.

What makes each mutual fund different is the fund's *objective* that is explained in the prospectus. The objective of the fund outlines the intentions of the manager, including the type of investments he will be using as well as the different philosophies or strategies he will employ. This is the most important item in the prospectus to understand. The second most important item to look for is the list of restrictions. These guidelines are set up to help keep the fund manager focused and on track.

Mutual Funds Aren't Just for Small Accounts Anymore

Conventional wisdom might have you believe that mutual funds are designed to help investors diversify small amounts of money. It's certainly true that mutual funds offer a great deal of diversification, but they offer many other benefits that most investors completely overlook. Here is a list of what a portfolio of mutual funds offers the shareholder.

- Because you are able to virtually hire several money managers at one time, you benefit from the synergy of combining all their unique investment styles into your portfolio.
- Services such as automated checking account debit purchasing that makes it a lot easier to invest on a monthly basis.
- Since the management fees are so inexpensive compared to the expenses of hiring a private individual money manager, mutual funds offer an inexpensive way to hire a group of investment managers.

- A cost efficient method of investing all over the world, considering the high cost of foreign security commissions that are charged to individuals.
- The ability to diversify among hundreds of securities all over the world that would be almost impossible for an individual investor to do with a small amount of money and a limited amount of time to research.
- If you build a portfolio of several different funds, each manager may have a different investment philosophy that gives you even greater diversification in your portfolio.
- Because you can sell your mutual fund as quickly as a stock, funds offer a great deal of portfolio liquidity.
- Peace of mind that someone is watching the portfolio.

Mutual funds are not perfect. They do have their limitations and disadvantages. They do not apply to all funds, but this is a list of possible disadvantages. I'm sure you'll agree that the advantages certainly outweigh the disadvantages.

- High portfolio turnover can result in higher management fees.
- Some people think mutual funds are too limited because they can only invest in marketable securities.
- Loss of control over when taxable gains are taken.
- Poor performance during bear markets.
- Legal limitations of the fund manager that could affect performance.

Mutual funds aren't just for small accounts anymore. As investors learn more about what it takes to build wealth, they quickly realize the advantages mutual funds have to offer.

Open-Ended Funds

An open-ended fund is a mutual fund that continually offers new shares to investors. When an investor purchases shares, money is directly deposited into the fund. When the shareholder eventually redeems his shares (hopefully at a higher price than he paid), money is withdrawn directly from the fund.

You need to understand the costs involved before you purchase a mutual fund. There are two types of open-end funds: load and no-load. The term load refers to a commission. No-load means there is no commission to buy the fund. Therefore, the price you would pay would be the net asset value.

My parents taught me, "If something sounds too good to be true, it probably is," and this is the reaction most investors have when they first hear about no-load mutual funds. The first question that pops into their minds is, "What's the catch? How can these mutual funds make money when they don't charge anything?"

All funds have a management fee that is paid by the mutual fund shareholders. This fee can range from .01 percent to 3.00 percent per year. This fee goes directly to the fund manager and fund company for operating expenses.

However, some funds charge a "load" or commission, which is an additional charge levied at the time of purchase, at the time of redemption, or each year the fund is held. This commission is paid to the salesperson/broker who sold the fund and the brokerage firm that hired the salesperson.

The bottom line is that the commission, or load, pays for the broker. With a little homework, you can do it yourself—buy a no-load fund and save an enormous amount of money.

Many people think that the management fee on a no-load fund is higher than that of a loaded fund to compensate for the absence of commission. This is not always true. Many loaded funds have higher management fees than no-load funds.

Buying no-load funds is like buying direct from the manufacturer. This secret can save an investor up to 9.29 percent on every net invested dollar.

So why do people still buy loaded mutual funds? The two most common reasons are: 1) The investor is unaware of what a no-load fund can offer; or 2) The investor does not know how to find a no-load alternative to the loaded fund he has selected.

If you want to learn more about no-load funds, go to your local library. They should have several publications, such as, *Money, Kiplinger's Personal Finance, Fortune,* and *Forbes*. They regularly feature articles on subjects such as no-load funds. You can also call **Morningstar** ($395 per year, 1-800-876-5005). They have a $55 trial subscription. This is a small price to pay if you are serious about your research. You will get the entire past year's worth of information. This publication has updated information on most mutual funds and is presented in a format that enables you to easily compare one fund to another.

There are two ways to buy a no-load mutual fund: direct from the company or through a discount brokerage firm. If you want to buy direct, Morningstar will provide you with each fund company's phone number. If you want to buy the fund, just request a prospectus and new account application. If you decide to buy the fund, just fill out the application and send it back with a check made out to the name of the mutual fund company.

If you want to buy several different funds, it may be much easier to consolidate everything into one account at a discount brokerage firm. Charles Schwab and Co., the discount brokerage firm (800-435-4000), offers a unique service that allows investors to purchase over 300 different no-load mutual funds within the same account without any transaction fee. You may want to call and get more information on this service.

Open-end funds are normally divided by their objective or investment of choice. Here are a few different types:

- Aggressive Growth Funds
- Growth Funds
- International
- Global Equity Funds
- Growth and Income Funds
- Equity Income Funds
- Balanced Funds
- Flexible Portfolio Funds
- Index Funds
- Specialized Industry Funds

I would define each of the above categories, but it would be rather futile. Why? Because every magazine, every mutual fund service, and every author has a different definition, it makes no sense to include one here.

There are several different services that provide an extensive list of mutual fund indexes. Lipper Analytical and Morningstar are the two most popular. You can find many of their indexes listed in *The Wall Street Journal* and *Barrons*. Be sure to compare apples to apples when you measure a fund's performance to an index.

Closed-End Funds

One of the most overlooked investment vehicles is the closed-end fund. You know from the previous chapter not to buy these during an initial public offering because they are too expensive. However, once these funds make it to the secondary market, they can trade at a discount to their actual net asset value. Because they trade like a stock, their market price has little to do with the actual net asset value. I've seen some funds trade for as little as 65 cents on the dollar. This may be hard to believe, but it's true.

Just like open-end funds, closed-end funds can focus on many different sectors. Most of the closed-end equity funds focus on one individual country or geographic region. Therefore, closed-end funds can be a perfect way to invest in a specific country or region that you might be excited about.

Closed-end funds offer two unique advantages. There is certainly the advantage of having the opportunity to buy a mutual fund at a discount to its net asset value. However, the most important advantage is rarely ever discussed. What makes a closed-end fund so attractive is the fact that the manager doesn't have to worry about shareholders withdrawing money on a daily basis. Open-end fund managers have to worry about this everyday. Closed-end fund managers don't have to worry about this, which means they can focus single-mindedly on managing the portfolio.

There are very few closed-end fund indexes available for comparison. Therefore, most of the time you will have to compare performance to other similar closed-end funds. Often you might find other open-end funds that are also similar.

A Little Secret about Bond Funds

Bond funds, just like stock funds, do give the shareholder diversification into many different individual bond issues, which is a great benefit. However, if you are going to build a portfolio and you need to allocate money to bonds, you should first consider buying individual bonds. Unless you're dealing with junk bonds or small amounts of money, it may be more cost efficient to build your own portfolio of individual bonds. Why? What's wrong with a bond fund? Individual bonds are primarily purchased for their interest payments that are usually fixed at a given rate. Given today's current interest rates, these bonds don't pay a lot of money, and if they're purchased within a mutual fund, you're going to receive even less money in interest payments. Bond funds, just like all other mutual funds, have management fees. I've seen 1.35 percent management fees on a bond fund that only paid about 6 percent interest. The net interest payment to the shareholder was only 4.65 percent! That means that 22.5 percent of the interest payment went to management fees, which is crazy. And, people actually buy these things everyday! Just be aware of the details before you buy a bond fund.

The Best Tools of Wealth

I have found that most wealthy people use the same wealth building tools. The following is a list of the most lucrative tools.

Your Own Business Is the Best Tool

Equity in a fast growing company, preferably your own, is the best tool to use when attempting to achieve Wealth Levels 3, 4, and 5. Why? Because your own business may be the only way to get potential returns in excess of 10 percent. The value of the stock is tied to earnings growth of the underlying company. If earnings are growing at 50 percent, then the stock is likely to be growing at 50 percent. This is truly the only way to achieve consistent returns that exceed the stock market. You might be able to accomplish above average returns in the stock market, but you don't have the same control over that return unless it's your own company. We'll discuss starting your own business in Part 3.

A No-Load Mutual Fund Portfolio Is the Second Best Tool

After studying money management for almost 11 years, I've come to realize my own personal limitations and recognize the power of tapping into the greatest money management minds in the world. Sir Isaac Newton once said, "If I have seen further, it's because I stood on the shoulders of giants." When I heard this humble statement, I realized just how important it was to get help from others. By delegating the monumental task of following certain segments of the market, you stand a better chance of not only maintaining your own personal life, but also your financial future.

Would you rather invest in a stock representing a particular company in Mexico or invest in a mutual fund of Mexican stocks managed by an advisor who actually lives in Mexico and knows the country better than you ever will? Do the basics yourself, but delegate the most difficult and time-consuming task of investment management to the people who do it professionally. For an average management fee of one percent, they will follow industry trends, keep up with geopolitical events, visit the actual companies in person, and buy the individual securities for you. Can you do all this and spend less than one percent of your portfolio? The real question is this: Can you beat their portfolio performance?

The Perfect Portfolio

The optimal wealth building portfolio has these characteristics:

- The portfolio is built primarily of stocks and maybe some bonds in an automated account—the aggressive investor may not own any bonds, while the conservative investor may have 60 percent bonds.
- The stocks are globally diversified among the U.S., foreign developed countries, and foreign emerging market countries—the ideal percentage of foreign securities for a moderate risk investor is approximately 30 percent.
- It must be easy to skew the portfolio toward the best opportunities in different sectors such as countries and industries.
- The portfolio must be able to employ the greatest specialists in the world to manage each sector that results in a level of synergy and diversification of thought that would be impossible to achieve alone.
- When your portfolio needs more diversification, you must be able to switch from sector focus to a more broad-based focus.
- The portfolio can be quickly, easily, and cost-efficiently adjusted to take advantage of better opportunities.

The Perfect Specialist, When You Need One

If you want to manage your own portfolio—that's great. However, why not be a manager of fund managers? Why not build a portfolio of mutual funds that would give you a team of specialists who all work for you. What do you look for when you hire all these specialists? On the following page is a list of the most important requirements.

- These specialists must focus on the micro-economic picture allowing you to focus on the macro-economic picture.
- The specialists must be inexpensive, held accountable, and easily measured against each other on a daily if not weekly basis.
- You must be able to find and understand what makes each specialist unique or better than the others—what is their idiosyncratic advantage?
- The specialist must be independent of a brokerage firm.
- The specialists hired can be fired and re-hired with little to no emotion involved.

This would almost be impossible to do with individual stocks. However, no-load mutual funds enable the investor to achieve all of the above goals. They are the only investment vehicle that gives me all of the above characteristics along with the type of specialists I need. While I focus on what is going on in the world, I need other specialists to focus on what is going on in each individual country and industry. I realize I can't follow all the stocks in the world, but a team of specialists can for me.

No-load mutual funds give me the ability to combine the power of equity growth along with what I call the multiple manager concept that can result in an efficiently managed portfolio with potential returns exceeding 10 percent.

The Least You Need to Know

- Always look for the different kinds of hidden commissions and fees that can eat away at your portfolio like excessive 12b1 fees.
- Identify the possible conflicts of interest before you take any investment advice.
- If your goal is to maximize the growth of your portfolio, you're going to have to use stocks.
- The best portfolio for beginners to build is one that is diversified all over the world through no-load mutual funds managed by the greatest money managers in the world.

Chapter 9

Five Things You Must Know Before You Hire Professional Help

In This Chapter

- Where to look for an advisor
- What to look for in an advisor
- What you should avoid
- Questions you need to ask the advisor
- Questions you need to ask the advisor's clients

Once you have achieved the advanced stages of Wealth Level 2, where your return exceeds your target savings goal (TSG), you must pay close attention to the management of your portfolio. If investing is not a hobby or passion of yours, you need to eventually consider getting some help from a professional in the investment industry. Every investor has different needs, and every professional offers somewhat different services. This chapter will help you match your needs with the best professional available: a financial planner, full-service broker, or other professional.

Whatever professional you need, one thing they all can do for you is eliminate procrastination in your financial plan. They can keep you accountable and even make decisions for you. The key question is whether the advisor can do better than you. If you think an advisor can beat your performance at least by the amount of fees and commissions charged, then you should consider hiring that advisor. If you think you can do a better job, then try it yourself.

Will All the Great Advisors Please Stand Up?

The best place to start looking for an investment advisor is with friends. Find friends whose investment knowledge you respect the most, and ask who those friends recommend. You can also talk to your CPA or tax preparer, if you use either; these folks see brokerage statements every year and know firsthand which advisors make money for clients. Watch your local newspaper for investment seminars and workshops in your area. Otherwise, you may have to resort to the Yellow Pages.

That Reminds Me...

If you are just starting out with your portfolio and you have less than $20,000 to invest, you are in what I call the "gray zone." If you go look for help, you'll find very few quality investment brokers or advisors willing to spend any significant time with you. Why? Because the commission or fee income from $20,000 isn't usually enough to get most brokers or advisors excited. If you're in the gray zone, you need to be sure not to let an unscrupulous advisor steer you into a "commission trap" to make up for your lower portfolio size. The commission trap is any investment that charges above average commissions. If you don't understand the possible hidden commissions and fees, you'll be easy prey for this trap. The next chapter will help you through the gray zone.

The most difficult question an investor will ever have to answer is, "What kind of professional should I trust?" This decision is usually the first one to make and often the least researched. Many people in my workshops ask me to explain the difference between Fee-Only Investment Advisors, Investment Advisors, Money Managers, Brokers, and Certified Financial Planners. Therefore, I thought it might be useful to discuss the various titles that accompany these professionals in the investment industry. The primary differences to be aware of include services offered, source of compensation, how are they influenced, and who regulates them.

Full-Service Investment Brokers

The first and most widely known investment professional is the Full-Service Investment Broker (broker). Other titles that describe a broker include registered representative, financial consultant, investment banker, and even Vice President (usually awarded once certain levels of commission are achieved). Investment brokers are security salespeople who help investors buy and sell securities for a commission. Brokers seldom have fiduciary responsibility for client's accounts, so the clients must be contacted prior to and must agree to any investment transaction. Some brokers may also offer financial planning, estate planning, and retirement planning services.

> **Words of the Wealthy**
>
> A **fiduciary** is an advisor who has been authorized to buy and sell securities on behalf of the client, without the client's express permission. This authorization is given in the form of a limited power of attorney signed by the client. An advisor has *fiduciary responsibility* when he is responsible for buying and selling securities for the client.

Brokers are regulated by the Securities and Exchange Commission (SEC), your state's Securities Department, and the National Association of Securities Dealers. The primary advantage of using a full-service broker is the extensive research about investment decisions they can provide. However, many discount brokerage firms now offer the same research information. The full-service brokerage firm might have a team of security analysts, but they make mistakes, too. When selecting stocks and other securities, pay attention to facts, not the opinions of security analysts. With a little experience, your instincts may produce better results.

> **Wealth Warning**
>
> The primary influence over the broker is the investment firm's branch manager, who is also compensated based upon the amount of commissions and proprietary investment products sold. Proprietary investments are those that the broker's company underwrites and exclusively distributes or sells.

The primary disadvantage of working with a full-service broker involves the way they are compensated—via commission for each investment purchase or sale you make. Commissions usually range from 1.5 percent charges on stock trades to 8.5 percent charges on mutual funds and other packaged products. Many investors feel commission-based investment advice is a conflict of interest. When you have any investment planning done by a broker, make sure you know the full extent of the commissions involved in every recommendation.

Registered Investment Advisors

The second most popular type of investment professional is the Registered Investment Advisor (RIA). Investment advisors are typically independent and have fiduciary responsibility for their clients' portfolios, meaning they make the investment decisions on behalf of the client based upon the individual client's objectives. Advisors are paid in one of three ways: by fee-only (flat rate based on assets managed or time), by commission (based on the amount of your purchase), and by a combination of fees and commissions. Advisors who charge a commission or a combination of fees and commissions are sometimes called non-fee-only advisors.

What would be a fair fee rate? Fees charged by RIAs usually range from 1 to 4 percent depending upon the size of the account. The average fee rate today is about 1 percent. If your portfolio is less than $250,000, expect to pay a higher rate of 1.6 percent, and if your portfolio exceeds $1 million, your fee should be 1 percent or lower. Remember, all fees are somewhat negotiable.

There are two types of fee-only RIAs: money managers and financial planners. Fee-only money managers make investment decisions for clients based on the risk tolerances and goals of the client. They are paid a fee that is usually based upon the value of the account. No income is derived from commissions. Fee-only financial planners assist investors with budgeting, retirement planning, estate planning, taxes, investments, life insurance, and real estate. On smaller estates, they are paid a fee usually based on the amount of time it takes to complete the plan. These fees usually run about $200 per hour. Once you have achieved Wealth Level 3, you might want to pay a yearly retainer based upon the size of your estate or net worth. Retainers are negotiable, but usually range from .5 to 1 percent. Most importantly, they do not receive any commission from any investment or life insurance product they recommend.

Words of the Wealthy

Money manager is simply another name for a fee-only investment advisor.

Words of the Wealthy

A Fee-only Advisor is a money manager or financial planner who receives a fee for service that is usually based upon a percentage of assets under management or time. Fee-only advisors do not receive any commissions for any investment they recommend.

The primary advantage offered by fee-only advisors is the way they are compensated. Advice and commissions are separated. The only way a fee-only money manager can increase his or her own income is to increase the performance and therefore the size of the client's portfolio. This produces a "win-win" relationship for both the client and advisor. If the fee-only advisor is independent, there is no management influence or commissions quota to produce commissions. The only disadvantage here might be the experience of the advisor. The regulatory agencies that govern the advisor include both the SEC and the State Securities Department.

Non-fee only RIAs also manage portfolios for clients, but receive commissions and fees. Some offset their fees by the amount of the commissions charged to each account. The commissions can be somewhat disguised using a technique known as "Soft-Dollars." The broker used by the advisor for trading purposes will charge additional commission (a few cents per share) to each trade made in each client's account. The brokerage firm will pass along the additional commission to the advisor by paying for certain services that are normally part of the advisor's own overhead expenses, such as research, software, and market quotation services. Some non-fee-only RIAs offer financial planning.

The advantage of using an independent non-fee only RIA is the absence of influence from management normally experienced at full-service brokerage firms. The primary disadvantage involves how they are compensated. As is the case in dealing with investment brokers, many investors feel commission-based investment advice from a non-fee only RIA is a conflict of interest. When you have any investment planning done by a non-fee only RIA, make sure you know the full extent of commissions that will be involved in all the suggested investments. Non fee-only RIAs are regulated by the SEC, your state's Securities Department, and the National Association of Securities Dealers.

Certified Financial Planners

Certified Financial Planner (CFP) is the most confusing term you'll encounter. It is often a title used to disguise a commission-based broker. CFPs are people who have passed a set of comprehensive exams offered by the College of Financial Planning in Colorado. The course is structured as a three-year program, but it can be completed in one year. This is a great program; however, many investment professionals take advantage of the title. CFPs can be insurance agents, brokers, mutual fund salespeople, fee-only advisors, and non-fee-only advisors. All of these professionals want to sell you something for a commission, except for the fee-only CFP. The true fee-only CFP will profile your financial situation and goals and develop a comprehensive financial plan. Some will even implement this plan for you. The plan usually includes how much to save, how much to spend (budgeting), how much insurance you need, how you can save on income taxes, how to save for college expenses, and how you can protect your heirs from estate taxes. The fee for a plan is usually based upon the time spent repairing the plan and normally ranges from $100 to $200 per hour. A large comprehensive plan may even run up to $10,000. This might seem high, but the commission-based CFP could easily get a $10,000 in commissions if you were to purchase a $120,000 in heavily loaded mutual funds or insurance policies.

Words of the Wealthy

A Certified Financial Planner (CFP) is someone who has passed the comprehensive CFP exams administered by a company in Denver, Colorado called the College for Financial Planning (303-220-1200). CFP's can be brokers, insurance agents, salespeople, or fee-only advisors.

fee-only CFPs are rare because the commissions offered by loaded mutual funds and insurance products just seem to dwarf the average $200 per hour fee.

If you want to check for any past complaints regarding the CFP you are considering or if you have a complaint regarding your existing CFP, just call the Certified Financial Planning Board of Standards at 303-220-1200.

The advantages and disadvantages of using a CFP are similar to the RIA. If the CFP is fee-only, then there is no conflict of interest from commissions. However, some CFPs charge both fees and commissions, so be aware of their charges and motives.

That Reminds Me...

If you hire a CFP who is also an insurance agent, be careful. You may find yourself investing in insurance products with huge commissions. This is not conducive to the wealth building process. If you want to build wealth, you can't do it with insurance products. You might protect your wealth with them, but you won't build it. I believe in insurance products for insurance and estate planning reasons, but not for investment purposes.

Your Advisor

To make it easier, I will use the term "advisor" to refer to all of the different types of professionals I've mentioned in this chapter.

The Four Cs: Compatibility Questions You Should Ask Your Advisor

If you decide to hire an advisor to help you in your journey toward your next Wealth Level, you need to know what to look for and the right questions to ask. What you should envision is a relationship between you and your advisor that is based upon trust and compatibility. You need to focus on finding someone who will keep *your* best interest in mind and be rewarded for doing so. Your goal is not only to find the best advisor for you, it is also to gain a certain degree of respect from that advisor. Often, the amount of attention and service you get from the advisor is directly related to the amount of respect he has for you.

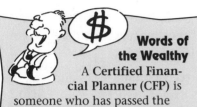

How do you gain that respect? First, by asking the right questions. There are four Cs of advisor-client compatibility: credentials, compensation, characteristics, and customer service. Your questions should at least cover these four areas. The rest of this section covers each area, including the key questions that you need to ask before you hire an advisor.

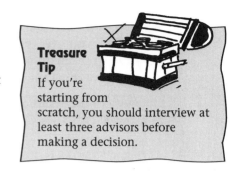

> **Treasure Tip**
> If you're starting from scratch, you should interview at least three advisors before making a decision.

Credentials

Just what exactly qualifies your advisor as a professional? Some advisors just hang a shingle outside their door and go to work. The following questions will help you to separate the wheat from the chaff.

1. **Who are you registered with?** The advisor should be registered with at least one of the following:

   - The Securities and Exchange Commission (SEC) 202-942-7040.
   - Your state securities department (usually found in your state capitol).
   - The National Association of Securities Dealers (if they are commission-based) 800-289-9999.

   If not, you should avoid doing business with the advisor. You might want to check their registration status and ask if there have been any complaints filed against them. Start with your state securities department, and then call the other agencies.

2. **Where did you graduate from college?** This might not be important to you, but it will sure answer the real question, which is, "Did you go to college and did you graduate?" If you doubt the answer you get, call the college and check. You shouldn't base your entire decision on whether or not the advisor finished college (I know several brilliant people who never went to college), but college is a test of tenacity. If the advisor you're interviewing didn't finish college, make sure they can show you at least five good years of investment experience.

3. **How long have you been in the investment business?** Don't be a guinea pig. If this is the advisor's first few years in the business, you might want to wait. Most advisors make their biggest mistakes during the first year in the business. If you do hire a neophyte advisor, start with a small amount of money. The best advisor is someone who has experienced at least one big market correction (a period where many securities "crashed," or went down in value) like 1987.

4. **Who was your previous employer?** You might even ask for a resume. If your advisor has jumped around from firm to firm a lot, you might want to reconsider.

If you were hiring an employee, would you hire someone who has jumped between jobs each year over the last several years? There are certainly exceptions to this rule. Ask why the advisor jumped around. He or she might have done it by design to learn more about the business before starting an investment firm.

5. **What certifications do you have?** The most important certification a money manager can possess is a CFA or Chartered Financial Analyst. This is a comprehensive three-year course developed and maintained by the Institute of Chartered Financial Analysts. It is not the most important thing to look for when hiring an advisor, but it is impressive. Comparing the CFA designation to the CFP is like comparing college to high school. The CFA is much more difficult and comprehensive than the CFP.

   The only possible problem with the CFA is that it can make your advisor too academic. Academic investors can sometimes be too rigid in their investment strategies, meaning they focus in on certain kinds of conventional portfolio strategies, but disregard others that also may be beneficial. Therefore, the most intelligent are not always the best money managers. As I will explain in Chapter 11, it takes much more than intelligence to be a successful portfolio manager.

6. **How many clients do you have?** The advisor can have too few or too many clients. Too few may imply that he has little experience. Too many may mean that he can't service all of them effectively. There is no magic number, and you'll just have to judge for yourself. The more clients the advisor has, the more experience she has. If you are hiring a money manager, you also may want to ask how much money she has under management. If the manager has over $30 million under management, she's built a significant business.

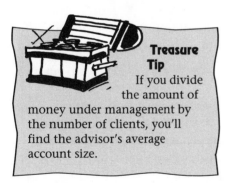

Treasure Tip

If you divide the amount of money under management by the number of clients, you'll find the advisor's average account size.

7. **Questions to ask yourself.** Are you impressed with this person? Are you comfortable with his credentials? Does he have enough experience to make you comfortable?

Compensation

The most respected professionals in the investment industry who do not work for full service brokerage firms or loaded mutual fund companies will tell you to focus on the fee-only advisor. Do-it-yourself investors would be the only exception to this rule. If investing is your hobby and you like to rely on a full-service brokerage firm's research, then by all means use these firms. They can be a great asset toward building wealth. However, if investing is not a hobby of yours, you should focus on fee-only advisors, who can't try to rack up commissions by steering novices into commission heavy investments.

You've got to fully understand the costs involved before you hire anyone to help you manage your money. As noted earlier, an advisor's method of compensation will dictate the conflicts of interest you may encounter. So, regardless of whether they are commission-based or fee-based, ask these questions:

1. **How are you compensated?** If the answer is "fee-only" then ask the percentage rate. Remember, it's not uncommon to pay 1.6 percent for an account less than $250,000. However, accounts that exceed $1 million should be no more than 1 percent. However, these fees are usually negotiable so don't be afraid to ask for discounts. Then compare these rates with the other fee-based advisors you interview. If the advisor is paid commission, it may be difficult to compare apples to apples because of all the different investment products they can sell. One way to do this is to compare the commission of 100 shares of stock at a hypothetical price of $25. Most brokerage firms also have minimum commission amounts. Be sure to compare these too. The most important thing to remember, if you hire a commission paid broker or salesperson, is that there is always a commission paid somewhere, somehow. Unfortunately, it's your job to ask about it. It's also your job to double check the accuracy of the answer you get. Numerous hidden costs can slowly eat away at your portfolio.

   One common hidden cost is the underwriting fee that is added to a new issue or investment product. If a newly issued stock, fund, or other investment product is offered to you by a broker with no commission charge, ask what the total underwriting fee adds up to be. Often you'll find these underwriting fees to be in excess of 6 percent. What amount is too much? You'll have to be the judge. I avoid these fees altogether.

   If a commission-based broker recommends to you a mutual fund, be sure to ask how you'll pay his commission. If he says the fund pays his commission, you should reply, "No, I'm paying your commission, just tell me how much it is and how I'm paying it." Listen to how he explains it. Ask him to explain the management fees and 12b1 fees. You might want to ask him to show you the explanation in the prospectus. If the fund has a 12b1 fee in excess of .5 percent (half of a percentage point), then this fund is a loaded fund and he should disclose that to you. The broker is paid to sell the fund, and keep you in it. Many of these funds, especially the proprietary funds, pay the broker "trailers" that are extra commission payments paid to the broker as incentive to keep clients in the funds. Always remember to ask what the total 12b1 fees will be each year before you buy any mutual fund from a broker or advisor. Your knowledge will certainly get their attention.

2. **Will you explain to me all the costs involved in each investment?** There are additional fees you need to be aware of that do not go to the broker or advisor. The most common are the management fees that are charged by mutual fund managers. The average domestic stock mutual fund management fee is approximately 1 percent. Foreign funds charge a slightly higher fee while bond funds charge lower fees. Another fee to look for is a custodian fee, which is normally charged by the brokerage firm for holding your account. If your advisor is paid a fee and uses a brokerage firm for trades, you also need to be aware of the commission and transaction fees charged by the brokerage firm.

3. **What if I want to change my mind and fire you?** Very few people think to ask this question. It may seem a bit harsh, but you need to ask it. If you are a positive person, firing the advisor may be the last thing on your mind, but you need to know the logistics and costs involved. You also need to know the cost of liquidating your account. Anything you buy should cost little to nothing to sell, and should have a secondary market where it can be easily sold.

   For example, most full service brokerage firms charge a 2 percent penalty (or $100 whichever is less) for transferring an IRA to another firm. You might not even realize this unless you read the fine print in the IRA agreement you signed when you opened the account. Many mutual funds have back-end loads that can add up to 6 percent if you decide to sell them within one year of purchase. As I pointed out in Chapter 7, most proprietary or packaged products will also have heavy commissions and fees hidden in them.

   Most of the hidden costs are listed somewhere in the agreement you signed to open an account or go with an advisor, or in the prospectus of the specific investment you bought. There are a few that aren't listed, but it would take another chapter to explain all of them. Just remember that nothing is free and that if it sounds too good to be true, it probably is.

4. **Questions to ask yourself.** After you have analyzed all the costs, do they seem reasonable? If you have hired a discretionary money manager, the total cost should not exceed 3 percent of your principal per year. Compare other money managers to see if they are more competitive. If your advisor's rates seem too high, ask for a discount. If you have hired a broker, compare the commission rates with other firms. If the rates seem too high, ask for a discount.

Characteristics

Each advisor has a unique personality that ultimately affects the contents and therefore, results of the portfolio. You need to understand this personality before you hire the advisor.

1. **What is your investment philosophy?** The advisor's investment philosophy is very important to your future. It dictates how your portfolio will be managed and therefore, how your wealth will be built and maintained. Most investment professionals either don't have a philosophy or they have difficulty explaining their investment philosophy within a few sentences. That frightens me. You want someone who can give you their philosophy easily, briefly, and with conviction. When you ask this question, look not only for these qualities, but also for understanding. Do you understand the philosophy? Are you comfortable with it? If you can't understand it, how will you know if you agree with what she thinks? How can you be comfortable with a philosophy you don't understand? For example, my investment philosophy reads: "Investment excellence is the synergy produced when you achieve high performance with global trend diversification, cost efficiency, convenience and the proper level of risk. This process often requires the investor to break down the walls of conventional wisdom."
2. **Do you focus on the domestic market, foreign markets, or both?** The answer should be both. Many advisors focus only on the domestic market, which is a shame. In order to establish the proper level of diversification, you must have both domestic and foreign securities in your portfolio. If the answer is both, ask if they use mutual funds or individual stocks for the foreign portion of the portfolio. If the answer is individual stocks, find someone else. There are only a few advisors in the world who can pick individual stocks and bonds all around the world successfully. If the advisor can show you a track record of success using both domestic and foreign stocks, then maybe you can consider working with him. For example, I think every investment portfolio should have both domestic and foreign stocks, as well as bonds. Instead of using individual stocks, I use mutual funds to accomplish this for my clients.
3. **Tell me a little about yourself.** Get to know your advisor as a person. You have to understand the person before you'll know whether or not she will be compatible with you and your needs. Ask her about her hobbies and interests. Ask her what motivates her. Ask where the advisor grew up.
4. **What is your specialty? What are you the best at?** You need to know what your advisor is good at. You need to know what she enjoys most about the investment business. What she enjoys most is what she will more than likely be the best at, and provide the best results in. My specialty, for example, is global portfolio management using no-load mutual funds.
5. **How do you view risk and how does your philosophy keep me within my risk tolerance?** Let the advisor explain how your risk tolerance is calculated and how your portfolio will be designed accordingly. Don't be afraid to ask questions here. The stock market can be volatile, so make sure you understand the risks involved.

6. **Questions to ask yourself.** You have to consider compatibility. Will you be comfortable with this person? What kind of attitude does he have? Is he patient with you or just trying to sell you something? Do you trust this person? Is he trying to confuse you with investment jargon? Will you worry about your money after you hire this advisor? Is this person a good listener? Did the advisor ask about your goals and objectives? You need to make certain that your advisor will help you achieve your goals. If you don't have any, then he should at least help you establish your expectations for risk and return.

Customer Service

If you pay close attention to the level of service offered by the advisors you interview, you'll more than likely find a large discrepancy. Most advisors offer a status quo level of service. However, as advisory firms and full service brokerage firms become more competitive, you will begin to see additional services such as monthly newsletters, quarterly market reports on audio tape, and detailed transaction explanations explaining why each trade was made.

1. **What services does your firm offer?** If you need a fee-only financial planner, ask what services are offered. The answer is different with each planner. The same is true with brokers and advisors in the money management business. The level of client services offered varies with each firm. Some firms are very competitive with the services they offer. Others don't seem to care. The following list of services will give you an idea of what advisors can offer you (if they want to), and the services you should ask about:
   - Quarterly, if not monthly, brokerage statements (ask to see an example).
   - Quarterly performance statements (ask to see an example).
   - Performance compared to a domestic index and a world index.
   - Advisor available by phone call.
   - A sufficient amount of client service people who can answer administrative questions.
   - Yearly one-on-one client reviews.
   - Yearly tax information statements to help you prepare your taxes.
2. **Where will my assets be held?** If you are considering an independent money manager, there should be an independent third-party custodian holding your assets for you. This custodian should be a brokerage firm that sends you statements every month. The money manager should have a limited power of attorney agreement with the brokerage firm that allows him to buy and sell securities for you, deduct his

fee quarterly, and get a copy of your monthly statement and daily account information. Having this independent firm separates your money manager from your account, and reduces the possibility of fraud.

That Reminds Me...

Years ago, in a small retirement community, one of my clients hired a man who called himself an advisor. She opened an account with the advisor and began receiving statements showing above average results. She began hearing other clients of his complain about not getting their monthly checks. Since she didn't need income from her account, she didn't have any problems—at least that's what she thought. The next thing she knew, the advisor had skipped town with her money. Every client this guy had was not only scared to death, they were furious and even embarrassed. How could this guy get away with this? It was easy! He was depositing the money in his own account and fraudulently producing his own statements. There was no independent third party producing a second statement. Approximately $10 million in client assets was lost. Therefore, when you open an account with an independent advisor, make your check out to the brokerage firm where your account is being held, not your advisor. Once your account is opened, call the brokerage firm and check your account number and balance. You should also receive a confirmation of the account being opened in the mail. Be sure to compare the statements you receive from the advisor with those of the brokerage firm.

3. **How accessible will he or she be?** It can be very frustrating to not have access to information or answers when you need them. Who do you call when your advisor is on vacation? Make sure the advisor has hired other advisors who can help you. This is called "depth." A firm has depth if it has employed more than one advisor.

4. **What has been your year to year performance vs. the S & P 500?** All advisors should be able to furnish you with a track record. This track record should be presented along with other relative indexes against which you can compare. It should reflect the combined performance of all the advisor's accounts and should mention that it was prepared using AIMR standards. The most common broad market indexes are:

   - The Standard & Poors 500 (S&P 500)
   - The Lipper Balanced Fund Index
   - The Morgan Stanley World Market Index

The best index to beat would be the last one because it represents an index of stocks diversified all around the world. If the advisor lagged all of these indexes, indicating lower than expected performance, you might want to ask why. Remember, don't base your entire decision on the advisor's past performance. Just because the advisor did well last year (or the past 10 years), doesn't mean you can expect the same performance this year. Be sure to consider the philosophy of the manager before you eliminate him just because his track record is bad. His philosophy might be right on target next year.

If you are hiring a commission-based broker, you will not get a track record. Brokerage firms do not offer track records on their individual broker's performances, nor on the client's individual account. You'll get individual performance data on your account if you are in a wrap account, but otherwise, you're on your own.

5. **What was your worst year? Best?** Wouldn't you like to know the advisor's worst year? Ask him what happened and listen to his answer. You want an advisor that takes responsibility for his results. If he defends his performance too much, he might not be willing to admit a mistake later. All advisors make mistakes. You want an advisor who's honest about it and willing to admit his mistakes. If he's willing to admit it, he's also more likely to correct it more quickly.

6. **Do you use AIMR Standards in reporting performance?** The best industry standard for reporting investment performance is the Association for Investment Management and Research (AIMR) Standard. These standards are intended to foster a fair representation and full disclosure of performance results. The second goal of these standards is to promote greater uniformity and comparability among performance presentations. The guidelines are strict and comprehensive. If your advisor does not claim to use these standards, you should ask him why he's not willing to comply with industry standards.

That Reminds Me...

The organization that administers the *Chartered Financial Analyst* (CFA) course and exam is the *Institute of Chartered Financial Analysts* (ICFP), which is a subsidiary of the *Association for Investment Management and Research* (AIMR). If your advisor is a CFA, his performance numbers must comply with AIMR standards. Otherwise he will lose his designation. The first objective of the AIMR standards is to establish a common, accepted set of ethical principles that ensure fair representation and full disclosure in investment managers' presentations of their results to clients and prospective clients. Their second objective is to achieve greater uniformity and comparability among such presentations. Without these standards, an advisor can manipulate his performance data to seem more attractive than it actually is. You can order AIMR's handbook of standards, titled *Performance Presentation Standards,* by calling 804-980-3647; Fax 804-977-0350. The cost is $20.

7. **Do you offer financial planning, money management, or both?** If you hire a financial planner, they need to know every aspect of planning, which includes spending control, retirement and estate planning, saving, asset protection, life insurance, and taxes. If you hire a money manager, they need to know every aspect of investment management, which includes investment strategy, global investment trends, domestic industry trends, interest rates, and a full knowledge of all the best investment products available.

   You may find that you need both a money manager and a financial planner. If you hire one person to do both, make sure you check their references. It's very difficult to be good at both. There are certainly exceptions to this rule. I personally know several advisors that do both well, but they are the exceptions, not the rule.

8. **Can you show me your client's portfolio performance each quarter for the last few years?** This is similar to numbers 4 and 5, but in more detail. These statistics might not be available, but if you can observe quarterly performance, you can get an idea of the volatility this manager has produced. Pay attention to the best and worst performing quarters. If you can't handle the kind of fluctuation you see in these numbers, don't hire this guy.

9. **How many clients did you lose last year? Why?** Every advisor loses clients each year for many different reasons. Before you hire an advisor, ask how many clients he lost and why. If he says none, you should be suspicious. There are many different reasons why advisors lose clients. It's a natural occurrence that cannot be prevented. I personally lost 12 clients out of 350 in 1995. Most of the reasons had nothing to do with me or my service. They either moved away, got scared of the market, or wanted to manage the money themselves. If the advisor says he's not lost a client, he might have lost several for reasons he doesn't want you to know.

Treasure Tip
You may find that most money managers will help you with the basics of financial planning. However, if you need more detail, find a fee-only financial planner who can help you. Make sure they spend time educating you so you can eventually do most of the planning yourself.

10. **Questions to ask yourself.** Do you feel that this firm will take care of your needs? Do they have a bias toward customer service? Are they open to your questions? Do they try to educate their clients? Find out specifically what makes this firm different. Do they have any unique services? Do they have sufficient staff to cover their clientele? How many advisors do they have that are registered? Do they have enough knowledgeable staff to cover their client's needs or are they understaffed?

Client References

It is standard procedure in almost any service business to ask for client references. The only thing different about the investment business is advisors have to ask a client's permission prior to using that client as a reference. Once the client agrees, the advisor can offer their name and phone number to other prospective clients who inquire. Some advisors don't offer references and when asked, they reply, "My clients are confidential." Don't accept this answer. It ought to be a warning signal. If the advisor has a legitimate business and does a good job, then his clients should be willing to be references. I did a survey of my clients in 1994, and asked them if they would allow me to use their name and phone number as a reference. Out of all the responses we received, only one declined. He said he was just too busy to take any calls.

Get at least three references that have been with the advisor longer than one year. You might ask for the client that has been with the advisor the longest. You need to talk to clients who have been with the advisor during bad market years like 1994 or even 1987. The advisor will naturally give you a list of his happiest clients, but you should still make the call. When you do talk to the references, assure them that their answers are confidential and that you have no intention of sharing them with anyone, including the advisor. Here are some questions you might ask:

1. **How long have you known (the advisor)?** I have clients that have known me since I was five years old. They know much more about me than a client that hired me just last year.

Wealth Warning

Don't accept the opinion of a client referral who is related to your advisor. Ask for one of the advisor's first clients. They can tell you the most about the advisor.

2. **What do you like best about (the advisor)? What do you like the least about (the advisor)?** These are my favorite questions. They are seldom asked, but they are probably the most powerful. The answers may tell you something about the advisor that you'd never otherwise know. You might find a personality trait that might make you feel more comfortable about working with the advisor. You might also find a monster in the closet! Whatever the case, the answers to these questions are usually by far the most interesting.

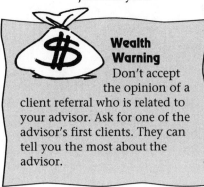

3. **Knowing what you know now, would you hire (the advisor) again today?** This is called zero based thinking. The question is whether or not the client would hire the advisor if he had to do it all over again. The answer often gives you more insight into how the client really feels about the advisor. If the answer is yes, you might even add, "Do you mind telling me why?"
4. **Has (the advisor) made you money?** You might want to be more specific and ask if the advisor has beaten the S&P 500 or other indexes important to you. You might also ask if the advisor achieved the return goal he set for his clients.
5. **Did (the advisor) do what he said he was going to do?** Did he make any promises he didn't keep? This is the ultimate question that sums it all up for you.

Background Check

Finally, before hiring any type of advisor, broker, or planner, you might even want to call your state's Securities Department to see if there have been any complaints filed on the advisor. If you want to get an idea of the kind of professional to avoid, just ask them about the most common complaints. Most consumer complaints involve financial planners, brokers, and advisors who earn their income solely by commissions, especially those advisors who represent only one company such as one mutual fund family.

The biggest scam in the investment business is the salesperson who calls himself a financial planner to disguise his true colors. If you hire a financial planner who charges you a fee for a financial plan and then gives you a plan with loaded (commissioned) mutual funds, you should run away as fast as you can. If the plan suggests proprietary funds (funds run by the firm the advisor works for), you should run even faster. This is one of the biggest conflicts of interest in the business.

The Least You Need to Know

- If investing is not your hobby or passion, you should consider hiring a fee-only advisor and avoid commission-based brokers.
- The best advisor to hire is a fee-only advisor who may be a money manager, financial planner, or both.
- Before you hire any professional, make sure he or she is compatible with your personality, risk tolerance, and financial goals.
- Make sure the advisor is registered with either the Securities and Exchange Commission, your state's Securities Department, or the National Association of Securities Dealers.
- Be sure to ask for references and call at least three of them.

Chapter 10

Getting Your Feet Wet with the First Decision

In This Chapter

- What to look for in your first investment
- How to avoid the commission trap
- Measuring your risk tolerance
- Setting up your return expectations
- Specific mutual fund ideas

In Wealth Level 1, when you make your first investment decision, you might feel somewhat overwhelmed. This chapter will help you narrow your focus considerably and get you started on the right track. The first mistake most investors make when they begin investing is procrastination. Most investors fear their first investment decision so much that they procrastinate, sometimes for years. They think they have to buy a stock or something complicated that requires days of study and research. If you follow the five questions in the first pages of Chapter 8, you'll instantly narrow down your choices considerably. Therefore, the first investment decision should actually be the easiest, and this chapter will give you a nudge in the right direction.

Most first-time investors are also so afraid of making a mistake that they actually become frozen in fear. Don't let this happen to you. Remember from Chapter 3 that the most important element initially is the amount of money you save, not total return. Your first investment decision is important, but the amount of money you save is much more important. Mistakes early in your journey can often be completely covered by one or two savings deposits down the line.

Don't Be a Sucker

Yes, the first investment for most people can be the most expensive. Why? Because the first-time investor usually knows the least, which means he falls pray to commission traps sold by brokers, insurance agents, and other salespeople. The typical first-time investor buys an insurance policy as an investment or a fully loaded mutual fund.

Some loaded mutual fund investments are sold as contracts that require monthly deposits, usually in the form of automatic checking account debits. The debit concept is great. Automatically, without any effort on the part of the investor, money is withdrawn from his checking account and invested for him. However, if you are buying a loaded fund, the commission usually bites heavily into the deposit before any money actually gets invested.

If you are a novice investor, it's difficult to prevent a smooth salesman from selling you an investment product with heavy commissions. They are trained to sell and they are wonderful at it. Your best defense is knowledge. Chapters 7 and 8 should have helped with the basics of the good and bad alternatives.

For your first investment, pass on anything that seems to have a high commission attached. Also, trust your gut and pass if the salesperson is using heavy-handed tactics or is trying to rush your decision.

That Reminds Me...

I have a client who was sold a mutual fund with a 50 percent commission charge on the first year's monthly deposits. This is still legal and promoted heavily in the armed forces by commission-paid salespeople. He was sold one of the most expensive investment products known to man. Fortunately for him, his tenacity and market performance prevailed and his account grew substantially as he continued his deposits. However, he said, "If I would have known there were such things as no-load mutual funds, my account might have performed a little better."

What Should Your First Investment Look Like?

If you understand the necessary characteristics of a properly diversified portfolio, you'll find that the list of investments is quite short. Because the list is so small, you may not need an advisor to help you. If you are uncomfortable with making a decision after reading this chapter, then you may want to get some help from a fee-only investment advisor, using the questions in Chapter 9 to help select one whom you're comfortable with.

Near the end of Chapter 8, I gave you a list of optimal wealth-building portfolio characteristics. Here's a reminder of the most important elements:

- The portfolio is built primarily of stocks.
- The stocks are diversified among many different countries and industries, to help maximize return while reducing risk.
- The portfolio can be cost-efficiently adjusted.

One stock can't meet all these characteristics. However, if you think the above characteristics are boring and you have your heart set on buying a stock or another investment idea, go ahead and try it. Make your mistakes now while they don't hurt so bad. Go with your gut and with a little luck, you might do well.

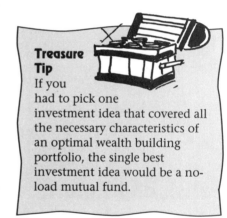

Treasure Tip
If you had to pick one investment idea that covered all the necessary characteristics of an optimal wealth building portfolio, the single best investment idea would be a no-load mutual fund.

The only way you can possibly design a portfolio of less than $100,000 using the portfolio characteristics listed above is with no-load mutual funds. Therefore, before you make your next investment decision, let's explore mutual funds again.

You Have to Meet the Minimums

All mutual funds have a minimum investment amount you must meet to initially buy shares in the fund. Therefore, you have to pay attention to minimums when you design your portfolio. If you have only $1,000 and want to get started with a mutual fund, you might have difficulty finding a fund. Some funds have a $25,000 minimum, but the average minimum investment is $1,000. If you have less than $1,000 to invest, you can either wait until you've saved that much or find a fund with low minimums. For example, **Twentieth Century Funds** (800-345-2021) offers a number of funds with low initial investment minimums. Some funds will accept less than $1,000 if you agree to purchase at least that amount over the course of a year using monthly deposits.

Narrowing the List

Your first step should be to buy a single fund that is globally diversified. You need a fund that invests not only in the U.S., but in other developed and emerging market countries. Very few funds do this well, so your list of alternatives is quite small.

If you're looking for a globally diversified fund (that invests in the U.S. and foreign countries), you may encounter some confusion. These funds go by different names depending upon which mutual fund rating service or publication you choose. The most common title is "International Funds," which include mutual funds that invest in the U.S. and foreign countries. You might also find the title "Global Funds," which should be the same. Regardless of what they say, make certain you know how these funds are allocated. Be sure not to mistake a foreign fund for an international fund. Foreign funds invest exclusively in foreign countries.

The following is a list of funds I personally like that are globally diversified:

Sogen International (low load)	800-334-2143
Founders Worldwide Growth	800-525-2440
Mutual Discovery (small caps)	800-553-3014
Scudder Global Discovery	800-225-2470
USAA World Growth	800-382-8722

Remember that these are just ideas to get your started. Please be sure to read the prospectuses before you buy these funds.

Risk and Return

The stock market lost almost 80 percent of its value in the crash of 1929. The market did come back, but it took a few years to do it. The possibility of a crash like this is highly unlikely today, however, the risk is there. The more likely scenario is a 10 or 20 percent drop in stock prices. Many investors refer to this as a stock market "correction." The question you need to ask yourself is whether or not you could handle the potential damage to your portfolio. If you can accept this risk, then you are what I consider to be an aggressive investor who should focus 100 percent on stocks or stock funds that are diversified throughout companies all over the world.

"To Thine Own Self Be True"

Most investors overestimate the level of risk they can actually handle. Their true risk tolerance is unmasked only when an actual correction is experienced. When this happens in Wealth Levels 3, 4, and 5, it may be too late to make any adjustments. Therefore, either lean a little more to the conservative side or accept the risk of a correction. Keep in mind that you are investing for the longrun.

What Kind of Return Do You Expect?

An aggressive investor should target investments with annual returns in excess of 15 percent, moderate investors should shoot for 12–15 percent, and conservative investors 8–12 percent. Don't try to hit home runs, no matter how much risk you think you can tolerate. Investing is like baseball. It's won with base hits, not home runs. The more home runs you attempt, the more you'll strike out. However, if you're bored with base hits, go for the fence now, early in your career. When you do make a mistake, learn from it. Spend some time learning why you failed. Ask yourself:

- What could you have done to prevent this loss?
- If you had to do it all again, what would you do differently?
- What will you do next time to improve your results?

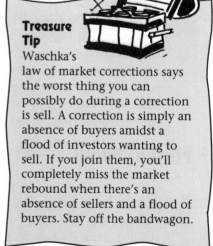

Take some time to learn from the loss, but don't let it discourage you. So many people take their mistakes personally. They say to themselves, "I guess that's just the kind of investor I am." I hear them say to me all the time, "If you want something to go down, just let me buy it." This is a horrible attitude to have, and ironically, it is very self-fulfilling. If you think this way, you better believe you'll lose money. But if you take the time to learn from your losses, you'll be all the wiser.

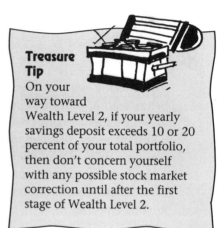

Treasure Tip
On your way toward Wealth Level 2, if your yearly savings deposit exceeds 10 or 20 percent of your total portfolio, then don't concern yourself with any possible stock market correction until after the first stage of Wealth Level 2.

Treasure Tip
Waschka's law of market corrections says the worst thing you can possibly do during a correction is sell. A correction is simply an absence of buyers amidst a flood of investors wanting to sell. If you join them, you'll completely miss the market rebound when there's an absence of sellers and a flood of buyers. Stay off the bandwagon.

Investment Ideas for the Confused and Bewildered

If you're starting to work on your portfolio, there are some key investment tools to consider: stocks, real estate, and mutual funds.

Individual Stocks

If your heart is set on individual stocks, that's great. Be sure to learn all you can about buying stocks. There are a number of books on stock picking that you might want to read. The two best authors I've found are Peter Lynch and Ben Graham. Check your local library or bookstore.

Real Estate

If you decide you want to try real estate, that's also fine. Be sure to learn all you can before buying your first rental property. Property management can be a nightmare. Waking up to a tenant's call at 3 a.m. because the toilet broken is not my idea of fun. If you want to speculate on undeveloped land, just remember—this is one of the riskiest investments available. Therefore, you better make real estate your business before you make a purchase. For example, if you are a licensed real estate appraiser, then by all means focus your attention on real estate as an investment. You'll see deals before anyone else does.

Real estate is just like any other industry or business. I don't believe real estate is a particularly better industry than any other. It has its good years and its bad just like other industries. In the late 70s, for example, we had double-digit property appreciation almost nationwide. Banks would loan money on almost any property. Those days are long gone and we don't have that environment available anymore. It's simply just another industry now—one that happens to be filled with con men on TV offering "no money down" books, cassettes, and videos that lead to very little actual success. However, many fortunes have been made in the real estate market, and if you expect to make your fortune this way—go for it. Just remember one thing: No matter what industry you decide to use to build your wealth, you better have a passion to be the best at it. Otherwise, you won't have the desire to learn all you can about it.

Mutual Funds

I prefer to use mutual funds. They require relatively less attention and offer a level of diversification beyond any other investment opportunity in the world. I've tried individual stocks, bonds, options, futures, real estate, and even dividend reinvestment plans (DRIPs). From the standpoint of balancing risk with returns, nothing builds wealth better than mutual funds.

Because of the ever-changing market, I hesitate to mention any specific mutual fund ideas, but I want to help you get started. You have to keep in mind that markets change, funds change, and that managers may leave the fund. You can't assume that any fund will remain profitable, will duplicate past performance, or will keep the same manager. However, the funds I'm suggesting next have seasoned managers that should be with the fund for a long time. They are only as good as their managers, and if the manager leaves the fund, you may want to find another fund.

Let me assure you that I receive nothing for mentioning these funds. I like the philosophies of the managers. They are all very unique and brilliant at what they do and I know they will take good care of your money.

- **Aggressive Risk.** Founders Worldwide Growth (800-525-2440) is known for its allocation toward foreign markets. This is truly a globally diversified fund with only about a third of its assets invested in the U.S. market. The fund has holdings in developed and emerging markets all over the world.
- **Moderate Risk.** Mutual Discovery (800-553-3014) is managed by Mike Price who focuses his attention on small-cap stocks (stocks for smaller companies) here in the U.S. and Europe. Mike focuses on special situations like mergers, corporate restructurings, subsidiary spin-offs, and bankruptcies. He tries to buy companies for 65 cents on the dollar and sell them at 95 cents to a dollar. What makes him unique is the active role he often takes with the management of the companies in which he chooses to invest. Out of the three Mutual Series Funds he manages, he claims that Discovery is his most conservative fund.
- **Conservative Risk.** Sogen International (800-334-2143) has a small load, but it is worth paying if you insist on a single conservatively managed fund. Jean Marie Eveillard has managed this fund for many years and has produced a combination of above-average returns along with relatively low price volatility. His portfolio is diversified among an eclectic mix of stocks all over the world. If I knew I was going to be stranded on a desert island for 10 years with no contact with the real world, I'd never worry a minute if all my money was invested with Jean Marie at Sogen International.

Don't Spend Too Much Time Monitoring Your Investment

If you are focusing on achieving Wealth Level 2, now is not the time to look at your investments every day. There are two much more important things to focus on now: your savings amount and investment knowledge. These are the two most important elements during your journey toward Wealth Levels 1 and 2.

The Tortoise and the Hare

Most beginning investors worry too much about picking the fastest growing investment. They focus too much on the market and not enough time on minimizing expenses or meeting their target savings goal. The result is portfolio mediocrity as their unbalanced portfolio never grows significantly in size. Such investors end up with a volatile portfolio that might be growing at a 15 percent rate, but it doesn't really matter. Because they didn't meet their target savings goal, their account never grew very big. It's the classic tortoise and the hare story. While the hare runs around frantically trying to buy the best performing stocks each month, the tortoise wins the race because he saved as much as he could each year. His returns might not be all that incredible, but his account value sure is. Try to be the tortoise, not the hare.

Invest Automatically

Most mutual funds offer an automatic debit service from your checking account. This is a no-brainer, yet so few people take advantage of it. Over half of the people I suggest this to are afraid of it. I've narrowed down the list of fears most people have of the automatic debit service:

- Fear of the mutual fund company taking advantage of them
- Fear of an invasion of privacy
- Fear of losing control
- Fear of forgetting to record the deposit in the check register

Treasure Tip

Waschka's law of savings says save automatically by letting a mutual fund debit your checking account each month.

First, the mutual fund can't take advantage of you. Why would they jeopardize their registration with the SEC just to get a few more dollars out of your account? Second, the mutual fund can only debit a certain amount, not check your balance! Third, this service is a way to gain control over spending, not lose control. Fourth, write a big note where you pay your bills to record the debit each month. The debit service is too easy and powerful not to take advantage of it.

Where to Put the First Investment

Your first investment could be purchased within an IRA, which would allow it to grow tax-deferred. It doesn't matter whether or not you can deduct the deposit; what's important is the tax deferred growth and the almost unlimited investment alternatives to choose from. Therefore, consider your first $2,000 investment going into an IRA. Any of the types of investments listed here in this chapter can be purchased within an IRA.

An IRA is simply an investment account. An IRA at a bank may be invested in a CD, but it is actually an account. They may restrict you to CDs only, but it is still an account. Brokerage firms (full service and discount) offer the same account. However, they will allow you to put several different securities or funds within that same IRA account. This is a confusing topic. Just remember, you can have as many different IRA accounts as you want. You might decide to do business directly with several different no-load mutual fund companies. That's fine. Each one will open an IRA account for you.

You could also start out by investing in your 401k from your employer. In a 401k, you're probably not going to find an international fund as an alternative. More than likely you'll find a foreign fund that could be combined with a domestic stock fund to achieve a global balance.

You could also start your own investment account for yourself (and your spouse). The first decision you'll have to make is whether or not to buy directly from a mutual fund or through a discount brokerage firm. For now, as long as you are buying only one or two funds, going with the discount brokerage firm doesn't give you much of an advantage. Later, when you own three or more funds, the discount brokerage firm will let you consolidate your portfolio into one account. This is a real time-saver. Investing directly with several different funds can be time-consuming. To buy a fund, you have to call for an application, wait for the application to arrive, fill it out, send it in, wait for them to receive it, and then they purchase the fund for you. This could take ten days. This entire procedure can take place the same day if you have an account with a brokerage firm that offers no-load funds. Instead of getting many different statements in the mail, the brokerage firm will consolidate all your mutual funds on one statement. Instead of getting several different 1099s at the end of the year, you get one.

Remember, discount brokerage firms are somewhat limited in their list of available funds. Therefore, your favorite fund might not be on their list. You can call the firm and ask if they plan to add that fund, or you can just go directly to the fund itself.

Graduating to More Than One Fund

The best advice I can give any novice investor who's looking to do more is to learn all you can. Graduating from one fund to two or three requires a little more knowledge and confidence, which are easily attainable from books and investment classes. If you want to learn more about mutual funds, read *The Complete Idiot's Guide to Mutual Funds*. If you just can't stand this stuff, get a fee-only advisor to help you get started.

Words of the Wealthy
A **value-oriented** manager searches for undervalued stocks that are priced below what the manager actually thinks they're worth. The goal of the value manager is to sell at a profit once the market realizes the stock's true value.

Words of the Wealthy
A **growth-oriented** manager searches for stocks with high earnings growth. Investors are willing to pay relatively higher prices for these stocks for the chance that they may be even higher later.

Graduating to Two Funds

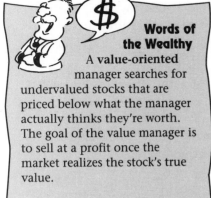

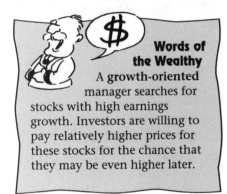

Assuming you chose one mutual fund in your investment portfolio, sooner or later you're going to have enough money to diversify into two, three, or more funds. There's no magic amount to begin this split, it's all a matter of preference and whether or not you can meet the minimums on the funds you have selected. You want to be sure to build a mix of domestic and foreign invested funds. If you tend to be a little conservative, focus on stock funds that buy off relatively large companies using a value-oriented philosophy. You might also keep your foreign fund allocation at or below the 30 percent level, which leaves 70 percent of your money domestically invested.

If you are an aggressive investor, you might want to focus on stock funds that buy stocks of relatively small companies using a growth oriented philosophy. Your foreign allocation could be as high as 50 percent.

When you select each fund, look for a fund manager that thinks like you do. The only way to find this out is by reading the manager's objective and philosophy in the prospectus. You might get lucky and find an article or television interview, but chances are you're going to have to do some searching. Don't worry; the next six chapters should make the search a little easier.

Graduating to Three Funds

You might consider three funds once your portfolio grows beyond $15,000. If you are a moderate-risk investor, your three-fund portfolio should look something like this:

35%—Small-cap domestic stock fund

30%—Mid-cap domestic stock fund

35%—Foreign stock fund

Basically, you would be adding a small-cap fund to your portfolio at this point. If you are conservative, you can still use a value manager with a 30 percent or less foreign allocation. Aggressive investors can use a growth oriented manager and up to 50 percent foreign.

You don't really need any more than 12 mutual funds in a portfolio. Graduating beyond the three-fund portfolio takes more time and effort. The next six chapters will help you be more effective and efficient in that effort.

The Least You Need to Know

- Your first investment should meet basic portfolio characteristics, which should include a focus on stocks (a stock mutual fund) that are diversified globally, and managed cost-efficiently.
- Don't let a smooth-talking salesperson take advantage of you by selling you an expensive investment product.
- Learn as much as you can from your mistakes by asking yourself what you will do next time to improve your results.
- If you are a conservative investor, focus on value-oriented mutual funds, and if you are aggressive, focus on growth-oriented mutual funds.
- On your way to Wealth Level 1, don't monitor your investment every day—focus on learning more about he market and maximizing your savings amount.

Chapter 11

The Investment Management Cycle

In This Chapter

- Real-life asset allocation strategy
- The most important portfolio management strategy
- When you should sell

This chapter is designed to teach you the cycle of building wealth through the use of your investment portfolio. If you understand the principals in this cycle, you will be able to achieve any wealth level you desire. Once your portfolio exceeds approximately $10,000, which is large enough to easily diversify among more than three mutual funds, you're ready to take advantage of another level of opportunity called multi-fund portfolio management. You now have the ability to add additional layers of diversification to your portfolio, hire a team of investment specialists, and build a synergistically profitable portfolio.

But how do you select the investments to build this portfolio? Most investors use past performance. All the fine print says not to do this, but investors do it anyway. Markets do change, meaning that your investment strategies should reflect these changes. That's what this chapter is all about, incorporating a portfolio management cycle that keeps up with the changing markets.

This chapter primarily refers to mutual funds, because that's where I spend most of my time helping my clients. However, you can use the same principles in this chapter for stock investing. It's a lot more difficult to do, but it can be done if you have the time and passion necessary.

The Portfolio Management Cycle Asset Allocation.

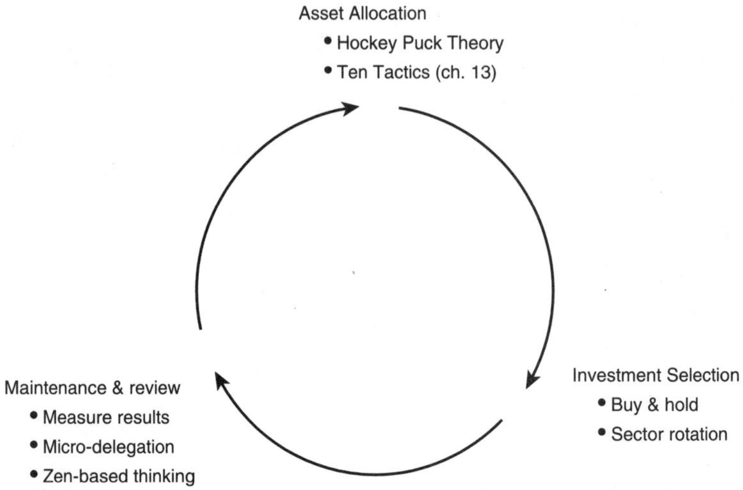
Asset Allocation
• Hockey Puck Theory
• Ten Tactics (ch. 13)
Investment Selection
• Buy & hold
• Sector rotation
Maintenance & review
• Measure results
• Micro-delegation
• Zen-based thinking

Asset Allocation

The first step in the portfolio management cycle is asset allocation, which is simply dividing your assets among several different types of investments or asset classes for the purpose of diversification and profit. An asset class can be stocks, bonds, money markets, gold, or even real estate. The theory of asset allocation is based upon the idea that a portfolio diversified among many different asset classes will incur less risk than a portfolio invested in only one class.

Throw Away Your Asset Allocation Software

There are also several very expensive software programs available that will calculate your "optimal" asset allocation based upon your risk tolerances. Unfortunately, the outcome is based upon years of past performances of each asset class. This means that the allocation you get assumes that the future will be very similar to the past, which is one thing that is simply not true. Therefore, don't waste money on these programs.

Don't Base It on Your Age

How do you know how much to place in each asset class? Most brokers and investment advisors use some type of rule to decide how an investors assets should be allocated. The rule is usually pretty dogmatic. For example, many of them believe that an investor's bond allocation should be based upon age. If you are 25, then 25 percent of your portfolio should be in bonds and 75 percent should be in stocks. If you are 80, then 80 percent of your portfolio should be in bonds and 20 percent in stocks. Remember this: The market doesn't care how old you are, it will take your head off whether you are 25 years old or 80. If you had 80 percent of your money in bonds in 1994, your portfolio got hammered.

Instead, your allocation in any type of investment should be based upon your risk tolerance and how you feel about that investment, as well as the risk you are willing to assume to meet the goals you want to achieve. You can also take into account the Hockey Puck Theory, described next.

Base Your Asset Allocation Upon the Hockey Puck Theory

It's said that Wayne Gretzky, the most popular hockey player in the world and definitely one of the best, was asked by a reporter one day, "Wayne, I don't get it. Why are you so much better than your teammates and opponents? You are not a faster skater. You are not a quicker puck handler. You're not even any meaner. What makes you so much better?"

Wayne stopped a minute and said, "Well, most of my teammates and players skate to where the hockey puck is. I skate to where I think the hockey puck is going to be." This has nothing to do with investing, but it has everything to do with excellence in portfolio management. If you think about it for a minute, most investors don't even invest where the market is. They invest where? Where the market has been, right? So, your goal should be to invest where the market is going, and not where it has been. You must be willing to invest your money based upon what you think is going to happen. To do that, you have to understand trends. A trend is a three, five, or ten year series of events that affect a niche of the world economically, politically, and socially. The most dramatic trends go on to affect the entire world.

The whole idea behind investing for profits is to position your money to take advantage of the best investment opportunities available. These opportunities are best found by focusing your attention on trends, especially the ones indicated by small revolutionary changes in the world that have the potential to:

- Spawn new products and maybe new industries
- Improve the health and lifestyles of people all over the world
- Help emerging countries catch up with the modern world
- Help corporations be more productive and profitable

Therefore, instead of allocating assets the conventional way—using different asset classes—position your assets to take advantage of trends. By diversifying your money among several different unrelated trends, you dramatically increase your potential for returns and reduce your risk of loss.

That Reminds Me...

If you really want to find examples of the most dramatic trends in the world, just pick up a copy of *The Economist.* Its "Survey Of The Software Industry" (May 25, 1996, p. 4) said that John Doerr, one of Silicon Valley's leading venture capitalists, has calculated that the introduction of the PC caused the largest creation of wealth in the history of the planet. The article also said that Morgan Stanley's Mary Meeker, one of the computer industry's most respected analysts, reckons that the Internet has the potential to become even bigger. This is a TREND with a capital "T."

If you are going to forecast trends, you have to be able to develop scenarios based upon events that are currently unfolding. This requires some knowledge, imagination, and a heavy reliance on the latest flow of economic data. You need all this to provide some hint of a realistic prediction of the future. Your prediction doesn't really have to be exactly on target, you just have to be close. It's a little like landing an airplane using only your instruments in the midst of a hurricane. It may be difficult, but it certainly beats flying completely blind.

So the first thing you do is find the most dramatic trends in the world. You can start simply by asking your spouse or parents what they new things they are spending money on. You can also find trends in the news media. Instead of just listening to the news, spend time thinking about how you could profit from the events being covered. Look for statistics whenever you can (like the number of people using cellular phones or beepers, for example). Select the three to six best trends you can find and design your portfolio to take advantage of these trends. If you select unrelated trends, your portfolio will have a certain amount of diversification. You have to expect to be wrong to some degree. At least one of these trends might not develop the way you anticipated. If you diversify among several trends, your mistake won't hurt so bad. You can divide evenly among the trends or over-weight some trends more than others. What does a trend look like and how do you find one? Chapter 13 will help you easily identify these trends.

Second, find ways to exploit those trends. You can do this with individual stocks and bonds or mutual funds. The most convenient method would involve mutual funds.

While the mutual fund manager focuses on the micro view of the corporate world, you have more time to focus on the macro view of the world. If you allocate your assets among these funds according to the amount of confidence you have in the trends you've selected, your portfolio will be more customized to your personality and beliefs. That's the way it should be. You should invest in what you believe in.

Why not take a minute to write down the five most influential trends in your life. Observe what you have purchased in the last several months. Look at the magazines you read, especially any trade magazines you might use in your business. What's new? What changes do you see in the future? Here's a list to get you started:

- Advances in healthcare the aging babyboomers who'll need it
- Advances in communications via cellular phones and pagers
- The growth of emerging market countries and their communications industries
- The aging babyboomers and their desire to travel more for pleasure as they approach the age of 50

This method of asset allocation is what I call real-life asset allocation. Most investment professional and professors will argue that it doesn't work because it's not based on specific procedures, has no equations or formulas, and doesn't have any set guidelines for use. However, neither does the market!

Because of the market's tendency to continuously change, you can't expect quantifiable logic to work. If the market was quantifiable and easy to profit from, everyone would be rich! But that's not the case. Therefore, if you want to flow with the market and make any money, you have to escape from conventional wisdom and remain flexible in your strategies. Your success will be directly related to your ability to stay flexible and adapt to the changes.

Investment Selection

The second part of the portfolio management cycle is investment selection. Most people just pick stocks or mutual funds without any thought to allocation. They grab a magazine from the shelf at the grocery store checkout stand, pick a great performing fund off the "Top Picks" list, call the company, and just like that—they're invested. As soon as their fund is off the "Top Ten List," they swap into another fund. This is the scary truth about investors today. They spend more time cleaning their car than they do planning their investment portfolio.

There are basically three types of fund selection strategies. These strategies work, but you cannot be dogmatic with them. You have to be flexible and adaptable to change. The market is not dogmatic, and neither should you be when investing in it. You are also going to be wrong a certain percentage of the time. When you make a mistake, first you have to be willing to admit it without taking it personally. Then, you must be proactive enough to correct your mistake.

> **Treasure Tip**
>
> Morningstar (800-876-5005) is a company in Chicago that produces printed and computer-based research that will make your mutual fund selection process much easier. They offer a $55 trial subscription of their printed product which is normally $395 per year. They also have trial offers on their computer-based products including CD-ROMs. I don't pay attention to their opinions or fund ratings because they are based on several years of past performance. But I do use the factual information they offer.

Each selection strategy is used in conjunction with your asset allocation decision. If you have decided to devote 20 percent of your portfolio to technology stocks, then you need to select one or two technology funds to fill that 20 percent allocation. These selection techniques will help you do that. There are three investment selection strategies: buy and hold, market timing, and sector rotation.

Buy and Hold Strategy

This is the single most common strategy used by mutual fund investors. It simply is what it says: Buy a security and hold it through good times and bad. But this strategy should only be part of your investment selection strategy. You should use the buy and hold strategy to build the core of your portfolio which should deliver stability to your over-all portfolio. Core funds are rarely traded, and are usually held two to four years.

When using this strategy to purchase mutual funds, the most important thing is the manager. You want the fund to go with the flow of the market. If the market is overpriced, then you want the manager to take action toward protecting the fund from a possible correction. Whatever the market conditions are, you want the fund manager to be able to react properly and invest in almost anything he sees fit to buy. Therefore, you want the manager to have few restrictions. You can find a list of these restrictions in the prospectus. If you give someone few restrictions, you need to demand a lot of experience.

Make sure to look for funds that have a relatively steady track record in good times and bad. Don't overlook new funds. Most investors shy away from new funds because there is no three, five or ten year track record. The manager might have a great record at another fund that you can easily research.

The best fund managers in the world are interviewed regularly in publications such as *Barrons* and *Forbes*. They are truly giants in the industry. Here are a few of my favorites and the funds they manage:

- Mike Price, Mutual Series Funds, 800-553-3014
- Robert Sanborn, Oakmark Fund, 800-grow oak
- Don Yacktman, ("Yok-man") Yacktman Fund, 800-525-8258
- Eric Ryback, Lindner Dividend, 314-727-5305
- Carlene Murphy Zieglar, Artisan Small Cap, 800-344-1770
- Jean-Marie Eveillard, Sogen Funds (low load), 800-334-2143
- Chris Browne, Tweedy Browne Global Value, 800-432-4789

Don't just buy one of these funds because it is listed here. Get their prospectus and annual report and do some research (your own fundamental analysis). Chart the funds using the software listed in Chapter 12 and select the fund with the best performance but least volatility.

Words of the Wealthy

Fundamental analysis is the study of the basic facts that determine a security's value. A fundamental analysis of a mutual fund includes the study of the securities within the fund, the manager, the philosophy, expenses, and average P/E ratio.

Market Timing

Market timing is simply the strategy of being in the market when it is going up and out when it's going down. This is quite a seductive strategy, but it's almost impossible to accomplish consistently over time. Market timing is also known as technical analysis which includes primarily the study of information in the form of charts. Technical analysts attempt to predict the movement of a particular market or security based upon past behavior in similar market circumstances.

Words of the Wealthy

Using charts to read the price history and other statistical patterns of stocks or mutual funds is known as **technical analysis.** Many investors and most professionals use these charts to make investment decisions. A technical analyst is also known as a "chartist."

Be careful not to take this strategy to the extreme. One of my clients called me just recently and asked me to sell every mutual fund he owned and buy a money market fund. This is the extreme. I use money market funds to a certain degree for market timing purposes, but the biggest position I've ever held for any length of time is 45 percent.

Sector Rotation

Many investors use this strategy for selecting investments without even realizing what it's called or how it actually works. It's a strategy based upon several theories. First, is the theory that there are many markets or sectors of the market that can act independently of each other. These sectors can be industries, countries, or any specific type of security. The second theory of sector rotation is the assumption that there will always be opportunity in the market. As my friend Dave Muller says, "There's always a bull market somewhere." He writes a little known monthly investment newsletter titled, *Foreign Markets Advisory* (P.O. Box 75, Fairfax Station, VA 22039 or fax 703-425-6263,$197 annually). In his newsletter, Dave uses a graphic illustration that compares the performances of each country's stock market to one another. When I want to compare the stock market trends of different countries, this newsletter is invaluable. If the theory is correct that there's always a bull market somewhere, this newsletter helps me find it. The third theory behind sector rotation assumes that an investor is able to be invested in the sectors that are performing well, and can get out quickly before the trend changes direction for the worse. The fourth theory of sector rotation says that by maintaining a portfolio focused on the best performing sectors, you'll be able to beat the market over time.

> **Treasure Tip**
> Some funds are managed by a committee instead of one manager. I prefer to have a single manager because they are usually more decisive and efficient than a committee. However, there are certainly exceptions to this rule.

The illustration in this section shows how the theory of sector rotation works in a perfect world. After identifying a major trend and investing in the corresponding sector, the investor rides the growth of one sector (or trend) and rotates to another sector (or trend) before growth begins to slow. You can ride the growth of a sector by using mutual funds that focus on that particular sector, or you can use individual stocks. This process is hopefully repeated over time to produce above average returns. This strategy does require a lot of work, but it can be very profitable.

Sector Rotation

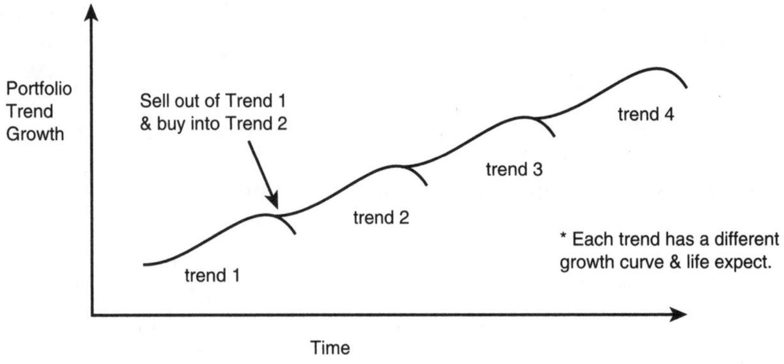

You can compare this strategy of sector rotation to surfing in the ocean. First you find just the right wave, then you position yourself to take advantage of it. Before the wave crashes you against the beach or rocks, turn back and go find another wave. This strategy may seem very seductive, but it is very difficult. It is a game of numbers, which means that you will fail part of the time. But with patience, research and diversification, your winnings will cover your losses. It is not a question of "if you will lose?" It is a question of "when you will lose?," and "to what extent?" If you can win more than you lose, your portfolio will prosper. The only way to win is to buy an investment (from someone else) that you think is worth more than the money you paid. Then you must hold that investment until someone is willing to pay you more than you feel the investment is worth. Both transactions involve other people being wrong. What you are in fact saying each time you buy and sell is that the other person is wrong. That's pretty bold, wouldn't you agree? But this is only half of the boldness required. In order to increase your chances of profit, you have to increase your chances that the other person is wrong. The more wrong they are, the cheaper you can buy and that means more profit for you. There are several ways to increase those chances:

1. Buy the sector that has fallen or corrected the most—what everyone hates
2. Buy the sector that everyone fears—usually a sector that is somewhat new to the market
3. Buy the sector that has the most negative media coverage—what does the media hate?

The objective is to find the most hated or feared sectors, wait until they have hit a bottom, and then buy. It's hard to know exactly when the bottom is hit without a chart. You don't need a three year chart to do this. A 6 to 12 month chart usually works better. Make sure the fund's price chart verifies this bottom. What does a bottom look like? It doesn't really matter. What's important is whether or not the fund is trending upward after a long period of falling. Don't try to invest at the exact bottom. Buy the fund when you see the price trending upward.

Hold the fund until it hits a top. That's usually when everyone is talking about it or when it hits the front pages of *Time* or *Newsweek*. Then sell it and find another sector. Make sure the fund's price chart verifies this top. What does a top look like? Again, it doesn't really matter. What's important is whether or not the fund is trending downward after a long period of rising. Don't try to sell at the exact top. Sell when you see the price begin to trend downward. As funds top-out and are sold, it's important to have other funds available to buy. The perfect scenario would be to have another sector available to rotate into immediately. Therefore, you should always be on the look-out for other sectors that are beginning to trend upward.

The Flower Portfolio

All three fund selection strategies are best illustrated by the flower portfolio diagram in this section. The buy and hold strategy is used to build the core of your portfolio. They are rarely traded and therefore make the base of the flower. The market timing and sector rotation strategies are used to build the next layer of sector type funds, represented by the petals. As market trends change, so does the portfolio. If the market is under-priced or in a bull phase, the flower may have many petals. If the market is over-priced or in a bear phase, you may only see one or two petals. The core funds tend to be somewhat of a safe-haven when the markets are over-priced. While the core remains in tact, the petals fall off occasionally and are sometimes replaced with different petals. Therefore, the flower does change its design as the seasons of the market change. The only problem is that the seasons don't always repeat themselves each year. Core funds are normally held two to four years.

The second layer of funds (sector related) in the portfolio should be purchased based upon the hockey puck theory. They are selected based upon their potential ability to take advantage of a particular trend. These funds are normally held six to eighteen months.

The Flower Portfolio.

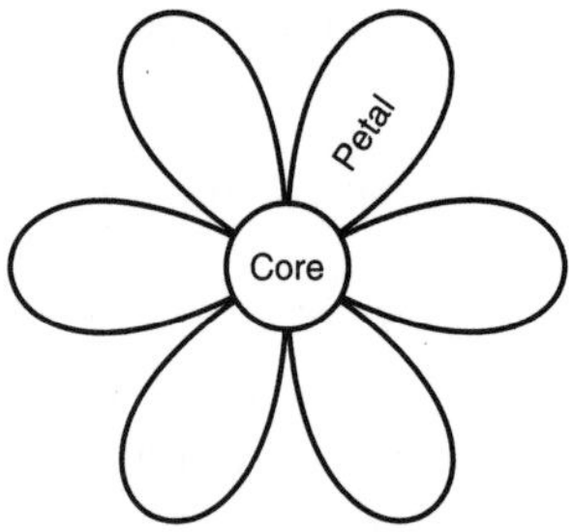

That Reminds Me...

When using the hockey puck theory and sector rotation, the funds I tend to use usually focus on one particular industry, country, or specific security type. I call them "Orville Redenbacher Funds." Have you ever seen an Orville Redenbacher commercial? The company motto is "Do one thing and do it better than anybody else." They do one thing—popcorn—and they do it better than anybody. That's what a specific objective fund manager can do for you. The manager concentrates on only one industry, country, or specific security type—nothing else. This focus enables them to be a true specialist in that particular area. They do one thing and do it better than anybody else.

Maintenance and Review

The third phase of the portfolio management cycle, maintenance and review, is most often neglected by investors. For example, most investors have no idea how well their portfolio is performing. They try to do everything and rarely ever make transactions when they should.

Measurement of Results

At least once a quarter, youneed to measure and review your portfolio's percentage performance. This can be a very difficult calculation if you are making regular deposits (or withdrawals). The easiest way to calculate your portfolio's performance for a particular period is to subtract your beginning balance from your ending balance and divide the result by your beginning balance. This will give you a simple rate of return for that period. If you've made deposits each month into your account, instead of using the beginning balance in your calculation, use an average balance. To calculate your average balance, just add up the beginning balances for each month and divide the total by the number of months. These are short-cuts you can use. There are many more accurate, yet complicated ways to calculate your total return. These will do for now.

Once you've done this, be sure to compare your performance to the S&P 500 market index, as well as the Morgan Stanley World Market Index. Both indexes can be found every business day in the *Wall Street Journal.* Record these indexes as often as you measure your portfolio results so you can keep track of the index.

Your individual funds should also be compared to relatively similar funds. You don't have to constantly switch back and forth between the best performing funds, but if your funds consistently under-perform other similar funds, then you may want to make a change. Also if other similar funds in a sector you're heavy in begin to slow down and head south, it might mean that the trend is changing. Your fund may still be going strong, but all the other similar funds could be going down. If you knew this, you could get out before your fund follows.

The Most Important Investment Strategy: Micro-Delegation

The macro-view is the study of major trends around the world, while the micro-view is the study of the specific stocks that take advantage of these trends. Most of the major trends can be exploited using mutual funds. If you want to focus on technology for example, there are many funds that do so. If you do additional research, you'll find that some focus on hardware and some on software. Depending upon your particular interests, you can usually find a fund that matches your specific goals. If you can't find a mutual fund that takes advantage of the trend you choose, then select several stocks that will.

Even if your passion is investing, the amount of time you have to research the world markets and the fine details that go along with them is very limited. Recognizing this limitation changed my entire outlook on investing. It brought me to the most powerful investment strategy I've ever used. I call it micro-delegation. If I'm going to really focus on world-wide trends, how could I expect to be able to have the time to thoroughly study individual stocks and bonds? I couldn't answer this question, so I began to delegate the micro-view responsibility to mutual fund managers. The simple purchase of a mutual fund automatically means that you have delegated the micro-view responsibility to the fund manager. Since I made the decision to exclusively use mutual funds in January of 1992, the benefits have been incredible. The most important benefit went to my clients who now have a higher potential for returns at much lower risk levels.

Words of the Wealthy

Micro-delegation is simply the delegation of the micro-view responsibilities to other professionals. This strategy enables you to focus on the big picture. It also allows you to delegate the details to other people who are often better at them than you.

Outlined in the next chapter, your efforts in keeping up with the world markets and different economies will be rewarded. The ten portfolio management tactics in Chapter 13 will help you interpret and exploit the information and market changes you'll encounter, which in turn will help you maintain the proper asset allocations necessary to beat the market averages.

Zero-Based Thinking

As I've mentioned earlier in the book, all sell decisions should start with this question: If your portfolio were all in cash today, would you buy what you own? If the answer is no, then make the changes necessary to get to where you want to be. If the answer is yes, do nothing. Your decision should be based upon your continued research of world markets and trends.

The Least You Need to Know

- Use the Wayne Gretzky asset allocation theory to allocate your assets among several different trends in the world.
- Build your portfolio by using several different mutual funds that position themselves to profit from the trends you feel the strongest about.
- Maintain your portfolio by focusing on the macro-view of the world while rotating portions of your portfolio to take advantage of the changing market conditions.
- Always ask yourself, "if your portfolio were all in cash today, would you buy what you own?", If the answer is no, make the necessary changes.

Chapter 12

Six Things You Must Have to Be a Successful Portfolio Manager

In This Chapter

- A quick look at economic theory
- The best sources of investment information
- Charting mutual funds
- Unreasonable thinking

You've achieved the first stage of Wealth Level 2 and your portfolio's return now exceeds your Target Savings Goal. It's here that portfolio management becomes vital to the wealth building process. If portfolio management is your passion and you decide to manage your own money, there are a few things you must know. You need six traits to successfully manage your investments. They are easy to obtain and utilize, and they are the keys to unlocking the world of high performance investing as you build your portfolio beyond two or three mutual funds or other types of investments, as described in Chapter 10.

I do not claim to be any smarter than you, nor do I have access to information that you don't have. The traits listed in this chapter have more to do with common sense than they do with genius. After you read this , you should have a different perspective on doing research and making investment decisions. This may be just what you need.

You've Got to Know the Markets and World Economy

To really do well in the stock market, you must understand the basics of economic theory. There are many books available on this subject. For example, Steven Landsburg, an associate professor of economics at the University of Rochester, wrote an interesting book titled *The Armchair Economist* (published by The Free Press, a division of Macmillan, Inc.). It's easy to understand if you'll just take a little time to study it. A basic understanding of economics will help you make so many decisions in life including when to buy a house, when to borrow money to start a business, and when to buy a stock or bond. It will also help to clarify the three most important aspects of economics: inflation, interest rates and corporate earnings growth.

Inflation and Interest Rates

You need a basic understanding of inflation and its effect on interest rates. A basic economics book will teach you the details, if you want to get into them.

The key thing you need to understand is that the expectation of higher inflation will spur higher interest rates and vice versa. Why? If investors anticipate inflation, they know that higher interest rates will follow, which will cause bond prices to fall. Therefore, they sell their bonds. Bond prices work on the age old principal of supply and demand. No matter what inflation does, if a large number of investors sell their bonds at the same time, interest rates go up and bond prices fall. This is especially true for long-term treasury bonds. However, once interest rates on treasury bonds or corporate bonds approach an 8 to 10 percent yield, investors tend to sell stocks and buy bonds. Why? Think of it logically. Why would you want to own risky stocks that might (historically) have paid only 10 percent when you can get a guaranteed 8 to 10 percent with a bond? How do you anticipate inflation and interest rate movements? Just watch the producer price index each month along with the consumer price index. (These are usually announced in major newspapers and on the national news.) The former will tell you how the latter will move in the future. We'll talk more about this in Chapter 13.

Earnings Growth Is the Key to Making Money in Stocks

You also need to understand how corporate earnings can affect the stock market. Stock markets move primarily in response to anticipated earnings growth of different companies. If the economy does well and corporations here in the U.S. are able to produce a higher amount of profit (earnings) than last year, then the stock market should do well.

The same applies to other countries around the world and their stock markets. If investors anticipate a country will grow economically, or if they see companies beginning to improve their earnings, they will buy stocks in that country. You can make a lot of money investing in these countries if you get there before everybody else does. How do you anticipate the earnings growth of a country? Watch the economic growth which is measured by the gross domestic product (GDP) growth rate. My most favorite magazine is the *Economist.* The *Economist* will show you current and anticipated GDP growth rates each week. The best scenario is to look for a country that is turning around from slow or negative growth to faster, positive growth. Don't try to buy foreign stocks individually. They should only be purchased through mutual funds. If you want to focus on a particular country, look at the closed-end funds that invest there exclusively.

Treasure Tip

In your efforts to do research, don't spend too much money on subscriptions and on-line services. Visit your local library and see what publications are available there. You may find *Value Line* which covers most stocks and *Morningstar* which covers most mutual funds.

Information Is the Key to Wealth

You must have access to economic and market data worldwide. You can do this with a few publications or tap into the Internet. If you'll do this at least once a week, you should be fine. When the market is volatile, you'll naturally want to check more often.

The best investment Web sites are:

Pawws Financial Network	http://www.pawws.com
Lombard Institutional Brokerage	http://www.lombard.com
Investools	http://www.investools.com
Zacks Investment Research	http://aw.zacks.com
The Motley Fool	http://fool.web.aol.com/fool_mn.htm
Fund Link	http://www.webcom.com/fundlink
Fund Atlas	http://networth.galt.com/www/home/mutual/fund_atlas/fund_atlas.html
GNN Personal Finance Center	http://gnn.com/meta/finance
National Council of Individual Investors ($49 per year)	http://com.promenet.com/nci
SEC's Office of Investor Education and Assistance	http://www.sec.gov/consumer/abotoiea.htm

The best investment publications are:

The Wall Street Journal
800-568-7625
$164 per year
daily (except Sat., Sun., and legal holidays)
Market data and news

Investors Business Daily
800-831-2525
$189 per year
daily (except Sat., Sun., and legal holidays)
Market data and news

Barrons
800-544-0422
$140 per year
Weekly
Market data and news

The Economist
800-456-6086
$125 per year
Weekly
World news

Forbes
800-888-9896
$57 per year
Bi-monthly
Domestic news

Business Week
800-635-1200
$49.95 per year
Weekly
Domestic news

A Chart Tells a Thousand Words

A picture tells a thousand words and so does a chart. You can't pick a fund just by looking at its performance numbers. So what if it's up 20 percent for the year. Its price might be trending downward and it could still be up 20 percent for the year. The only way to know this is to see a chart of its price over the past year or so. The pros use charts before buying, why can't you? It's easy. All you need is a computer and some specialized software. Here are three charting services that can help you. Call and get a trial disk from each one. Try them out for 30 days and see what you think. Be careful, once you see how fun this is, you may never leave home.

- **Telescan** (713-588-9700) is relatively inexpensive and easy to operate. The company allows you to download prices daily into your software which produces price graphs for you. Telescan lets you chart almost all domestic stocks and mutual funds.
- **Livewire**, produced by Cablesoft (530 West Ojai Ave., Suite 109, Ojai, Ca., 93023, 805-646-0094), costs $295 for the software. The data feed is $100 every six months. They do offer a 45 day trial for only $45. What makes Livewire unique is that it allows you to overlay up to three different graphs on top of each other to show relative performance. Livewire lets you chart almost all domestic stocks and mutual funds.
- **Monocle**, produced by Manhattan Analytics, (PO Box 1795, Manhattan Beach, Ca., 90266, 800-251-3863) costs $149 for the software and monthly downloads are $20. It may take some time to learn, but it is the best software I can find to chart mutual

funds. The primary advantage of this software is its ability to calculate and chart the relative strength of one fund versus any other fund or index. The only disadvantage is that they only have data on 1,500 funds. However, the program is so good it makes up for this disadvantage in many different ways.

There are charts available in publications such as *Morningstar*. However, they are usually at least one month old, and that's just too old. The charting services listed previously offer current, up to date data. That's what you'll need.

Basically, you want to look at three things in a chart: the general direction of price movement, how it relates to a market index, and volatility. First, you want to look at the general direction of the price movement. Is the stock or fund going up or down? Obviously, you want a security that is going up. Maybe it has trended downward for quite some time, but is now turning back up. This might indicate a turn-around opportunity. Second, you want to compare the stock or fund's price movement to a market index like the S & P 500. Is the fund more volatile? Does it move with the market? Or does it move somewhat independently? If you think the market is too high, you might want to find investments that move independently of the market. Third, how volatile is the security? Does the price move inconsistently up and down or steadily across the page? If you are a conservative investor, you'll want to avoid the volatility and focus on stocks or funds that move steadily upwards. If you want to learn more about charting, you might want to read William O'Neil's book, *How To Make Money In Stocks* (McGraw-Hill, Inc.).

Words of the Wealthy

Relative Strength is a graphic illustration of the percentage (or fractional) difference between the price of a security and an index (or any other security). If the security and index rise and fall equally at the same time, the graph would be a straight line.

The Time Commitment

It takes time to make money in the market. The time you choose to spend will depend upon your passion for and interest in investing. Therefore, if you find yourself not taking the time, get some help. You don't have to watch the market every day, but you do have to watch it at least every week. As your portfolio grows, you'll need more time for research and decision making. The majority of your time should be spent reading publications and thinking. You need to follow inflation, interest rates, the stock markets, and other trends which I'll explain in more detail in the next chapter. The publications I mentioned earlier will help you do this. The charting software I mentioned will help you keep an eye on your funds as well as others you may be interested in.

A Little Discipline Goes a Long Way

You must have a certain amount of discipline to be a successful portfolio manager. You need the discipline to research, know when to sell, know when to buy, and know when to hold.

Take the Time to Research

The changes in the market aren't always big enough to catch your attention. You have to see them take place gradually. If you don't watch the world markets and trends consistently (at least on a weekly basis), you may not see the gradual changes. If you are working on achieving Wealth Level 1 or 2, then don't worry too much about the economy—focus on your savings target. However, once you reach Wealth Level 2 and you decide to manage your own money, you must pay attention to the world economy and stock markets. If you enjoy doing this and make this a hobby, it's easier than you think. All you have to do is read a few publications each month. *The Economist* will help you keep up with world-wide stock markets and trends. You don't have to read the entire magazine, just read what interests you. *The Wall Street Journal* and *Forbes* will help you keep up with the U.S. markets.

Sell When It's Time to Sell

This is the most difficult thing to do. It's easy to know when to buy, but it's really difficult to know when to sell. Here's an easy discipline to try. Look at your portfolio at least once a week and ask yourself if your entire portfolio was in cash today, would you buy what you own today? If your answer is no, make the changes necessary. Maybe you need money for another project or maybe you have a better investment idea—whatever the case, make the necessary changes. If your answer is yes, then don't make any moves. This is what I call zero-based thinking. I came up with this idea at lunch one day with Brian Tracy, who produced the tape series *The Psychology of Achievement*. It has helped me develop my own sell discipline.

Another helpful sell discipline I use is the last half of Sir John Templeton's second law of investing. He said, "sell at the point of most optimism." Most people call this contrary thinking. Whatever you want to call it, just do it. The investment game is won by those willing to sell when everyone else is buying like crazy.

Buy When It's Time to Buy

The best time to buy is when everyone else is selling. The first half of Sir John Templeton's second law of investing reads, "Buy at the point of most pessimism." If you have the discipline to follow this advice, you can make a lot of money in the stock market. Unfortunately, only a few investors have the guts or discipline to do it. Those who think and invest this way are called contrarians. What excites them the most is bad news because they know investors will over-react and as a result, certain stock prices will fall lower than they should. That's when they buy.

> **Words of the Wealthy**
> **Contrarian** investors are those who invest contrary to everyone else. They buy when the market is correcting and sell when the market reaches new highs.

Stick with Your Decision

Make your decision and stick with it until the reasons why you bought the investment change. You don't have to trade a lot to achieve an above average return. This is especially true with mutual funds.

Imagination Is More Important than You Think

Albert Einstein said, "Imagination is more important than knowledge." Why do so many academically advanced investors do so poorly in the market? Do they know too much? Maybe they develop their brain but not their gut. Why do so many high school students beat investment pros in stock market contests? Your ability to process knowledge and data with an open-mind is the first key to successful investment decisions. But, an investor can know too much. If your knowledge limits your ability to objectively see all the possibilities, you know too much.

You Have to Be a Little Unreasonable to Be Any Good

George Bernard Shaw once said, "All progress depends on the unreasonable man." He deduced that the reasonable person adapts himself to the world. The unreasonable person tries to adapt the world to himself, and therefore improves the world for everyone. It is my belief that to be a successful investor, you must also be a little unreasonable.

First, the changes that are taking place in the world today are quite unlike the changes we've experienced in the past. They are unreasonable. They include social, economic, and political trends that most people don't even understand until they hit the local community. These changes often involve highly advanced technology that didn't even exist last year. Second, these unreasonable changes will transform the way we work, live and think. Never before has it been so important to pay attention to what the future can bring. Third, if these changes are unreasonable, then our thinking must be unreasonable to deal with them. We're going to have turn our normal patterns of thinking upside down, even if such thinking seems outrageous.

Companies today can design a product and put it on the shelf faster than ever and they're getting even faster everyday. This means that the software or appliance you are using today will most likely be obsolete in 12 months. Someone, somewhere will come up with a better idea. That means that the company or even industry that produced the "old" product is at risk. If they don't stay in touch with their customer and the changes in the product, they are dead. I'm saying that more than ever, complete industries are now subject to forced "re-engineering" at a moments notice. Re-engineering to some might be a new advanced product line to compete with the new model that was just introduced. Re-engineering might also mean lay-offs and plant closings because no one saw the trend or paid any attention to the customer. This scenario applies to all products and no one is safe from it. The possibilities are endless. The best defense for most companies would be to distinguish themselves with outrageous customer service and extensive in-house research work done by very open-minded people.

That Reminds Me...

What if a company chooses to ignore these new changes or continues to think the old way? After years of extensive research and analysis, scientists have found that if you put a live frog in a pan of cold water and very slowly apply heat, the frog will not budge. Even after the water gets to a boiling point, the frog will not budge! It just sits there and dies. Why? Why doesn't the frog react? "Because each change in temperature is so slight that the frog continues to adjust to the water. It fails to realize that the net result of these changes should be an abrupt, energetic change in its behavior——a new approach to new conditions." How many reasonable investors do you know that have been boiled alive as small changes in the market occurred over time while no action was taken?

To achieve investment excellence, unreasonable thinking must be used. Successful investors today can no longer ignore the small market changes. They must be able to interpret the seemingly insignificant in order to beat the street.

George Bernard Shaw also said, "The only person who behaves sensibly is my tailor. He takes new measurements every time he sees me. All the rest go on with their old measurements." Take new measurements often and don't be afraid to be a little unreasonable.

You Have to Be Able to Think Creatively

Sometimes thinking differently means applying completely different logic. I like to use the phrase, 'creative thinking.' For example, imagine you wanted to travel exactly two miles while averaging 60 miles per hour. (You may want to write this down.) If you averaged 30 mph during the first mile, how fast would you have to travel during the second mile in order to average 60 mph? Let's take out acceleration and deceleration to make it easier.

I've asked this question in my workshops for over four years. Almost everyone answers "90 mph." They add 30 and 90 to get 120 which when divided by two, equals 60 mph. However, this is incorrect. In this case, it is impossible to average 60 mph no matter how fast you travel. During the first mile, if averaged at 30 miles per hour, two minutes are used, which is the exact required time needed to average 60 mph over the entire two miles. The problem here is that most people try to apply addition/division to a time/distance problem. Therefore, the answer can never be solved. Investors do the same thing everyday. They try to apply three, five and ten year past performance histories to a not continuously changing investment world. In order to beat the stock market averages in this world, you often have to ignore past performance and use creative thinking instead.

In order to be a successful investor, you have to look at very current data (i.e., 3, 6, and 9 month economic data) and then project into the future any possible trends this data might show. Investment selection techniques must now be based upon these trend projections. To be any good at this, you must have a great imagination and be willing to make decisions that often go directly in the face of conventional wisdom.

Desire and Passion Will Make You Very Wealthy

Show me an investor with passion and I'll show you someone who's more than likely beating the market.

Those that do well in the market have a passion for it. They love the research and study investing requires. They are natural sponges of information. They soak it all in and make decisions from the gut. They're confident and take responsibility for their mistakes. They know that mistakes are necessary for learning and improving their work. Here is a list of the most common desires I've found among wealthy people:

- A desire to learn
- A desire to be a proactive investor
- A desire to learn from mistakes
- A desire to beat the market
- A desire to manage risk

You can't force yourself to have these desires. Your interests may lie in a completely different field. If this is the case, don't worry about it. Just find someone who does have these desires and hire them to help you manage your portfolio.

The Least You Need to Know

- In order to be a successful portfolio manager, you must understand the basics of economic theory.
- Focus on the best business publications and take advantage of the information available to you on the Internet.
- Use charting services to observe and compare fund performances with one another.
- Develop the discipline it takes to sell at the point of most optimism and buy at the point of most pessimism.
- Knowledge is important, but your imagination will make you more money.

Chapter 13

My Ten Favorite Portfolio Management Tactics

In This Chapter

- Using interest rates to predict bond prices
- Taking advantage of panic attacks
- How the economic cycle can make you money
- The baby boom generation and stock market boom
- Natural and forced market inefficiency

If you ever want to achieve Wealth Level 3 using your investment portfolio, you need to be better than the average investor. This chapter will show you ten tactics that will give you a certain advantage over most other investors. These tactics are primarily mental mindsets. They are like binoculars through which you can view the investment world.

In our society today, knowledge is power. For all practical purposes, it has become the most powerful tool in the world. Very few people realize this, however, and much less understand it. It's been proven throughout history that whoever knows how to harness and use the most powerful tools has the potential to be wealthy beyond their dreams. Therefore, you must first focus on harnessing knowledge and information (which I covered in Chapter 11). Then you have to know how to use it. Specifically, you have to know how to think, and that's what this chapter is all about.

I have designed ten portfolio management tactics that are essentially ten different ways of looking at information. These are simply ways of thinking or methods of looking at the world. They are also funnels of thought through which information is poured and processed into a more useful form. Their purpose is to help you discover and better understand the magnitude of specific trends in the world. These tactics will also help you see each individual trend from many different perspectives. The more you understand these trends, the better chance you have of profiting from them to contribute to your ongoing efforts to build wealth.

With the growth of the Internet and the growth of other forms of media like cable television, never before in the history of time has information been more easily accessible. That's exciting. However, accessing the information isn't enough. You have to know how to process it. Your mind can be your greatest asset. It can also be your greatest liability. Here are ten tactics to improve your investment mind.

Interest Rate Tactic

Bonds produce a fixed rate of cash-flow (income) that investors are willing to buy for a certain amount of money. For example, if you bought a newly issued 30 year treasury bond at $1,000 and it yields 7 percent, you would get a $70 yearly fixed cash-flow until the bond matures. If inflation dropped dramatically, interest rates would also fall. Therefore, let's say the government a year later is issuing the same 30 year treasury bond, but now it's paying a yield of only 5 percent, which is a $50 yearly fixed cash-flow. If the same bond is only paying $50 now, what would *your* 7 percent bond be worth? It's paying two percentage points higher (or $20 more per year), so it's got to be worth more, right? Yes sir, your bond's worth more money. If you sold it, you would receive more than the principal you invested. How much more? By using certain yield-to-maturity formulas or a simple "bond yield book," you can calculate how much more. You can find bond yield books at your local bookstore or library. Bonds do fluctuate in price over time; however, at maturity, that price fluctuation stops and the bond matures at its face value.

The most important thing to understand is how bond prices are affected by changes in interest rates. Let me explain using a seesaw. If you put interest rates on one side of the seesaw and bond prices on the other, you can get a better understanding of how bonds can fluctuate in price. When interest rates go up, prices of bonds currently trading in the market go down, and vice versa.

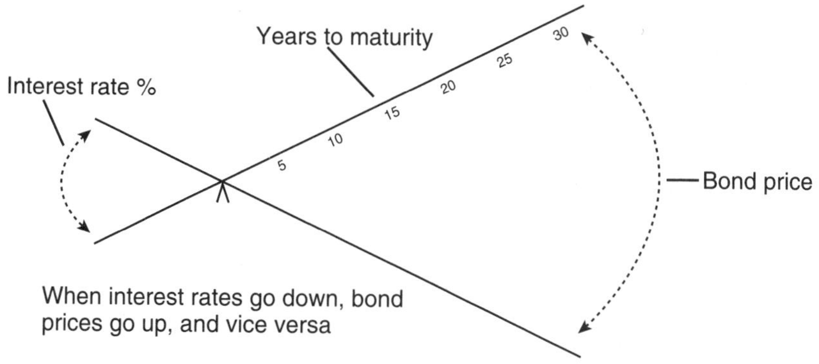

Interest Rate Seesaw.

Notice how the seesaw is lop-sided. This is to show the effect interest rates have on bonds with different maturities. A five year bond (a bond that will mature in just five years) will fluctuate much less in price than a 30 year bond. The longer the maturity, the bigger the potential swing in price.

Now that you understand this tactic, what do you think interest rates will do in the next 12 to 18 months? If you think they will fall, you might want to invest in the longest term treasury bond or bond fund you can find. However, if you think rates will rise, you might want to avoid longer-term bonds altogether and invest in very short-term bonds (or even a money market fund, which is considered to be the "shortest" short-term bond fund). If you are investing for the long-term, don't worry about the maturity of the bond. Regardless of whether you select a 30 year bond or a one year bond, these are liquid securities or tools that can be used to profit from short-term moves in interest rates. For the purposes of this tactic, they are never bought with the intention of holding until maturity. Interest rates normally trend up (or down) over a period of at least a year. Therefore, I'm not suggesting that you make trades much more often than once a year.

That Reminds Me...

One of the most important and influential forces in the stock and bond markets is the rate of interest paid on the 30 year treasury bonds, which are bonds issued by the U.S. Government that mature in 30 years. When you hear someone mention the "bond market," they are specifically referring to the price movements of this particular bond. All other bonds seem to fluctuate in price according to the movements of the 30 year treasury bond. Interest rates such as mortgage, CD, and money market rates also are influenced by the 30 year treasury bond.

That Reminds Me...

One of the best places to be when interest rates fall is in *zero-coupon treasury bonds,* which are also known as strips or zeros. These are bonds that are sold at a discount to their maturity; that is, you buy the bond at a particular price, then receive its full value when the bond matures. The zeros with longer term maturities are the most volatile because they offer no interest and only a principal payment at maturity. It is cheaper to buy these bonds individually, but you can also purchase them through a mutual fund. The Benham Group offers a Target 2020 Fund, which is a portfolio of zero-coupon bonds that mature in the year 2020. Remember that these bonds are also the worst place to be if interest rates go up.

Panic Cycle Tactic

The stock market has taught us over the years that its movements can rarely be explained or justified. The knee-jerk movements in the market (especially in 1987) have very little to do with logical fundamental calculations. The most important discovery I have made during my 14 years of investing has been that emotion has more to do with market movements than rational thinking.

I often refer to the market as "Mr. Market." When you go to Mr. Market's house, you never know what to expect. He's emotional, temperamental, and subject to wild mood swings. The headlines one week may be negative on interest rates. The next week it might be the trade deficit. Most major news coverage with a negative outlook causes Mr. Market to think a crash is coming. If you rely on Mr. Market for advice, as most people do, you'll follow in his footsteps and you'll be persuaded to sell.

Then, out of the blue, good news will appear. It may be an earnings announcement or lower interest rates. It doesn't really matter, it's good news and that's what counts. Mr. Market jumps for joy and buys stocks like crazy. Most investors, just like clockwork, jump right in with him. Hey, the market's going up—can you blame them?

There's just one small problem with this story. Mr. Market and his followers never make much money. At best, if they are lucky, they might equal the averages. The biggest reason is that most stocks seem to be bought at their high. Plus, the excessive transactions necessary for this strategy cost a lot of money.

The irony here is that the true way to make money and build wealth is to do just the opposite of Mr. Market. Whatever he hates or whatever he is selling is more than likely what you need to be buying. This will help ensure that you are buying at the lower price.

Remember, Mr. Market has loads of money. If you can buy what he might want later, you will be rewarded. The reverse is also true. Once everyone in his gang is buying, you need to be selling. This will help ensure that you are selling at the higher price.

Also known as the contrarian theory, I call this tactic of doing the opposite of what Mr. Market does the panic cycle tactic. It's the most powerful tactic in this chapter because it offers the most potential for profit. It also requires the largest amount of guts and faith because it flies directly in the face of conventional wisdom.

First, being able to identify the point of most pessimism (panic) or optimism (euphoria) is almost impossible. However, you don't have to be exact, you only have to be close.

Second, when you really get close to the point of most pessimism, buying what everyone tells you not to isn't exactly easy. The last thing your friends or advisors are going to do at that time is suggest that you buy. The opposite is also true. When you get close to the point of most optimism, when everyone is buying like crazy and telling you to do the same, the last thing you're going to want to do is sell. (However, you might want to sell and take a profit, especially if you bought at a much lower price.)

The pendulum illustration in this section clarifies how the panic cycle works. You can apply this to individual stocks, bonds, industry sectors, countries, geographic regions, and styles of investing. You can even apply it to real estate. The market pendulum swings between panic and euphoria. The middle, equilibrium position of the pendulum represents fair value. Because investors tend to overreact, securities tend to be over- or underpriced.

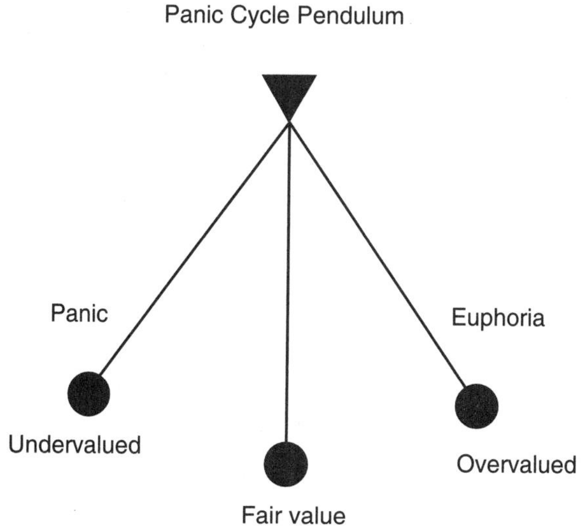

Securities in the market swing back and forth from an undervalued position to an overvalued position as investors overreact both ways.

When investors panicked in 1990 over banks possibly having the same trouble as the savings and loan industry, bank stocks fell dramatically in price. I purchased a closed-end bank fund in 1991. In less than two years, I made a 100 percent profit for many of my clients.

So ask yourself this question: "What is everyone panicking over today? What does everyone hate to invest in now?" It's not always easy to find something everyone hates. It may take some time, but you'll find it eventually.

Industry and Country Growth Tactic

This tactic involves the search for industries or countries that indicate new growth prospects, and the search for stocks or mutual funds that can profit accordingly. What you want to find is an industry or country that is in the early stages of a new wave of growth. Here is a list of the best industry growth opportunities:

- New industries in their early growth stages
- Mature industries that develop new products
- Mature industries going through a financial reorganization
- Mature industries going through a mission reorganization
- Mature industries going through a management reorganization

An example of the first is certainly the Internet, which has the possibility to make more people wealthy than any other industry in the history of the world.

Here is a list of the best country or regional growth opportunities:

- Emerging market countries in their early growth stages
- Emerging market countries adopting capitalism
- Developed countries experiencing economic cycle changes
- Countries establishing new governments
- Countries with falling inflation and economic growth

A great example of the first opportunity is China. Each one of these growth opportunities is also an example of a trend, and you can take advantage of almost every single one of them by using mutual funds. Most of these growth trends are long-term, which means you often have plenty of time to take advantage of them.

Economic Cycle Tactic

This tactic is based on the cycle of economic expansion and contraction. It requires you to estimate the economy's current condition and the most likely future condition. You can do this by estimating the growth of the Gross Domestic Product, which is announced monthly in most financial newspapers. The actual growth rate tells you what happened. You have to guess what you think will happen. This is not an exact science, but you can make estimates using certain economic data. An economic expansion is made up of increased employment, consumer spending, increased corporate borrowing, and corporate earnings growth. An economic contraction (recession) is the opposite of this scenario. The easiest way to predict economic expansions and contractions is to watch the monthly index of leading indicators. This index is made up of 12 leading economic indicators that move in advance of the business or economic cycle. If the index is rising, you can more than likely expect a growing economy. The opposite is also true.

Once you've made estimates, then you make asset allocation decisions (deciding what percentages of your portfolio to put in which types of investments) based upon where you think we are in the economic cycle. The economic cycle is best illustrated by plotting the growth rate of the gross domestic product (GDP). In the illustration in this section, you can see what this cycle looks like in a somewhat-perfect world.

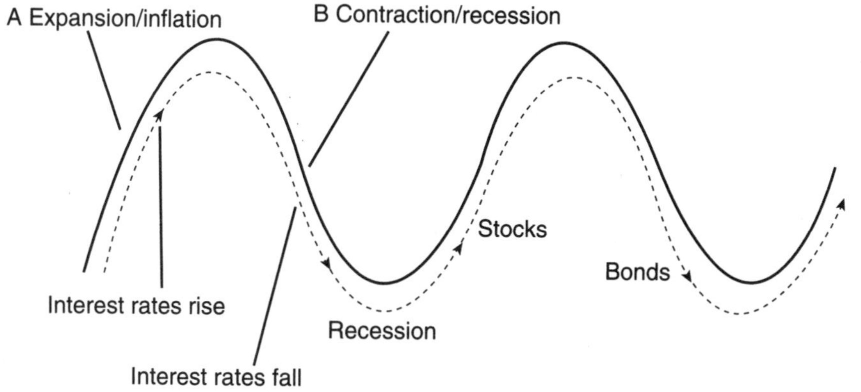

The Economic or GDP Cycle.

As you can see, at certain points in the cycle bonds perform well, and at others stocks do well. If you know the current position of the economy on this curve and understand how different securities react to certain points in the cycle, you know how to allocate your portfolio.

For example, when the economy expands (area A), interest rates usually go up and bond prices fall. Therefore, you may not want to own long-term bonds. At a certain point in the expansion as interest rates on bonds become more attractive, stock investors tend to sell stocks and buy bonds. This may cause the stock market to do poorly. Therefore, at some point you might want to build a position in money market funds.

> **Words of the Wealthy**
> The **gross domestic product (GDP)** is the total value of goods and services produced by a country during a year. The GDP's rate of growth is much more popular in the news than the actual total GDP number. When plotted on a graph, this growth rate illustrates the country's economic cycle.

When the economy contracts (area B), interest rates fall and bond prices rise, which would be a great time to own long-term bonds. At some point during the contraction, stock investors will anticipate a turn-around in the economy and begin to buy stocks—even as the economy continues to do poorly.

So when is a good time to own stocks? When a contracting economy is predicted to turn expansionary, stocks tend to do very well. They continue to do well until interest rates are predicted to go up. Notice that in both cases, I said "predicted." Investors usually don't wait to see the actual economic change. They make moves in anticipation of these economic changes. Therefore, stocks prices often move well in advance of economic data.

Market Cycle Tactic

At any given point in time, the overall stock market can be considered too high, too low or just right. There are a lot of ways to measure this specifically. It's not enough to just say the market is up 25 percent in 10 months. Relative to 10 months ago, yes, the market could be too high. However, relative to corporate earnings, the market prices could be low.

How do you measure the market's price relative to corporate earnings? You have to look at the average P/E ratio of the S & P 500 Index each week in publications such as *Barrons*. This is the average P/E of the market, and it's listed under "P/Es & Yields" in the "Market Week" section. When the average P/E of the market exceeds 20, the market is believed to be a little overpriced. Investors tend to get a little nervous. At this level, they seem to want to sit on the sidelines and let earnings catch up with stock prices. If earnings are predicted not to grow fast enough to catch up, investors will sell and cause a correction. Therefore, the average P/E ratio of the market is very important to watch when you're investing in stocks and stock mutual funds.

> **Words of the Wealthy**
> The **P/E ratio** is the price of a stock divided by the yearly earnings per share. It is the price of a stock relative to its earnings, which is important to know when you compare one stock to another. It is also important in determining if a stock is under- or overpriced relative to other stocks.

If you consider the market to be overpriced, you might want to be conservative and focus on value-oriented stocks—stocks that have already corrected or fallen in value. This strategy is very conservative—when stock prices fall, value-oriented stocks seem to fall less than the average. You might even begin building a position in a money market account. Why? If you are right and the market makes a correction, you will have some of your assets protected in the money market account, and you'll have money to invest at lower prices. If you are wrong and the market doesn't correct, you'll still be participating. If you consider the market to be underpriced or fairly valued, you want to be fully invested.

There are other ways to measure the market such as the average market to book and the average dividend yield of the market indexes. I don't use them much, but they are also listed in *Barrons* under "P/Es & Yields" within their "Market Week" section.

Demographic Tactic

Demographics affect the market more than most realize. One of the most significant demographic concepts this century has been the effect of the baby boom generation on our economy. It is important to understand the ripple effect this wave of births has caused. The baby boom generation is 80 million strong.

And it wasn't just one wave, it was three—two small waves and one big one. The first peak is 1942, the second 1946, and the big third wave 1955. If you knew when these people statistically spent the most money, you would be able to predict a super strong economy once the average baby boomer reached that age.

According to the U.S. Bureau of Labor Statistics' *Consumer Expenditures Survey*, conducted in 1987, the average American family spends the most money per year between the ages of 44 and 46. Harry Dent, author of *The Great Boom Ahead* (1996) took the graph of baby boomer birth year peaks and moved it out 46 years to see when each particular segment of the boomer population would reach 46. If you add 46 to each of the peaks, you would know when these people would be theoretically spending the most money—1989, 1993, and 2007. This would also have an affect on the stock market. Dent says, "The correlation between spending and the stock market is remarkable, and it's no accident." He says that consumer spending trends and the stock market have moved together historically time after time. He predicts that as the huge third wave of babyboomers approach the average age of 46 (2007), we will experience the greatest bull market in history.

What do these people buy? Vacation homes, durable goods, entertainment items, and cruises. These people also now have money to invest for retirement. Where do they invest? The stock market! Why not get there before they do?

But what happens later when this segment slows their spending? The economy will slow also. This should take place approximately the year 2010. Where do you want to be invested? Probably in long-term treasury bonds. If interest rates fall as I predict they will, bond prices will rise.

Information Gap Tactic

The information gap is the gap in time between when a newsworthy event occurs and when the general public recognizes the event. The wider the gap, the bigger the profit potential. Whether you invest in the market or own a business, you have to make educated assumptions based on information.

Successful investors know the cycle of research:

1. You study information that you gather.
2. Make assumptions about the future.
3. Test your assumptions.
4. Measure results.
5. Gather more information.
6. Make adjustments.
7. Test again.
8. Measure results.
9. Gather more information.
10. Test again....

The quality of information you gather can significantly affect your outcome. Therefore, your goal must be to continually put yourself in front of the best quality information available.

Knowledge of this gap alone gives you several advantages. First, we know that mainstream media enjoys covering blood, guts, and conflict. Stories like the North American Free Trade Agreement (NAFTA), the Turkish Stock market up over 200 percent in 1993, and post healthcare reform in 1995 were all given a much lower priority.

Second, we know that the general public tends to focus their attention on poor quality media—usually sensational journalism. People seem more interested in the two-headed Martian baby than in the economic events taking place in Singapore. Only a fraction of the general public read high quality publications such as *The Economist, Barrons,* or *Forbes*. They are the only ones who get to take advantage of this knowledge. The reality in my opinion is that even fewer people take the time or have the imagination to project this knowledge into the future.

The goal therefore is to narrow your gap by being an avid reader of high quality information. Narrowing your information gap is all about getting the information first, before the general public sees it. To profit from narrowing the gap, you must act. Remember that not acting can often be a good idea too.

Technology Gap Tactic

The technology gap is the gap between the best technology available today and the technology currently in use today. The bigger the gap, the bigger the profit potential. The technology gap can be applied to countries, industries, and individual companies. Technology in its simplest definition is the key to efficiency and ultimately profits. The profitability of most companies today has a lot to do with the level of technological sophistication in place. If a company, industry, or country installs or incorporates a higher level of technology, its efficiency should improve and increased profitability should follow. Therefore, if you identify companies, industries, or countries who are (for whatever reason) using out-of-date technology, you might find an opportunity.

The key is to invest in entities that can benefit the most from improved technology. Small improvements in technology can exponentially increase production and efficiency. This is the name of the game in the '90s. Where are the biggest gaps right now? They could be in the following areas:

- **Technology industry.** Consumers who are not connected to the Internet. The technology is there, but the majority of consumers are still not connected.
- **Healthcare.** New drug therapies. We have the technology to cure so many diseases, yet certain areas of the world like the emerging market countries are just now getting the benefits of these drugs.
- **Entertainment.** Surround sound, virtual reality. We now have the technology to produce theater quality sound in every living room, and the price of the equipment is dropping dramatically. Yet the percentage of homes with these systems is quite low.
- **Emerging market countries.** Building infrastructure and basic industries. We have the technology to build extensive infrastructures and basic industries for cities and countries, yet many of the emerging market countries have yet to build them.

Inefficient Market Gap Tactic

Whether you agree or not, all investment markets, to some degree, are inefficient. The inefficient market gap measures this level of inefficiency. This is not an exact measurement, but more of a relative measurement. Specifically, the inefficient market gap is the difference between a market's current level of efficiency and its ideal level of efficiency. This is of course impossible to measure exactly. I'm referring to a more subjective measurement—certainly quantifiable I'm sure. But for our purposes here, I want to stay relatively simple.

The efficiency I'm referring to is the ease by which information upon which investment decisions are made flows to the public. If there was an even distribution of all relative information about a particular market to the entire investing public, you would have a perfectly efficient market.

An efficient market assumes first that there is an even distribution of all relative information to the public. Second, that the public can make investment decisions based on this information quickly and efficiently. Third, that these decisions can be made with no restrictions.

As you can probably imagine, a perfectly efficient market is not only hard to profit from, but also quite boring. If it's perfectly efficient, there's no way you can strategically take advantage of the market. Therefore, your chance of return is the same as anyone else's. You want to look for pockets of inefficiency—where you can strategically take advantage of a market.

There are two basic types of inefficiencies: natural and forced. Natural inefficiency occurs in the market when information is distributed chaotically. Improper information distribution can include:

- Distorted or exaggerated information
- Lack of information
- Incorrect information
- Misunderstood information

The most commonly occurring natural inefficiency I see in the market is the obscure and forgotten stocks. These stocks are followed very little by the big multi-national brokerage firms and followed even less by the media (at least positively). There are many of these stocks out there, but only a few are worth investing in.

The best way to take advantage of these is to hire the best value-oriented stock pickers in the world. With all the mutual funds available now, this is relatively easy to do (see the "Buy And Hold Strategy" section of Chapter 12 for these managers).

The second type of inefficiency is Forced Inefficiency. There are very few examples of this, but I have a feeling that with more government regulations, there will be many forced inefficiencies coming this decade.

The best example I can give you would be the Junk Bond market in the early 1990s. Back in the days of Michael Milken and Drexal Burnam Lambert, (the late '80s) junk bonds were considered evil. Once loved by many insurance companies, these bonds became the enemy of all insurance companies and many institutional investors.

Have you seen the commercial showing a wrecking ball swinging toward a building while a voice says, "back in the '80s most insurance companies invested in junk bonds." The ball hits a building and takes an enormous hunk of concrete and steel with it. In the next scene, the same ball is falling toward a similar building while the voice says, "However, we only invested in investment grade bonds." Then the ball hits the building and explodes while the building stays perfectly intact.

This is an illustration of forced inefficiency. Because of events in the past and the resulting new written policies, most (if not all) insurance companies cannot purchase noninvestment grade corporate bonds otherwise known as junk bonds. But you can! And, the minute your junk bond becomes investment grade, insurance companies will trip over themselves to buy it. Therefore, once the junk bond gets a more attractive credit rating, the market for the bond is much more efficient. But until that point, the inefficiency is there.

Words of the Wealthy

A **junk bond,** also known as a high yield bond, represents an IOU issued by a company whose ability to repay its interest and principal in a timely manner depends upon the economy and its ability to sell its products or services. Standard & Poors as well as Moody's Investment services offer corporate bond ratings. A junk bond is any bond with a rating below BBB or Baa.

That Reminds Me...

You don't have to buy individual junk bonds any more. All you have to do is find a good junk bond fund. My favorite is a little known no-load junk bond fund called Northeast Investors Trust. It is still managed by Ernie Monrad and his son Bruce. This fund was not only the top performing junk bond fund, it was also the top performing overall bond fund in 1994. It was one of the few bond funds with a positive return that year. If you ever see an opportunity in the junk bond market, be sure to include Northeast Investors Trust in your research.

The Weekly Top 10 Tactic

I personally believe that a list of the top performing mutual funds in the past 10 years is useless information. The world economy is completely different from what it was 10 years ago. However, I do keep an eye on the top 10 list for the week. By watching the top performing funds and stocks list each week, I get an idea of both the leading and laggard industries or sectors in the market. Why is this important?

If a mutual fund or stock from a particular sector is new to the leader's list, it may indicate an opportunity. This is especially true if this same sector has been on the laggard list in the recent past. Likewise, if an industry that was previously growing is new to the laggard list consistently for a few weeks, it might indicate a correction in that industry.

I also use these lists to compare my sector fund's performance to other similar sector funds. If I see a fund in a similar sector hit the laggard list, I immediately begin to watch other similar funds. As other funds in the same sector begin to correct, I tend to sell in anticipation of a correction in that industry. Because the funds with less quality management tend to fall first, you may have a chance to sell before the correction.

Where can you find a list of the top performing funds last week? You can't find it in your grocery store, I can promise you that! But you can find in on the Internet. In Chapter 11, under "Investment Web Sites" you'll find a site called "Fund Atlas." This site will allow you to keep up with the top 25 funds for the past week, month, three months, etc. This can be a powerful tool for your wealth-building arsenal.

The Least You Need to Know

- Keep your eyes on the economic cycle, interest rates, and the market's feeling toward inflation.
- Look for what most investors are panicking about and consider investing in it.
- When you think the market is overpriced, put some money in a money market fund.
- Unless something totally unexpected takes place, the baby boom generation should support the stock market at least until the year 2004.

Chapter 14

The Laws of Successful Portfolio Management

In This Chapter

- What ten years of investment experience can teach you
- The investment laws that can make you rich
- What it takes to be a successful investor
- The secret to wealth
- A special note to brokers and advisors
- Eliminating all unnecessary fees and commissions.

It takes years to learn how to be a successful investor. Some people rely strictly on their own experience. Others read books and learn from others. I've found that the most successful investors do a little of both. By studying the experiences of others, you can save a lot of valuable time.

Learning from others who have gone before you can help speed up the learning process and prevent years of mistakes. I know this from experience. I've always said that if you want to be good at anything, go find the people who are the best at it and model after them. I may not be the best investor, but I sure have learned a lot from some of the best investors in the world. This chapter is a list of investment laws I've learned from others, as well as on my own. I've also summarized a few laws I've mentioned in earlier chapters.

Waschka's Laws of Investing

These strategies and philosophies have taken me over 10 years to find, refine, and develop. I hope they are as profitable for you as they have been for me and my clients.

Know When You're Being Sold

About 90 percent of the investment advice you will hear or read in your lifetime is marketing related. As in most businesses today, most people in the investment industry want to sell you something. It may be a subscription, a security, or an insurance policy. Whatever it is, just be careful to evaluate the facts and disregard the marketing fluff before buying.

Stand on the Shoulders of Giants

I've said this before, but it's so important. Take advantage of other people's talents when you can. At the very least, learn from them. Sir Isaac Newton once said, "If I have seen further, it is because I stood on the shoulders of giants." He was giving credit to all the mentors and philosophers that came before him. I do the same thing as an advisor and investor. I first select specific themes that I think will be profitable during the next five years. Then I hire Orville Redenbackers (fund managers) to help. Remember Orville Redenbacker's wisdom, "Do one thing and do it better than anyone else." The fund manager who is targeting Hong Kong, Malaysia, and Singapore will know more than you and I will about that region. He travels there, knows the language, and will find opportunities years before we will here in the U.S.

What You Don't Know Can Really Hurt You

If you don't know that the investment you're making will cost you 8.5 percent and there's no secondary market for it, it's going to hurt. If you don't do your homework, you may not realize it until it's too late.

If It Sounds Too Good to Be True, It Probably Is

This just says it all. How many times have you been suckered into something that turned out really bad? I know I've fallen victim more than a few times.

If you want to substantially reduce the chance of getting your financial hide skinned, learn to separate the wheat from the chaff before you invest. Look for all the possible signs of deception: hidden fees, misleading information, absence of disclosure documents, and conflicts of interest.

Accept Risk, but Learn How to Manage It

Risk managed properly can be your key to wealth. Return is what you get for your willingness to assume risk. Learn how to manage it through diversification and market knowledge.

Always Be Prepared for the Stock Market to Go Down

Most investors live in fear of a correction. Some worry about it more than others. The successful investors I know focus on the long-term and seem to welcome an occasional correction. They see corrections as buying opportunities.

Be Proactive

Don't just throw your money in a fund. Do some of your own research and make investing your hobby. If not, consider getting some help from a fee-based advisor if you have to.

Treasure Tip

One of the ironies of the investment world is that if you really are a long-term investor who regularly puts money in the market, you should hope the market stays down until the year you need all of your money. The whole idea is to buy low and sell high, right?

Know the Difference between Rumor and Reality

Don't use rumors to invest. Most of them are wrong. If they are even remotely close to factual, it's probably too late to do anything. Do your own research first before you invest any money.

Recognize Conflicts of Interest When You See Them

Find out how your source of advice or information gets paid. Unless you are an experienced do-it-yourself investor, don't pay for investment advice with commission. Pay for it with a fee so that you don't have any possible conflicts of interest.

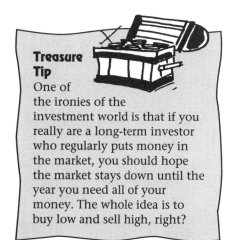

Wealth Warning

You may think you're paying a fee, but does your advisor benefit from your purchase directly or indirectly? Be sure to look at all the disclosure documents available such as the advisor's ADV or the broker's fund prospectus.

Focus First on Value, Then Costs

A great deal of this book has been dedicated to reducing your investment costs. However, it would be a shame for you to know the cost of every investment, yet completely overlook the value they offer.

Some funds may have larger than average fees, but may well be worth the extra expense due to the management's experience or specialty. Sogen International is a great example. It is a loaded fund, but it's worth it to get the management expertise of the manager, Jean-Marie Eveillard.

Treasure Tip

Yes, there are loaded mutual funds that are worth the load. Yes, there are brokers who are worth the commissions you pay. And, someday there will be a variable annuity with enough investment alternatives to make it worth investing in. Don't overlook the value of an investment just because of the cost.

Focus on What You Can Control

There are two sets of variables in the world of wealth/investing: Those we can control and those we cannot.

We cannot control the price of a stock in our portfolio, but we can control the amount of money we save/invest or spend. Most investors focus on the stock market, which is completely out of our control, while only a few focus on what they can control. The few that focus primarily on controlling their savings/investment and spending dollars tend to be increasingly wealthier.

Don't Sell in a Quick Correction

The worst thing you can possibly do during a brief stock market correction is sell. A correction is simply an absence of buyers amidst a flood of investors wanting to sell. If you join them, you'll completely miss the market rebound when there's an absence of sellers and a flood of buyers.

A Note to Brokers and Advisors

Some great advice for brokers and advisors, which I always keep in mind: Your clients and prospective clients aren't idiots. They are your parents, your relatives, and your friends and they are the sharpest investors in the world. At first glance, they may not seem all that experienced, but if you try to feed them a bunch of garbage, they'll know it. Treat them with the respect they deserve. Teach them all you can, and take good care of them. If you do, you'll be rewarded with success beyond your wildest dreams.

Avoid Custodian Fees

A custodian fee is a yearly expense charged to your account by the brokerage firm (or custodian) simply for having the account open. Not all firms charge custodian fees, especially the discount brokerage firms, if you keep a certain minimum balance. The brokerage firms justify the fee by offering services such as cash management accounts. These accounts allow the investor to hold all securities in one account, which can include a money market account, into which all credit balances (extra cash) are automatically swept into a money market fund (or interest bearing account). This usually happens on a weekly, if not daily, basis. This is called the "automated feature" of the account. Cash management accounts also feature a checkbook and debit Visa card with which you can withdraw money. Remember here, the Visa card is not a credit card. It directly debits money from the account.

The last main feature of the account is margin capability. If your cash management account has securities but no available cash/money market balance, you can still write a check and borrow against (margin) your securities. You'll pay interest on that loan, but the rate is usually reasonable.

Before you open an IRA account with a brokerage firm, you might also want to inquire about custodian fees. Often you'll find brokerage firms offering to waive the fee if the account exceeds a certain balance. If you are a do-it-yourselfer, be sure to shop and compare the custodial fees for these kinds of accounts at varying discount brokerage firms. The discount companies offer all the bells and whistles of the full service brokerage firm accounts without the heavy custodian fees.

> **Wealth Warning**
> If you do business at a full service brokerage firm and you decide to take your IRA to another firm, be aware of any exit or transfer fees that might be charged to your IRA account. These fees can add up to as much as $200 or 2% of your account, whichever is less. This may seem expensive, but don't let this fee keep you from going to a better opportunity at another firm.

Buy Closed-End Funds That Sell at a Discount

Closed-end funds are mutual funds that offer a set amount of shares when they are initially offered, after which they are openly traded like stocks on the stock exchanges. What makes them so unique is the difference between their market price and actual net asset value price (NAV—what they are actually worth per share). If the market price is higher than the actual NAV, then the fund is selling at a premium. If the market price is lower than the actual NAV, the fund is selling at a discount. If you want more information about these funds, look back in Chapter 8 under "Closed-End Funds."

Any premium you pay on a closed-end mutual fund is like adding another potential expense item to your portfolio. Therefore, only buy them when they offer a discount to their net asset value. Since these mutual funds are traded like stocks on the exchanges, they don't necessarily trade at their actual net asset value. Due to the emotional nature of the stock market, these funds often trade at prices below the actual value of the fund portfolio. They also can trade at prices above their net asset value—that's when you want to avoid them. These funds give the internationally-minded investor access to most of the world's individual stock markets, often at bargain basement prices (discounts). For example, the Latin American Discovery Fund (LDF) traded at an average 96 cents on the dollar in 1993, and had a total return of 112 percent for the year. That's very nice.

Avoid Limited Partnerships

Stay away from investment products such as limited partnerships or anything not traded on the open market. They are typically illiquid, very expensive, and difficult to accurately price. The successful investors I know avoid these—you should, too.

Avoid Buying on Margin for Extended Time Periods

Brokerage firms will allow you to borrow money against your securities. The rate of interest you will pay is usually competitive with bank rates. This service can be very handy if you are fully invested and need money on a short-term basis. However, on a long-term basis, it's not such a great idea. Borrowing money to invest in the stock and bond markets over a long period of time is not a good idea. It's too expensive and just not worth the risk.

Never, Never, Never Invest Just for the Tax Savings

If you have doubt in my wisdom, just ask any wealthy individual over the age of 45 about tax sheltered investing and limited partnerships. Your first and second priorities of investing should be profit and proper management of risk (or capital preservation). My first long-run priority has to be not to lose my client's money. My second priority—a very close second—is profit. If you manage your own money, you might reverse the order of these two. However, never make tax savings one of the top two priorities. Until we have absolutely zero tax shelters or loopholes, there will always be a "tax advantaged investment product" that will offer to save you tax dollars. They are usually very expensive and have little to no profit potential. Avoid these like the plague.

Don't Buy from Strangers

Never buy an investment over the phone from someone you do not know. If the investment sounds good, ask for references and do your homework.

> **Wealth Warning**
> If anyone tries to sell you a variable annuity in an IRA, take your portfolio, turn around, and run.

Variable Annuities Don't Go in IRAs

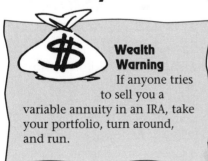

Run, do not walk, from anyone in the investment business who tries to sell you a variable annuity within an IRA or qualified retirement plan. I covered variable annuities in Chapter 7. If the gains and income in the IRA are already tax deferred, why would anyone buy a variable annuity? I'll tell you why. Because a money grubbing commission-based salesperson sold it to them. I've seen it happen and it's ugly. The penalty to correct this scam is expensive.

That Reminds Me...

A prospective client came to one of my workshops years ago and decided he wanted to open a $450,000 IRA account with my firm. He said that his money was currently with a full service brokerage firm. I asked him what he was currently invested in. He said a money market fund, but before he came to the workshop, his plan was to buy a variable annuity. This made the hair on the back of my neck stand up. I asked why he wanted to include that in his IRA when it was already tax deferred. He said, "because the broker suggested it." I explained that the broker's commission would have been at least $27,000. This nearly blew his mind. Not only was the annuity expensive, but it also had only five investment alternatives to choose from. Buying this annuity would have been an expensive nightmare.

Take Advantage of Breakpoints

Focus on largertransactions when possible for breakpoint discounts. For example, if you have to buy a loaded mutual fund, ask at what amount of investment your commission rate falls; it may require a purchase of several thousand dollars or a few hundred shares. If you know you're going to eventually put enough money in the fund to meet one of the breakpoints, ask for a "letter of intent." This will say that you intend to invest enough to exceed the discount and therefore, will get you the breakpoint discount.

Wealth Warning

The more you invest in a loaded fund, the cheaper the commission will be. The dollar amounts at which this commission rate falls are called breakpoints.

Other Investment Laws Revisited

This second section of this chapter is designed to summarize other key investment laws presented earlier in the book. They are vital to the wealth building process and I thought you might enjoy having them listed again for review.

There's Always a Bull Market Somewhere

There are too many investments doing well to stay in something going down.

The Market Is Full of Inefficiency

Where there's inefficiency, there is profit potential.

Be an Unreasonable Investor

Try to think differently with more imagination and creativity than other investors.

Your First Investment Must Do It All

If you are investing less than $5,000, can accept some volatility, and can do without the money for at least four years, you should start with a mutual fund that invests all over the world. Choose the one investment that meets all your criteria.

Understand No-Load Mutual Funds vs. Loaded Funds

There are two kinds of open-end mutual funds—those that have commissions or "loads" and those that do not. All mutual funds have management fees (average is about one percent), but only loaded funds have extra commission charges attached to pay the broker or pay for advertising. By doing a little more of the legwork yourself, you can save as much as 8.5 percent on your purchase. Avoiding a commission means more of your dollars are actually invested.

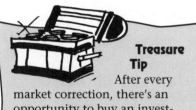

Treasure Tip

After every market correction, there's an opportunity to buy an investment at an undervalued price. And vice versa, after every major market rally, there is an opportunity to sell and take a profit. Most investors overreact as much in a negative direction as they do in a positive direction. For example, what is hated the most often seems to be quite popular later. Inefficiency breeds opportunity.

One type of hidden commission is the 12(b)1 fee. I covered this in Chapter 7, but it's important to the wealth building process that you understand how 12(b)1 fees work. It doesn't matter if your fund says it's no-load, check the prospectus's expense chapter for 12(b)1 fees. Be sure to avoid 12(b)1 fees in excess of .25 percent. If the 12(b)1 fee is higher than .25 percent, the fund is somewhat of a loaded fund. *12(b)1* is a securities regulation that allows mutual funds to charge a fee in addition to the management fee for such things as "marketing expenses, distribution expenses, or sales expenses." In reality, these expenses disguise the commission, which is either paid in advance to the salesperson, each quarter, or a combination of both.

Avoid Loaded Variable Annuities

Loaded variable annuities are one of the most exciting things for a broker to sell—they make in excess of 6 percent commission on these. Vanguard's (800-462-2391) true no-load variable annuity is the most inexpensive variable annuity I have found with only 1.08 percent in yearly expenses. Here are other companies that offer no-load variable annuities:

- Charles Schwab & Co.
- Fidelity

If you want to research the mutual funds within these variable annuities, call *Morningstar* (800-876-5005), which offers research on the mutual funds of variable annuities.

> **Wealth Warning**
> Just because a variable annuity is inexpensive, it doesn't mean that it's a good investment idea. If you're limited to only a handful of investment alternatives, the chances of your portfolio performing well is also limited.

Account Consolidation

If you like buying no-load funds, but you don't like multiple statements, multiple phone numbers, and doing business by mail, you may want to contact a discount brokerage firm.

Consider Starting a Simplified Employee Pension (SEP)

If you are self-employed this is certainly the least expensive qualified retirement plan to start and maintain.

Never Use Life Insurance for Investment Purposes

Life insurance policies were never intended for investment purposes.

Be Careful Purchasing Mutual Funds in December

Most mutual funds issue capital gains distributions in the month of December. If you own the fund the day of record (the official day the shareholder is given the dividend), you are given the capital gain—which means you pay the tax on a gain from which you might not have benefited.

Check Twice for All the Fees and Commissions

When you purchase anything from a full service broker, investment advisor, insurance agent, or anyone in the financial industry, ask at least twice about all the costs and fees you will be charged.

Educate Yourself with Free or Low Cost Resources

Attend local investment workshops and seminars. Call your local college and ask if there are any non-credit investment courses offered.

If Interest Rates Are Rising, Don't Buy Long Bonds

Remember, when interest rates rise, bond prices fall. Therefore, avoid intermediate and long term bond funds when interest rates are rising. The best time to be in these bonds is when rates are falling. You can do this directly by investing in individual treasury securities or use a mutual fund. One of the best funds you can buy when interest rates are falling is Vanguard's Long Term U.S. Treasury Fund (800-662-7447). With a management fee of only .2%, it is the most inexpensive long term U.S. Treasury bond fund available. You can also buy individual treasury bonds directly from the Federal Reserve with no commission.

Don't Buy Proprietary Products

Avoid loaded proprietary mutual funds, loaded annuities, and packaged products like UITs.

Don't Be a Trader

You don't have to trade often to make money in the market, especially if you are using mutual funds.

Utilize "No Transaction Fee Programs" (NTF)

When you can, take advantage of the NTF programs available at discount brokerage firms.

Don't Buy Individual Foreign Stocks or Bonds

If you are a "do-it-yourselfer," don't buy individual foreign stocks and bonds—use foreign mutual funds instead.

Ask for a Discount

It's all negotiable, so ask your broker or advisor how you can get breaks on commissions and fees.

Eliminate as Many Barriers or Limitations as You Can

Make certain you can purchase any type of investment you want from your brokerage firm, including no-load mutual funds.

Demand Liquidity

Stick with marketable securities that have available secondary markets.

The Secret to Successful Portfolio Management Is to Make It a Passion

If portfolio management is your passion, you'll work at it harder, smarter, and longer than most people. The end result will be wisdom and profits. If your passion lies somewhere else, find someone to help you who has a passion for portfolio management.

That Reminds Me...

The happiest wealthy people I know focused on having fun at work. Most people don't enjoy their work. That's why most people don't get rich. Their attitude prevents them from ever getting anywhere in life. So many of them hate their job, their boss, and their coworkers. They bring this frustration home and it can result in divorce and even abuse. This is a cycle of misery that eventually affects every aspect of a person's life. The only way out is by change of attitude—away from selfishness and toward helping others and getting along with others, including the boss.

My hope is that these ideas will help you achieve investment excellence—the cost efficient balancing of risk and return.

The Least You Need to Know

- You must be able to identify the difference between real unbiased investment advice and marketing related advice.
- If an investment sounds too good to be true, it probably is.
- Profits are your reward for accepting risk and learning how to manage it properly.
- Focus on the things you can control like the amount of money you spend and save.
- Always study the costs of doing business before you invest in anything.

Chapter 15

The Most Common Mistakes Made by Investors

In This Chapter

- The crazy things investors do
- What makes investors procrastinate?
- The investment traps people put themselves in
- The weird reasons why people buy bad investments
- How to prevent the most common investment mistakes

If you plan on reaching Wealth Level 3 or above, you're more than likely going to make some serious mistakes along the way. This chapter is designed to prevent most of them from taking place. The best way to learn anything is by trial and error. Unfortunately, we seem to learn the most valuable lessons from our mistakes. Even the most successful investors make mistakes. In fact, investment management could also be called "the management of mistakes." If you are an investor, you're going to be wrong some of the time. It's not a question of if you're going to be wrong, it's a question of when. The key to the investment game is to try to be right more than you are wrong.

The good news is that you can learn just as much from the mistakes of others as you can from your own. Learning from your own mistakes takes a lot of time and money.

Learning from other people's mistakes saves you time and money, and can catapult you far ahead of your natural learning process. That's what this chapter is all about, learning from the mistakes of others. You'll recognize some of these mistakes because they are the opposite of what I've suggested in other chapters.

Common Mistakes Made by Beginning Investors

If you are a beginner at investing, this section will help you prevent some of the most common mistakes. There are certainly many more possibilities—this is just a list of the most common ones I've seen (or experienced first hand).

- **I just met a broker over the phone, and he's great.** Brokers still make cold-calls every day. Some day this practice will be against the law. Until then, be careful.
- **I bought the fund because it had a great year last year.** The most common mistake investors make is investing where the market hockey puck has been. No matter how well a fund did last year, it is a new year now and everyone (including the fund manager) is faced with completely different circumstances—completely different markets. Investing is a forward thinking game. You place a series of diversified bets on your best judgment of the future, watch your bets, make changes when necessary, and maintain watch on the world for more new bets.
- **I'm not willing to take any risk.** Many investors don't understand that risk is something you accept and manage. If you avoid it, your assets will be subject to inflation risk (meaning, you'll make interest, but that interest won't help your investment grow faster than inflation). Most people unwilling to take risk become lenders. They lend money to banks and the government in exchange for interest payments on their CDs and bonds. What they don't realize is that in order to build wealth, you have to be an owner. You have to buy stocks or start your own company.

Wealth Warning

How far could you get in your car (in a forward direction) if you had to look in your rearview mirror 95% of the time? The same theory applies to using long-term past performance of mutual funds to make investment decisions. If markets repeated themselves, past performance would give you an indication of future returns. Unfortunately, the market changes on a daily basis.

Treasure Tip

Unless you know exactly when you are going to pass away, you don't know how much time you have or exactly how much money you'll need. The perfect financial life would consist of exactly enough money to live on until the day we die. Unfortunately, because of all the variables, there is no perfect financial life. Therefore, you have to plan for an uncertain future. How do you do it? Start saving now!

- **I've got plenty of time to start saving money.** This is definitely one of the most common mistakes Americans make today. They put off saving money until some arbitrary date in the future when their ship supposedly comes in. They honestly believe that in order to make it worthwhile, they have to save big amounts. But that's not true. It's the habit of saving that's important, and that the little amounts over time add up.
- **It's too late to start saving money.** This is the opposite of the last mistake. People wait until they have enough money to save (which to them is never), and wind up believing that they don't have enough time to save the amount of money they need. This is double jeopardy. They feel like they're stuck between a rock and a hard place. However, it's never too late to start saving money.

Common Mistakes Made by Intermediate Investors

An intermediate investor is someone who has been managing their own portfolio for more than a year. As your wealth grows and you become more aware of the basics of investing, you'll begin to make subtle errors that you might not realize for years. Here is a list of a few common errors I see intermediate investors make.

- **I picked a good mutual fund family.** Since discount brokerage firms began offering hundreds of no-load mutual funds to their clients, it makes absolutely no sense to do business with one mutual fund family. Buying exclusively from one mutual fund family is like saying all the funds that start with "P" are the best. You're destined for mediocrity with one fund family. Why limit yourself? Give yourself the opportunity to invest in at least 1,000 different funds by using the discount brokerage firms I mentioned in Chapter 10.
- **It's OK to have this much money in one stock.** Too much money in one stock is a typical problem for those who work or who have worked for a publicly traded company, particularly one that offers a 401(k) or employee stock option program. Granted, an employee might know a great deal more about that company than most other investors. But, if one small thing goes wrong with the company and the stock price plummets as a result, their portfolio will also plummet. It's not worth the risk. Do what it takes to diversify your portfolio. If you have a huge capital gain and you hesitate because of taxes, sell off some of your stock each year and spread out the tax. Consider gifts to charities. Talk to a tax attorney about setting up a charitable remainder trust (CRT).
- **My account's so big, I need five brokerage firms to do business.** Many investors get spread out among several different brokerage firms. They get so many statements each month that they have to add up and recalculate their portfolio allocation.

They get several 1099s at the end of the year. If they want to make a trade and they have only a little money in each account, they have to write several checks or transfer money from one account into another. To check their account between statements, they have to call each firm and get the numbers. Basically they live in a busy nightmare. Why not keep it simple? I have yet to see why anyone needs more than two brokerage firms.

- **Look at this great yield in the paper!** Don't be fooled by what I call "yield bait." An ad in the paper last month read, "Free conversion of your low interest IRA to our eight percent IRA. No equity risk. Call our IRA help desk without obligation." CD and treasury bond rates last month were well below eight percent on all maturities. With interest rates as low as they are, how can this company offer "eight percent," "no equity risk," and give you "free conversion?" Answer: They are selling an annuity with a one year guaranteed rate only. The penalty if you sell the annuity the first year is approximately six percent, and it declines to zero after six years. The annuity company will take the money invested and more than likely purchase corporate and long term government bonds. If unsuspecting investors buy this IRA and keep it for a year, one of three things is likely to happen:

  1. They will be happy with the new yield declared each year and keep the annuity,
  2. They will be unhappy with the yield and will want out, or
  3. They will find a better opportunity and will want to get out.

  Yield bait is a term I came up with to describe the many different tools (i.e. annuities, bond funds, and proprietary investment products) commission-based firms use to attract unsuspecting investors who need income. These investments are normally advertised as high paying investments with little or no risk. Most of the time, investors purchase these investments without any idea of the expenses and possible penalties involved. The moment they try to sell or get out, BOOM! Reality sets in. They immediately see how expensive the investment actually is, but the withdrawal penalty will more than likely prevent any change. In the case above regarding the annuity, the real question is, "Why do you want to limit your alternatives when you don't have to?" Why not purchase individual bonds or a no-load bond fund that costs little or nothing to sell next year if you want out? Remember, both fixed and variable annuities have sharp hooks with barbs. Once you get in, you're limited to whatever the annuity company offers you regardless of other possible opportunities. They may attract you with the yield as bait, but the consequences can be heavy commission charges or fees. The most dangerous yield bait today is the long term (10–30 year) government or municipal bond fund. If rates continue to go up, the fund's price will fall. Most of these government and municipal bonds funds are bought with safety of principal in mind. "Full faith and credit of the U.S. Government" means little to someone who loses 15 percent of principal on their government bond fund after only a one percent rise in rates. Remember, not all funds are bad. Just be smart and do your homework before buying any bond fund. This is especially important when buying any fixed income security from a commissioned broker or insurance salesperson. If you buy, they can make commission income of 8.5 percent off your money. It's what you don't know that will hurt you.

- **I heard a rumor.** Using rumors for investment research is like playing Russian roulette. One might be good every now and then, but the odds are against you making money. Typically, if the rumor has any truth to it at all, by the time you hear it, it's much too late.

That Reminds Me...

Where do rumors start? I have a theory. There are many people in the world who have entirely too much free time on their hands. Free time can often result in insecurity. Victims of insecurity spend a lot of time talking, trying to prove to others and themselves that their insecurities don't exist. One way these people disguise financial insecurity is to talk about everything they've heard, most of which is insignificant, yet easy to sensationalize. Abraham Lincoln once said, "It's better to keep one's mouth shut and be thought a fool than to open it and resolve all doubt."

- **The fund's up 10 percent this month, I think I'll take some profits.** Regardless of whether you use stocks or mutual funds, you don't have to trade very often to make money. If fact, most of the wealthy investors I know maintain a long-term outlook. They hold most of their securities over the long-term in good times and bad. For the most part, they don't try to time the market. They consistently add money to their portfolio or at least let some of the gains be reinvested, knowing that in the long-run they will be rewarded for their patience. However, when they feel an investment is no longer worth keeping, they sell it—so they do some trading, but not a lot.
- **I bought a no-load fund from a broker.** I was driving down the street last year and saw a full service brokerage firm advertisement on a sign that read, "Ask us about our no-load funds." Some brokers advertise (unlawfully) their 12(b)1 mutual funds with declining back-loads as "no-load funds." They say that they are "no-load" after six (or so) years when the back-load disappears. Don't be fooled. If there is a 12(b)1 fee in excess of .25 percent, then the fund is loaded. Where do you find the 12(b)1 fee? Ask the broker (this will surprise him), and then look in the prospectus under "Expenses."

- **I'm waiting for the market to go down.** Many investors try to time the market. Many wait to buy or sell in anticipation of a market drop. But, no one knows when the market will correct. It's a guessing game that I guarantee you'll lose if you play it short-term. You can only play long-term. It's the only way to win. If you really are convinced that the market is too high, divide your portfolio into four pieces. Invest each piece at a different time. You could invest once each month for four months, or once each quarter over a period of a year. Either way, you win. If the market does correct, you will be purchasing at lower prices. If the market continues higher, you are participating.

That Reminds Me...

A client recently hired me to manage a piece of his portfolio. He had been waiting for a correction since 1990 to invest. For almost 6 years, his $5 million portfolio has been sitting in CDs and money market funds. This is a long time to wait, especially if you consider that the market is up over 70 percent since 1990. As you can imagine, he's spent a lot of time beating himself up over this. He kept thinking about all the money he could have made if he had invested in the market back in 1990. I asked him, "If you had $3.5 million more in your portfolio, would it change your life?" He said, "No. You're right. I don't need to look back anymore."

- **I can't sell yet, I've got a loss and I'm waiting for the fund (or stock) to break even.** This is one of the craziest statements I've ever heard. What difference does it make whether the stock goes back up to the price at which it was purchased? While you're waiting, your money could've been in another investment, making money. What's important is whether or not you would be willing to buy the stock today if you had your money in cash. If not, sell it, even if you do so at a loss.
- **I can't sell now, my capital gain is too big.** So many people forget that this is a profit game, not a tax game. If you base your decisions on how much tax you're going to pay, you will lose. Zero based thinking again should be used to make this kind of decision. No matter how much tax you have to pay, if the investment is bad, sell it or give it away to charity.
- **I don't need any help, I can do this myself.** Many investors make the mistake of not delegating any of their work. This is OK to an extent. But, I've seen some pretty stubborn investors who sacrifice profits for pride.

Common Mistakes Made by Advanced Investors

An advanced investor is someone who has been managing their own money for more than five years. Even they make mistakes. This section is a list of the most common ones I've seen in the last several years.

- **My bond allocation should match my age.** I've covered this before, but it's worth repeating. I don't know who started this garbage, but it sure is a common theory. Just because you're 50 years old doesn't mean that your portfolio should be 50% in bonds. The percentage of money you put in bonds should be based upon two variables: your risk tolerance and what you think interest rates will do in the next 12 months. If you are a very conservative investor, you might want to keep a large portion of your portfolio in short-term bonds. If you are a moderate risk investor who thinks interest rates will fall in the next 12 months, you might want to build a position in long-term treasury bonds or zero-coupon bonds.

Treasure Tip

An irrational investor might say that the stock market moves with expected earnings, inflation, and interest rates. An irrational man might say that the stock market moves with the whims of human emotion. The irony is that they are both correct.

- **I know what I'm doing.** Many investors think they know too much and don't follow their own instincts. They get a "big head" because they follow all the market data and think that quantitative measurements win the investment game. I can certainly tell you from experience, they don't. If they did, everyone who could operate a computer would consistently beat the market. Quantitative measurement is important, but the market moves more on the basis of emotion than anything else. Learn all you can, then listen to your gut and go with your instincts.

- **If you need income, you must have mutual funds and stocks that produce big dividends.** This is the most common misconception among retired investors today. They shun capital gains in search of interest income and dividends. Why? There are two reasons. First, using interest and dividends is the traditional

Words of the Wealthy

Financial quantitative analysis involves the study of numerical information for the basis of decision making. Under the idea of quantitative theory, everything is expressed in measurable form and therefore also predictable. Investors who use this theory believe that by studying specific market data, they can accurately predict the market's movements.

way to produce income for the retired person. Second, most investment professionals think that interest and dividend producing securities are necessary for income seeking investors. They all seem to live in a world where capital gains never take place. It's as if they don't exist. But, there's a better way. It's almost so simple, it's stupid to even mention. A better way to furnish income would be to harvest not only the regular cash-flow from income and dividends, but also some capital gains (by selling selected shares for a security that's up). I've done this for many years and my clients are very happy about it.

- **I've made too much money, and I've got to stop paying so much in taxes.** I've actually had clients that told me that I made them too much money. No kidding! Two years ago, I called one of my favorite clients. She is retired, single, and lives in a small town here in Arkansas. She lives a very simple life, yet she loves to travel with friends both here in the U.S. and abroad. I explained to her that her account performed very well this year. For the 12 months in 1993, her account grew 25.5 percent (total weighted average). Remember what should follow any statement like this—"past performance is not indicative of future results." She made $104,844 on a beginning balance of $433,707. During the year she wrote checks totaling $42,149, which still left her $62,695. To anyone else on the planet, this would have been music to their ears. However, this was not exactly the case. Her reply was, "Larry, you made me too much money!"

  I told her, "You know, I don't think any client has ever told me that." She said, "You might have put me in a higher tax bracket." This could be true considering the fact that she also received income that year from timber being sold on her farm. I said, "You may be right, but I also made you enough money to pay the additional taxes. I also made you an additional $25,000 that was reinvested back into your account." She paused a minute and said, "Well, I guess I should be happy." To which I replied, "Yes ma'am."

  This client worries too much about taxes. When I met her, her account was 90 percent municipal bonds with maturities beyond 15 years. Her goal in working with me was to diversify and increase her return. She wanted a 10 percent return with very minimal fluctuation on the downside. I exceeded her return goal without coming close to her downside limit. But, all she could think about was the tax she would have to pay. Don't be blind to profits when you're faced with taxes.

The Least You Need to Know

- Don't buy an investment from a stranger over the phone or in person.
- Don't just settle for a good track record, do some homework and ask yourself what could happen in the future with the investment.
- Keep your investment life simple, get some help, diversify your portfolio, learn how to invest with your gut and instinct, and be a little irrational.
- It's never too late to start saving money—do it now and make it a habit for life.

Part 3

Achieving Wealth Levels 4 and 5 with Your Own Business

You can achieve Wealth Level 3 easily if you use the practices I've shared with you so far in Parts 1 and 2. However, achieving Wealth Levels 4 and 5 may require some extra work. Many of the people I know made it to this level using their own business. They used the same principles of saving monthly and investing, but their business gave them an extra boost both in terms of additional income and growing equity value. These are the two keys to building your wealth with your own business: salary or dividend income and equity value. If you build a business that can be sold in the future, you have the potential to build your wealth as fast as the business grows. Small businesses have the potential to grow very fast because they are nimble, flexible, and easily modified to meet customers' needs. Therefore, a fast-growing small business could be just the ticket to getting you to the upper Wealth Levels. This part will teach you the basics of getting started on your venture.

First, I'll help you select a business to start that you'll enjoy. Second, I'll explain what you can expect working for yourself. Third, you'll learn just how important a CPA can be to the wealth-building process. Fourth, I explain how important a good banking relationship can be. Fifth, you'll learn the most common mistakes made by business owners. Sixth, I'll share with you one of the hardest things I've ever experienced—finding good employees and delegating. Lastly, you'll learn the keys to building a profitable business that can be sold in the future.

Chapter 16

Can You Supplement Your Income with Your Hobby?

In This Chapter

- Why start a business?
- Designing your dream business
- Writing a business plan that works
- The best business plan software

Can you imagine starting your own business with one of your favorite hobbies? It's a dream that only a very few people realize. Why? First of all, most people don't even think it's possible. They think you have to be extremely talented, rich, or famous to start a business. Second, they think that making money should be hard. One of my employees loves to do research and after spending days at the library, she said that she feels guilty because she doesn't feel like she's working. She thinks work must be hard. It's simply not true. Your work should be enjoyable. It's okay to have fun at work. The third reason most people don't start a business doing what they enjoy is because they haven't taken the time to figure out what they enjoy doing, much less make a plan to implement it. This chapter begins to explore how your own business can be part of a plan to achieve the wealth level you want to achieve using a hobby or career that you enjoy.

If your target is Wealth Level 4, you're going to have to accumulate enough assets to produce a total return sufficient enough to substantially increase your desired lifestyle, and keep up with inflation. That may seem overwhelming at first—it was for me. However, once I started my own business and saw the dividends and equity growth, I realized just how fast a business can build wealth. And, if you want to achieve Wealth Level 5, starting your own business is almost a requirement.

Why Do People Start Their Own Businesses?

Here is a list of the most common reasons why people want to start their own business:

- To pursue their dream job doing what they enjoy.
- To achieve financial independence.
- To escape corporate bureaucracy.
- To achieve creative independence.
- To achieve a more flexible schedule.
- To build wealth.

Do any of these apply to you? Have you ever asked yourself why you want to start your own business? Now is a good time to do it. Ask yourself these questions, and if the answers are positive, you should definitely explore business opportunities:

- Why do you want to start your own business?
- Would you enjoy working for yourself? Why?

What Business Will You Start?

This is the hardest question for some people to answer, once they've decided that they do want to start a business. Unless you have had a burning desire to start a particular type of business, you may get stuck here. But I'm going to coach you through this process and make it a lot easier for you.

The first step is to review your answers to the three questions in Chapter 5 under the subheading "A Passion for What You Do." Here they are:

1. Your doctor calls you and tells you that in exactly 6 months, you will die a peaceful death due to a weird unknown virus. What would you do during this 6 month period? Who would you spend time with? What activities would you spend time doing? What would be important to you? (List at least 20 answers.)

2. An unknown relative died and left you a portfolio of cash totaling $2,000,000. What would you do? Who would you spend time with? What activities would you spend time doing? What would be important to you? Would you quit work? How would you spend your money? (List at least 20 answers.)
3. What three great endeavors would you dare to attempt if you were guaranteed you could not fail?

If you have not answered those questions, do it now. This simple exercise may just change your life for the better. Remember the rules:

- Sit in solitude
- Find a quiet place outside in a natural setting
- There's no such thing as a stupid answer
- Anything is possible—don't judge your answers yet
- Complete at least 20 answers to the first two questions
- Complete at least 3 answers to the last question

Please do not read any further until you have completed this exercise. The answers to these questions should give you a clear picture of your goals and values in life. Basically, you have just listed your passions and dreams. Use them to find and design the business of your dreams.

If you don't see a business idea coming right off the page, you might want to take some time and use the answers to at least design the parameters of the business you're going to start. For example, if you enjoy spending time at home, you might declare this as one of your business parameters. If you know and enjoy working with computers, this might be a key parameter also. If you will continue listing your desired parameters, it will be much easier to select the perfect business for you.

After you have a list of parameters, your next step is to screen every business idea you have. The perfect business might not meet every parameter for you, but

Wealth Warning

Most people think that to start a business they need some incredible new invention or product that will change the world. It would certainly help if you did have such a product, but it is in no way a requirement to start a business. All you need is a passion for producing a product or service and a customer who will buy it from you.

Treasure Tip

The primary key to success in your own business is to be passionate about what you are doing. Passion creates tenacity, and if you're tenacious enough to give it everything you've got, the money will follow.

it should satisfy at least your top three. Therefore, it is necessary to prioritize your parameters. Which one is the most important to you? Which is second? Third?

That Reminds Me...

Everyone's parameters are different. I wanted to be able to manage money for people, live anywhere, hire others to run the company for me and manage them, focus on what I enjoy (money management), take vacations, build a source of residual income, keep clients for life, work even if I was physically disabled, and continue working until I was 80 years old if I wanted to. Once I decided upon these parameters, it was very easy to make a decision.

If you are still having trouble finding the perfect business, here are some extra questions that might help you:

- What do you enjoy doing in your free time?
- What do you like to read in your free time?
- What do you excel in? What are you good at?
- What do others say you are good at?

Whatever you decided to do, make sure your business enables you to achieve at least your top three priorities. If not, you might not be able to maintain the necessary passion you'll need to be successful. If this is the case, redesign the business concept to meet your goals.

Once you have decided upon the business idea(s) that fit your parameters, you need to focus your market (potential customers). Who will buy your product or service? Do some research to find a market willing to buy from you. Here are some questions to ask yourself about your market:

- Will your business fill a need (of your customer)?
- Who is your competition?
- What is your strategic advantage over your competition?
- What makes your product or service better?
- How can you create a demand for your product or service?

How to Write a Winning Business Plan

Before you get started building your wealth further with your business, make sure to take time out to design and plan exactly what you're going to do. Some people hate business plans. I'm crazy about them. I did over 15 different business plans before I found my dream business—a money management firm. Planning is the most important part of starting a successful business. Your success will not necessarily depend on whether or not you complete a business plan, but it sure does help. In order to write a good business plan, you'll have to do some research. The following is my business plan outline. This business plan was not only used to help plan and develop my business, it was also used to secure a $100,000 loan from a local bank. I was 31 years old at the time and had very little collateral. I'm convinced the bank gave me the money primarily because of the organization of the plan. Use this outline to help you organize your plan. Record the outline on paper or in your computer and fill in the blanks, adding in the supporting documents where needed.

Part I: The Proposal

What is Waschka Capital Investments or WCI?

Loan Request and Purpose (Estimated Start-Up Costs).

Method and Terms of Repayment.

Part II: History Of WCI And The Investment Advisory Business.

History of WCI and Larry Waschka.

Mission Statement and Investment Philosophy.

Ownership and Corporate Structure.

Description of Services.

The Investment Industry.

What Makes WCI Different from the Competition?

Part III: Marketing Plan—How We Build Our Business.

Who Is Our Market?

Marketing and Advertising Strategy.

Pricing Strategy.

The Competition.

Economic Overview.

continues

continued

Part IV: Management

Principals and Key Associates.

Organizational Chart.

Research and Development.

Part V: Financials (this is a view of the beginning)

(pro-forma) Balance Sheets

(pro-forma) Income Statements (Profit & Loss Statement)

(pro-forma) Statements of Cash Flow

Ratio Analysis (if you are an existing business)

Part VI: Financial Projections—Short Range (First Year)

Assumptions

Projected Income Statements (Profit & Loss Statement)

Projected Cash Flow Statements

Projected Balance Sheets

Projected Ratio Analysis

Part VII: Financial Projections—Long Range (3 Years)

Assumptions

Projected Income Statements (Profit & Loss Statement)

Projected Cash Flow Statements

Projected Balance Sheets

Projected Ratio Analysis

Part VIII: Supporting Documents

Gross Income Projections on a Worse Case Scenario

Related Estimates for Expenses, Payroll, and Net Income

Graphs & Data

Gross Income Projections on a Best Case Scenario

Related Estimates for Expenses, Payroll, and Net Income

Graphs & Data

Gross Income Projections on an Outrageous Case Scenario

Related Estimates for Expenses, Payroll, and Net Income

Graphs & Data

Part IX: Appendix

Principal Resumes

Job Descriptions for All Associates

Business Advisors and References

Client References

New Office Lease

New Office Improvement List

Automobile, Equipment, and Furniture List

Results of Recent Client Survey

Larry Waschka's Personal Financial Statement

Personal Budget

Copy of Life Insurance Policy on Larry Waschka

Every business plan is different so some of the titles in this plan may not apply to you. This is just an example of a plan that worked. Where necessary, I have inserted optional items that you might consider. The bottom-line question is: Will your company make money?

My business plan filled a three ring binder. I explained every assumption and added all the necessary supporting documents. It was (and still is) a blueprint of my business. Some of my friends told me that my plan was too long—it was overkill. After I got my $100,000 loan and my net income grew by 1,000 percent the next year, I knew that the plan was just right!

If the task of writing your business plan and doing your financial statements seems overwhelming, buy one of the many business plan software packages available.

Business Plan Software

There are several business plan software packages available that can make this a whole lot easier for you. Make sure your package will do what you want it to. If you need good pro-forma financial statements, make sure the software will provide them for you. If not, a good CPA will help you. Remember that no single software package will ever completely personalize your plan. Automation is great, but if you take it too far, especially in building your business plan, the results may disappoint you. Make sure you do all you can to personalize your end product. Get your CPA or a friend to read it before you go to bank with it.

Here are a few of the best:

BizPlan Builder
800-827-0597
$129.00
Produced by JIAN
Also available:

Employee Manual Builder	$129
Safety Plan Builder	$129
Marketing Plan Builder	$129

PlanMaker
800-955-3337
$129.00
Produced by Power Solutions, St. Louis, Mo

Business Plan Pro
800-229-7526
$149.00
Produced by Palo Alto Software, Eugene, OR
Also available:
Marketing Plan Pro
Decision Maker

Business Planning Advisor
800-441-4132
$129.95
Produced by Enterprise Support Systems, Norcross, GA
Also available:
Situation Assessment Advisor
Product Planning Advisor
And several books by William B. Rouse

Before you select one of these packages, do some homework. Use the grid shown next to compare features in each of the programs.

Wealth Warning

Pro-forma financial statements are used to project the estimated financial results of a new company. They consist of an income statement, balance sheet, and cash-flow statement.

Competitive Analysis For Business Plan Software

	Business Planning Advisor	Business Plan Pro	BizPlan Builder
Formats - Dos Mac Windows?	Windows Only	Windows Only	Dos/Win Mac
Has complete financial statement analysis?	YES	YES	YES
Requires other software?	NO	NO	NO
On-screen sample business plans?	YES	YES	YES
Quickstart Manual	YES	NO	YES
Can create multiple business plans simultaneously?	YES	YES	YES
100% mouse support?	YES	YES	YES
Has text formatting?	YES	YES	YES
Has spell checker?	YES	YES	NO
Computes amortization and paydown schedules?	NO	YES	YES
Factors Loan paydowns into projections?	NO	YES	YES
Calculates depreciation and factors into projections?	NO	YES	YES
Computes payroll costs and includes in projections?	YES	YES	YES
On screen help feature?	YES	YES	YES
Includes tech support?	YES	YES	YES
Can accommodate separate sales categories into projections?	NO	YES	YES
Offers complete financial statements?	YES	YES	YES
30 day money back guarantee?	YES	YES	YES
Can tech support handle business oriented questions?	YES	NO	YES

The Pro-Forma Financial Statements

If you plan to achieve Wealth Level 4 or 5 using your own business, you're going to have to understand financial statements. They are the key measuring tool of your business efficiency and profitability. The first critical element in your financial statements is your return on investment. Before you start a business, you need to make sure your business passes the return on investment (ROI) test. Many business owners don't understand this test. They jump into a business without even considering (or knowing) what their ROI will be. In order to pass the ROI test, you must prove to yourself that your return on investment can exceed the historical returns of the stock market (which have been over 10% for the last several years). Your ROI can be calculated by dividing your net income by the amount of capital you've invested in your company. The obvious goal of your business should be to maximize ROI, and this can be done two ways: reducing expenses or increasing gross income.

Why is ROI so important? If you can't beat the stock market's return, why start a business when you can invest your money in the stock market? Why work so hard in your own business when you can invest money in the stock market from the comforts of your own home without any employees?

How do you know what your ROI will be? You'll need to prepare pro-forma financial statements using accurate or best judgment data. Pro-forma statements are simply estimated financial statements based on several assumptions. They enable you to answer questions such as: Given a certain amount of estimated sales and expenses, how much profit can be produced by your business? The easiest way to complete these statements is with software or a good CPA. Understanding how these statements work can make or break you in the first few years. Take some time to learn the basics of how these statements work and how to read them. You may hate accounting, but I promise, you'll hate failure and bankruptcy much worse.

That Reminds Me...

A 61 year old business owner told me one day that he wasn't in business to make money. He was trying to say that his focus was more on the welfare of his employees and customers. I couldn't believe his statement. This guy was either full of garbage or had his priorities completely backwards. I quickly responded, "The very best thing you can do for your employees and customers is make money. If you don't, there will be no business, no salary for your employees, and no service for your customers."

A critical element of your pro-forma statements is cash-flow management, which is measured using a "statement of cash-flow" or "cash-flow statement." This statement measures the actual beginning and ending balance of cash within a company. If you've never owned your own company, you may not realize how important cash-flow can be. I know businesses that grew over 100 percent per year in sales, but they went bankrupt because of poor cash-flow management. Since their clients didn't have to pay for the goods for 30 days, the business found itself with great sales growth but no cash to continue operating. The key is to plan in advance with estimated monthly cash-flow statements and know exactly how big your line of credit at the bank should be. I'll discuss bankers and how to get an adequate line of credit in Chapter 20. You and your banker will want to know where your break-even point will be. If you want to ensure success in business the first few years, take the time to learn all you can about cash-flow management. Buy a book or take a class if you have to. There are many tricks to the trade that can help you when you get into a crunch.

Treasure Tip
In a cash crunch, ask your suppliers and vendors to let you push payments back. Big companies do this all the time. Your supplier would rather be paid late than never.

Taking on a Partner

If you want to achieve Wealth Level 4 or 5, don't take on a partner unless you have to. The potential problems are extensive, but not insurmountable. The fight for control is the biggest problem. The second most common problem is trust and support. If one partner does most of the work, the other becomes resentful and loses trust in the other. The third biggest problem seems to be the inability to keep a single vision. If the two partners are both strong willed, they often will want to go in different directions.

Words of the Wealthy
Out-source is a new term that simply means to pay someone outside your firm to do a job for you. It's an alternative to directly putting someone on your payroll.

Try your best to hire or out-source everything you need to start your business. Only if you can't hire or out-source what you need, should you consider a partner. If it's money you lack and someone's offering you money for a partnership or equity, try every other angle first before you accept it. If at all

Treasure Tip
A great way to test your compatibility with a future partner is to go on a short vacation together. Don't bring the entire family. Just the two (or three) of you should go. You'll know in three days whether or not you can work together.

possible, don't trade control for money. You should always try to maintain control over your business. A partnership may take away from that control. However, there are exceptions. Not all partnerships are bad. Before considering one, get to know the person well. Ask yourself if you can work together in good times and bad.

A Last Minute Checklist

The following is a list of other items you might want to think about:

- Where will your business be located?
- What will be your legal structure? (see a CPA or attorney)
- What insurance coverage will you need?
- How will you compensate yourself? What is the minimum amount of salary you need each month?
- Will this business help you do more than make a decent living?
- Can you do this without a partner?
- Can you sell this business later?

Supplement Your Existing Income

If you want to achieve Wealth Level 4 using your own business, don't quit your existing job until you know that your venture can eventually produce an equal or higher income for you. Make sure you have adequate capital or income for the first year of living expenses. Be sure to finish your business plan, and then test your theory on a small scale before you jump out on you own. Don't get caught up in too much planning. Do a small scale test of your business. Test market your product, and test your production idea. Then learn from those tests. Don't go into a full scale business until you know your idea will work. I know from experience that this can save you hours of time and thousands of dollars later.

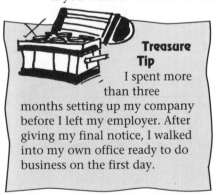

Treasure Tip

I spent more than three months setting up my company before I left my employer. After giving my final notice, I walked into my own office ready to do business on the first day.

How Do You Know When You've Made It?

It's when you reach the point where you can afford to spend a week every quarter on vacation somewhere in Europe or the Caribbean, but you don't because you're having too much fun at work! In 1995, my goal was to take a week of vacation every month. I did it for about four months and actually found myself missing my work. Once you reach this mind-set, achieving Wealth Level 4 is so much easier to do.

You also know you've made it when someone calls you on the phone and asks if you might be interested in selling your business. This just happened to me recently. This wasn't an accident. I built the business so that I could sell it later if I ever want to retire. I have no plans to do this, but the concept of building my wealth through the equity value of my company was done by design. It needs to be part of your plan too. Make sure you can sell your business one day. Find a way to build equity. Even if you offer a service, teach someone else how to do it. Hire an intern or apprentice who can take over later. I've hired 5 capable people in my firm who someday will be able to run my company without me. That's the ultimate dream. What will I do? I see myself being like Sam Walton, who continued to support his employees by helping them achieve their personal and business goals. He was like a cheerleader for his team. What a great job!

The Least You Need to Know

- Make sure your business allows you to achieve your wealth and personal goals and do what you love to do.
- All you need to start a business and achieve Wealth Level 4 or 5 is a passion for your work and a market for your product or service.
- Planning is the most important part of starting a successful business and a good business plan is the key to that planning process.
- Don't take on a partner unless you know you can't start the business without them.

Chapter 17

Working For The Perfect Boss—Yourself!

In This Chapter

- Managing all the overwhelming responsibilities
- Building your "Business Planning Notebook"
- Designing the systems and procedures of your business
- Focusing on marketing
- What to do when things go wrong
- Why business owners fail

The key to wealth is ownership of something unique and attractive that either produces income and/or capital gains, or has the potential to do so in the future. A successful business can do this for you faster than any other strategy because of the extraordinary growth rates that are possible.

There is a price to pay if you want to be your own boss. However, if you took my advice in Chapter 16 and you love what you do, the price will be easy to pay. When I started my money management firm in 1990, I didn't expect to take many vacations. I knew it would take a lot of work to be successful, but I didn't realize how much more time and money it would take. This chapter reviews the sweat equity you'll have to invest to build wealth through having your own business.

Words of the Wealthy

Sweat equity is the hard work you pour into your business, which results in equity value. It's just like buying a home and doing some of the remodeling yourself. The work you do actually increases the value of the house, and in this case your business.

Wearing All the Hats

With your own business, you are now your own boss, and you're faced with more responsibility than ever. But you love it because you are building your wealth doing what you love to do. To be profitable, you have to be able to single-mindedly focus on each area of your business. If you're not organized, you'll be stretched to the maximum every day of your business life. You're going to be overwhelmed with responsibility—some of which you haven't planned on. Many business owners get in this circle of overwhelming frustration and are never able to grow their business. They're too busy sawing the log to stop and sharpen the saw.

That Reminds Me...

A few years ago, I spent some time with a business consultant in San Diego. His name was Roger Lane and he taught me a lot about planning and goal setting for my business. Most of my friends know I'm a goal setting and planning nut. They thought I was crazy for spending the time and money I did with this guy. But, the results were incredible and worth every penny. He said that in order to have a successful business, I had to achieve two goals. First I had to achieve a 50% or better profit margin with a payroll that didn't exceed 20% of my operating income. Second, I had to develop a set of procedures and a staff that could run the business without me. These are good goals to start with. Once you achieve them, they are easy to maintain.

Therefore, you need a tool to help keep you on track. The best way to manage your business effectively is to build what I call a "Business Planning Notebook." This is just an extension or working model of your business plan. Simply take a large three ring notebook and divide your business plan into separate segments using titled dividers. Your business plan should already have identified these segments, but you may want to modify them a bit. Here is a list of the most common areas:

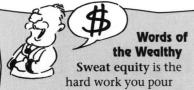

- Product/Service Development
- Marketing
- Management/Personnel
- Administration
- Financial
- Competition

Every business is different, and your segments will be different from mine. Just make sure you cover what's important to you. Within each segment, include the business plan copy that corresponds to that segment. You can even use different colored tabs to break down each area's heading into other additional segments. Marketing could be further divided into: pricing, target market, publicity, and advertising. Each segment should include at least these four basic items:

- Corresponding business plan copy.
- Goals in process.
- Future goals (ideas to consider in the future).
- The procedures to follow as the goal becomes a system.

If you will take the time to maintain this working business plan, you will keep your business and your life more on track. You'll also escape the inevitable overwhelming feeling that keeps most business owners running in circles.

Treasure Tip
Maintaining your business planner on computer will enable you to update and modify your plan more conveniently.

Designing Systems and Written Procedures

After you have designed your Business Planning Notebook, you need to take time each month to build the assembly lines or systems that make your business run successfully. If you take the time to do this, your business will not only run more efficiently, it will be better positioned to expand and grow. This in turn will help you build your wealth much faster as well.

Every business is different, but there is always some type of assembly line within each business. My assembly line produces diversified portfolios for my clients along with quarterly statements, monthly newsletters, and audio tapes. Each of these products is assembled using a separate assembly process. My responsibility is making sure my assembly lines run as efficiently and effectively as possible. One way to do this is by making sure my employees fully understand their role in this assembly process. These assembly lines are also called "systems" and they are the basic framework that all businesses are built upon.

That Reminds Me...

Why do you think a little local hamburger franchise like a McDonald's location can sell for as much as $1,000,000? Sure, the profit margins are great. But I think the main reason is because the systems and procedures are so efficient and well maintained that anyone could manage the franchise. Every task in that franchise, from pouring a drink to turning off the light at closing, is written down and delegated to an employee. That's what your goal should be. You should develop a procedures manual within your business plan notebook that everyone in your company can see and improve upon every day. That's what it takes to build a successful, profitable, and sellable business today.

Your job initially as a business owner is to identify and build your own systems. These systems must be designed and written in the form of a procedures manual. This is a working manual that must coincide with your business planning notebook. Every segment of your business has certain procedures that make up the assembly line of your business. These procedures are initially developed out of goals that have been set. Here are the steps to developing a procedure:

- Goal setting
- Brainstorming the tasks necessary to achieve the goal
- Listing tasks necessary
- Prioritizing the tasks—developing the procedure
- Implementing/testing the procedure
- Measuring results
- Improving the procedures
- Implementing/testing the tasks again
- Measuring results
- Improving the procedures...

This process goes on forever. Any business not dedicated to constant improvement is doomed. Eventually someone smarter will come along with a concept that is just a little improvement on your basic product or service. He or she will kick your rear-end right out of the game with some simple, stupid, idea that you should have come up with in the first place. How do you prevent this from happening? Develop a procedure for constant product/service improvement and dedicate yourself to enforcing it on a regular basis.

Written procedures do more than help you run your business. They will:

- Enable you to develop new products and services.
- Enable you to train new and promoted employees.
- Help you find procedures you can out-source.
- Help you find ways to automate your business.
- Enable you to see inefficiencies in your business.
- Enable your employees to cross-train each other.
- Make your business more attractive to potential buyers one day.

Once the procedures are built, you must focus your efforts on making them as efficient and effective as possible. You can't do this alone. This is best done with your employees. If you have no employees, get a friend, spouse, or supplier to help you. You can also call on other business people in your industry.

The next step is delegating all the procedures you can so you can focus on the most important ones. The key is to find the right employees who are responsible enough to take the ball and run with it. You don't want employees who just do the task, you want associates who are eager to help you improve your mouse trap. One way to do this is to reward them with little extra bonuses. This can be done individually, but it's best if you reward your whole team of employees. Any innovation or new idea that you implement can help your business for years to come. It's worth the expense.

Focus on Marketing

If you don't sell anything, you don't make any money. If you don't make any money, you can't save any money. Plus, the value of your business will decline as well as your wealth. Therefore, the most important segment or procedure of your business is marketing. Your business must have a marketing plan or procedure that you know will bring in business. How do you develop one? You follow the steps to building a procedure that were listed earlier.

The whole idea of marketing is to identify your target market and find the most cost effective way to sell to it. This is done by testing your approach or advertising. Continue testing until you find an approach or ad that works. Once you find one that works, use it. But don't stop trying to improve it. You must continue the process. If you stop improving, your market will change and you'll miss out.

That Reminds Me...

If you'll include your employees in your quest for constant improvement (and wealth), big things can happen. When I began teaching workshops in 1991, I advertised them with the title, "No-Load Funds, How To Build An All-Star Portfolio." The attendance was great, but after two years, it began to fall off. I changed the title to, "No-Load Funds, Top-Picks For 1994." Attendance rose, but fell off after a year. During a brainstorming session, I asked my employees for new title ideas. My associate Sharon, who is also a registered investment advisor, came up with a new title called, "How To Manage A Large Portfolio." Not only did attendance rise again, but those who attended were much better qualified. On average, they had more money to manage than the attendees of any of the other workshops I had taught. That title helped my company's gross income grow over 70% that year. Other money management firms all over the U.S. heard about our growth and our new workshop and began using the title. Little did they know that an advisor in Little Rock, Arkansas named Sharon came up with the idea. Thanks, Sharon!

Ten Marketing Questions You Need to Ask Yourself

Your marketing efforts are vital to the value of your business, and therefore your wealth. The following is a list of marketing questions for you to think about. They will enable you to develop your marketing procedure.

1. Can you explain and identify the demand for your product/service?
2. Who is your competition?
3. What are the distinct characteristics of your product or service?
4. Who exactly is your target market?
5. Where does your target market live?
6. How will you determine the price?

7. How will you advertise and get the message out?
8. How will you test your advertising on a small scale?
9. Can you describe in detail your advertising budget for the first year?
10. How will you deliver your product to your customer?

Treasure Tip
An advisor once told me that at least 50% of every business expense dollar should be spent on marketing and advertising during the first few years of business. His advice helped me increase my gross income over 100% per year for the first 4 years.

What If Things Go Wrong?

The wealthiest people I know seem to expect mistakes to happen occasionally. They learn from every mistake they make and do whatever they can to avoid letting it happen again. You're going to have to accept the fact that you will have failures in your business. No matter how much you plan, things are going to go wrong. If you're not experiencing some failure on a regular basis, you're probably not trying very hard to succeed. As a business owner, you are under the constant threat of sudden changes in the economy, competition, customer needs, and employee needs. You can take some preventative measures, but you'll still have to be ready for surprises.

How do you plan for things to go wrong? How do you prepare for it? First, imagine the worst things that could happen in your business. Sit down and design measures that could prevent these things from happening. Second, develop a "Damage Control Plan." The following is a Damage Control Plan I designed to use when things go wrong. Every problem is unique and every question may not apply, but it's a start.

- Separate the symptoms from the true problem.
- Describe the exact underlying problem in detail.
- What are the true obstacles?
- What elements can/cannot be controlled?
- How will you change the things you can control?
- What are the possible solutions? (list at least 10)
- Prioritize the best solutions and implement the best.
- How can you prevent this from happening again?

If you want some creative ways to solve your problem, get your employees involved. They may come up with ideas that you haven't even considered. If you don't have any employees, get a group of your friends or even your best customers if you have to. Don't give up without getting some ideas from other people.

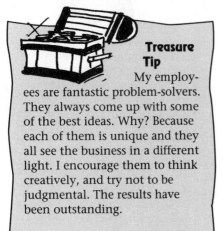

Treasure Tip

My employees are fantastic problem-solvers. They always come up with some of the best ideas. Why? Because each of them is unique and they all see the business in a different light. I encourage them to think creatively, and try not to be judgmental. The results have been outstanding.

If you have a cash-flow problem then you'll want to immediately preserve all cash. This can be done by pushing back payables, postponing expenses, expanding your line of credit, and giving customers discounts for early payment. Visit your banker immediately if you have to. If your banker is smart, he'll help you get through your problem. If the problem continues, examine all your expenses and cut back where you can. If you have to sell off assets to survive, do so. You could also ask your employees for help by allowing you to postpone payroll. They might be willing if the alternative is a lay-off. You could also offer equity in your business as a partial substitute for salary.

Taking Time Off

The wealth building process requires lots of motivation and creativity. The richest man in the world on his death bed would trade all his wealth for another pain-free and peaceful week of life. The cemeteries are full of wealthy business men and women who worked themselves to death. In order to maintain your motivation and creativity, you have to take time out from your business. When I started my business, I lived across the street from my office in a 500-square-foot apartment. For four years, I spent day, night, and weekends at my office working. My friends almost forgot about me. If it weren't for my desire to stay in shape and workout, I would have never left my office except to sleep or eat. Looking back, I could have been a bit more productive if I had taken a little time out to relax. But I simply felt guilty for not working. I had made a commitment to myself to be the best money manager in the state of Arkansas, and I knew that not one of my competitors was willing to work as hard as me.

Give yourself permission to take some time off occasionally. Spend that time in a relaxing atmosphere where you can rejuvenate yourself. Most business owners think that if you work hard all the time, you'll eventually be successful. This is not true! You have to work smart. This implies a lot of thinking and planning. Thinking and planning require time and a peaceful, relaxed mind. Without either of these two, your business cannot prosper. Therefore, don't forget to take some time out.

That Reminds Me...

The author and lecturer, Stephen Covey, told a story in one of his speeches about a man who walked up on a lumberjack who was sawing a log with a big hand saw. The lumberjack was sweating, panting, and sawing like crazy, but his saw was dull. He had made some progress, but at the rate he was going, he was more than likely going to be there all night sawing this log. The man asked the lumberjack, "What are you doing?" The lumberjack replied as he caught his breath, "I'm sawing this log." The man then asked, "Why don't you stop and sharpen your saw?" To which the lumberjack replied, "I can't. I'm too busy sawing."

The 22 Most Common Mistakes Business Owners Make—Why Businesses Fail

I've spent a lot of time talking to wealthy business owners about why statistically so many businesses fail. You've heard all the pessimism regarding new businesses. They say that over 90% of all new businesses fail. I've also been told that over 95% of new restaurants fail. But, the human spirit never ceases to amaze me. Regardless of all these horrible odds, new businesses start up every day.

What you need to understand is that most of the businesses that fail do so for very similar reasons. Knowing why they failed would be very important to someone who might be considering starting up a new business. Here are the 23 most common reasons why business owners fail:

- No clear goals or objectives
- They don't dream big enough
- Failure to plan or don't know how to plan
- Not enough discipline to follow the plan
- Can't manage their own attention
- Not enough cash
- Hiring bad employees
- Forgetting to test on a small scale
- Spending too much money personally

- Spending too much money on the start-up
- Starting a business just for the money
- Not knowing how to work with a banker
- Refusing to borrow money
- Not testing a big ticket item before buying
- Making hasty decisions that could—and should—have been researched
- Not making customer service top priority
- Not listening to the customer and empathizing
- Not listening to employees
- Ignoring industry trends and new product developments
- Starting a business in the wrong location
- Letting the competition steal your market
- Failure or the inability to delegate

The Least You Need to Know

- Using your business plan, build a "Business Planning Notebook" that has dividers for each segment or department of your business that can be used for goal planning.
- Use the goals you set and achieve to build a set of systems and procedures that will allow you to run your business more efficiently.
- Use these written procedures to delegate tasks to your employees so you can focus on the most important aspects of your business.
- Identify your target market and find the most cost effective way to sell to them by constantly testing new ads and different approaches.
- Plan on things going wrong by having a Damage Control Plan that will help you identify the problem, solve it quickly, and prevent it from happening again.
- Wealthy business owners learn from the mistakes of business owners who went before them and blazed a trail.

Chapter 18

Your CPA Is Your Friend

In This Chapter

- Why you must have a CPA
- Who's going to help you when the IRS audits you?
- What a good CPA can do for you
- The importance of financial statements
- How to get the most out of your CPA

Almost without exception, every wealthy individual I've ever met had a good CPA. Many business people still don't understand the value of a good CPA. I think it's because most people don't understand the value of measurement and accountability, which are vital to the success of a business. Most people think a CPA is someone who will fill out your income tax forms. However, a good CPA can do so much more than your taxes. They can help you solve problems, plan for your future, maintain financial statements, set goals, set up a financial plan, offer second opinions, and refer you to other professionals that can help you. They are in essence the coach and statistician in the wealth game. Best of all, they can be like a silent partner in your business venture assisting you with difficult financial decisions. I just don't know how to run a business without one.

Finding the Perfect CPA

The best way to find the perfect CPA is to get references from friends or business owners like you. If you don't own a business, I still recommend working with a CPA who can help you start one if you decide to later. If you are just starting your business, ask someone who has a small, growing, non-competing business that's only a few years old. Here are a few more sources of CPA references: family, friends, successful individuals, and the Yellow pages.

Don't hire the first CPA you meet. Interview at least three in person before you make your decision. Here are some questions you might want to ask them.

- **Are you a licensed CPA?** If you want an expert in accounting, make sure your accountant is a licensed Certified Public Accountant or CPA with a permit to practice. You might even ask to see his or her license. You might also ask if they have an undergraduate or master's degree.
- **What type of tax work do you specialize in?** You need a CPA that specializes in small businesses and tax work. You also need a CPA who understands the basics of corporations, partnerships, and investments.
- **How do you charge your fees? What is your hourly rate?** Every CPA is different. Most charge by the hour, but there are flat fees as well as fees based on a percentage of your return. I prefer an hourly fee for corporate work such as monthly financial statements and advising, but a flat fee for preparing my tax returns.
- **If I hire you, would you or someone else prepare my tax return?** If you are hiring a CPA, you want that CPA doing your work. It may not be a big deal to you, but at least have your CPA reviewing the work if it's done by others.
- **How long have you been in business?** Make sure your CPA has been a practicing accountant for at least five years and has experience in start-up and fast growing businesses.
- **How many employees do you have? CPAs?** It's nice to know how much depth your CPA's firm has. Does she have a qualified support team? Are there any other CPAs that work at the firm?

Wealth Warning

If at all possible, I would suggest not doing business with your competitor's CPA.

Treasure Tip

You may want to call your state's Board of Public Accountancy who can tell you if your prospective CPA is certified and has a permit to practice. You might also want to ask if there have been any complaints filed on her.

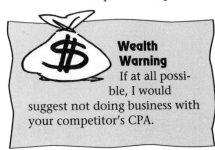

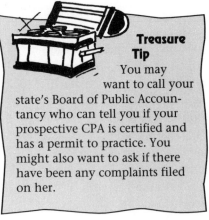

➤ **How accessible will you be for me?** This unfortunately might have to be a judgment call. You may never know how accessible your CPA will be until you need them. Ask her what she's doing to make herself available.

➤ **What percentage of your clients had to file extensions last year?** If the answer is more than 20 percent, the CPA probably has too much going on to take care of you. There may be a legitimate reason, so ask why. Her clients might have procrastinated and not sent their information in time.

Treasure Tip
Ask the prospective CPA for a list of client references. Call each one and ask how accessible the CPA has been for them.

➤ **How can you help me reduce my tax burden?** This may seem like a silly question, but it's a great way to see exactly how the CPA thinks. You might even ask about how she's helped her other clients reduce their taxes.

➤ **Will you furnish me with a letter of engagement?** This will list in detail all the services that will be performed for you, as well as the fees that will be charged.

Words of the Wealthy
A **letter of engagement** is a document prepared by the CPA that outlines in detail what they will do for you. The letter should also illustrate how the CPA will be compensated and at what rate.

➤ **Ask yourself if this person is a good listener.** It really bugs me when people don't listen to me. What I really enjoy is someone who not only listens, but also empathizes with me. I want my CPA to do just that. I want her to put herself in my shoes for a minute so she can better understand my situation. Will your CPA do that? If not, find someone who will.

Treasure Tip
There's a reason why God gave us one mouth and two ears.

➤ **Will you furnish me with a list of client references?** If the CPA is unwilling to furnish you with a list of client references, scratch her off your list. Once you do get references, call them and ask them what they like and dislike about the CPA. Ask them how accessible she's been.

Measuring Your Way to Wealth

I've learned that whatever is systematically measured seems to improve. Whenever I pay close attention to my financial statements, I see my weaknesses and I begin to focus on ways to improve my company. It's a natural tendency. If you don't get a chance to see your company financial statements on a monthly basis, you may be putting your head in the sand. If you want to be a successful company, you must measure your success at least every month. You can do this yourself with financial software, have someone in your office do it for you, or hire a CPA.

I chose the latter. Why? First, CPAs are Orville Redenbachers. They do one thing and (hopefully) they do it better than anybody—at least they do it better than me! I want someone who single-mindedly focuses on tax planning and financial statements. Second, there are too many tax code changes to keep up with yourself. Third, it's better to have someone outside your firm measuring your success. I think they will be more objective and unbiased. Fourth, if you'll pay a CPA to do what he does best while you continue to do what you do best, you'll both make more money in the long-run. Fifth, most creditors require audited financial statements prepared by a CPA. Your basic set of financial statements should include:

- Income Statement (profit and loss statement)
- Balance Sheet (assets, liabilities, and equity)
- Cash Flow Statement

That Reminds Me...

If you expect to build your wealth through your business, you need to understand the basics of financial statements. Take advantage of classes available at your local university. Some local banks also offer similar classes on cash management. If you can't find a class, go to the bookstore for help. This can be a boring subject, but it is vital to your success in business. If you can't read a financial statement, you won't know how well your company is performing.

A full service CPA can also help you with additional services and measurements such as:

- Pro-forma financial statements
- Financial Ratio Analysis

- Personal Financial Statements
- Financial statement forecasting
- Depreciation schedules
- Payroll management
- Business Valuation

If you have a good understanding of financial statements, you can do your own financial statement forecasting using several software packages that are available. Here are a few:

Profit Mentor
800-682-1908
$295.00
Produced by Management Advisory Services, Seattle, WA
Self-contained needing no additional software.
Windows version only.
30 day money-back guarantee

The Financial ToolKit
800-966-7797
$129.00
Produced by Money Soft, Phoenix, AZ
Stand alone DOS system—no Windows version available.
Self-contained needing no additional software.
30 day money-back guarantee

If you don't understand financial statements or just hate working with them, it might be better to ask your CPA to do your financial statement forecasting for you. It's worth the money each year to have this done. This kind of forecasting has three steps. First, you make a few key assumptions such as future sales growth and expense projections for the next several years. Second, using financial statement forecasting software, you enter your assumptions as well as your last several years of financial statements. Third, you let the computer compute the expected effect of the assumptions on your financial statements. If you don't like the desired effect, you can make certain changes in your assumptions. This kind of business forecasting not only allows you to find the optimal amount of sales growth for your company, it also gives you the opportunity to project your company's profitability. Therefore, if you can do this successfully, you also are able to measure, project, and keep track of your wealth.

> **That Reminds Me...**
>
> According to Management Advisory Services, over 163 Small Business Development Centers around the country currently use Profit Mentor software to help their start-up clients get funding from local banks. These centers are normally affiliated with local universities and colleges.

Having Someone Who Knows You When the IRS Calls

When the IRS calls you to set up an audit, the first thing you're going to want is some help. You're going to need someone who knows your business as well or better than you. Who's going to know you better financially than your CPA?

> **Wealth Warning**
>
> How do you prepare for an IRS audit? The best tool you have before, during, and after your audit is a good CPA who's been with you for years.

Call your CPA and have him go over with you verbally what you can expect from an IRS audit. Discuss what you two can do together to make it less likely to happen, and easier to handle if it does.

CPAs cannot do everything. If you need additional help in an audit situation, you may want to seek the council of a tax attorney with a lot of IRS audit experience. Find a firm that has a good track record. Make certain that they have defended clients from the IRS successfully.

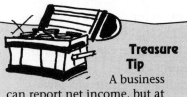

> **Treasure Tip**
>
> A business can report net income, but at the same time, may have a negative cash-flow. Without positive cash-flow, your business will more than likely go bankrupt over time. That's why I always remember the phrase, "Cash is king."

Problem Solving

The most common problem business owners face in their first 5 years of business is cash-flow. One of the single best solutions can be a good CPA. First, they can measure your cash-flow situation each month for you. Second, they can identify your problem faster using your company financial statements. Third, they can recommend ways to solve the problem quickly and they can show you ways to prevent further problems.

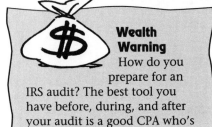

The second most common problem business owners face is maximizing the profit margin (the profits of the business divided by the revenues, which is the key measurement of profitability). Business owners and investors have a common problem. Most investors don't know their portfolio's yearly return, and believe it or not, many business owners don't even know their profit margin. If they don't know their margin, they don't know if they've maximized it either.

Goal Setting

Many business owners don't think about using their CPA when it comes to setting goals. They don't understand the value the CPA can add to the goal setting process. Not only do CPAs prepare your financial statements, they see things you don't. They have the capability of forecasting your financial success for you. Your CPA can help brainstorm and plan financial goals for your business. She can also help you achieve those goals by helping you monitor your progress each month.

> **Treasure Tip**
> Be sure to review your financial goals with your CPA. If he's aware of your goals, he'll be more likely to come up with ideas that can help you achieve them faster.

Basic Personal Financial Planning

Your CPA can also be a great source of basic personal financial planning. If you are ever going to achieve Wealth Level 3, 4, or 5, you must spend time maintaining your personal financial plan. The two obvious aspects of financial planning that a CPA can help you with the most are retirement planning and personal budgeting. Not all CPAs are good at this, but if you take the time to find a good quality CPA, they can be very instrumental in your wealth building process, which must include budgeting and retirement planning.

Retirement planning is key to the wealth building process and is simply a matter of planning to save and setting up the vehicle to save in. As a business owner, you can take advantage of one of the last great tax shelters—the qualified retirement plan. I'll discuss these further in Chapter 24. For now, it's important to know that your CPA can help you a great deal in deciding what plan is best for you and your company. If you don't have a retirement plan established, stop and do it now. Wealth Levels 3, 4, and 5 are almost impossible without one. They are without a doubt the most common denominator among all the wealthy people I've met.

> **Treasure Tip**
> Your CPA could be a key ingredient in your wealth building recipe. Be sure to ask her for help when you set up a budget or retirement plan. She may have some valuable ideas that you might have overlooked.

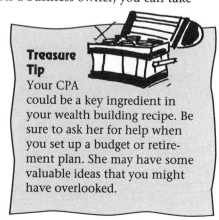

Budgeting is something most people naturally dread, but it can make you rich. A good CPA will help you budget your business expenses, as well as your personal expenses. Once they set you up initially, you can monitor yourself or use the CPA for accountability. If you know someone is monitoring your actions, you may be more inclined to make improvements.

Second Opinions

A good CPA is someone who knows you and your business and is willing to give you advice whenever you ask. During your wealth building journey, you are going to be faced with many decisions. Some will be quite easy, and some will be very difficult. A good CPA who knows your situation is like having a partner. Use this partner when you can to help you with the big decisions. My clients use their CPAs to help them with many different decisions. Here is a list of the most common:

- Business expansion
- Mergers & acquisitions
- Business deals with others
- Lease vs. Buy decisions
- Investment ideas & tax consequences
- Investment professionals
- Investment performance evaluation

Referrals to Other Professionals

If you are serious about reaching Wealth Levels 4 and 5, you're definitely going to need help from other professionals. Your CPA works with many other clients who have similar needs and problems. This can make them a great source of referrals. If you need help from other professionals, why not ask for a referral from your CPA? Be sure to ask for at least three referrals. Here is a list of different types of professionals your CPA should know:

- Investment advisors
- Investment brokers
- Financial planners (fee-only)
- Tax attorneys
- Insurance agents
- Bankers

Treasure Tip

Your CPA may even be a good source of information regarding prospective employees. Since she works with other businesses, she may know of an employee that might be looking for a promotion or other employment.

Helping You with Your Banker

Wealthy people have strong relationships with their bankers. Why? Because they are an excellent source of inexpensive capital that can be used to start or expand a business. Most business owners don't think of their CPA when it comes to banking. However, the banker does. Anyone who's ever borrowed money from a banker knows that good, accurate accounting is very important to a banker. Before you visit your bank looking for a loan, visit with your CPA. Make sure your personal financial statement is up to date. Get him to help you with your loan proposal. Get your financial statements in order, and consider bringing your CPA with you when your banker wants to discuss your loan proposal.

After you have started your business, you might also want to send copies of your financial statements each quarter to your banker—even if they're not required. This makes a banker feel good about you as a client.

Treasure Tip

If you decide to sell your business to retire or when you've acheived the wealth level you'd like, your CPA may know a potential buyer.

Setting Up Your Corporate Documents

A CPA can do most of the initial frame work involved in helping you decide how you want to legally set up your company. However, you may want to get additional assistance from an attorney who is experienced with all the different types of ways to incorporate.

Getting the Most from Your CPA

One of the best ways to minimize the cost involved in hiring a good CPA is to provide him with accurate and organized records. I know people who show up on their CPA's doorstep with a box of unorganized invoices and canceled checks. This is no way to run a business and no way to build wealth. Wealthy people keep their records organized and automate their accounting. Try to automate your business accounting from the beginning by utilizing one of the many accounting software packages available. Here is one:

QuickBooks Pro
$139.00
800-624-8742
Produced by Intuit, Palo Alto, CA
Self-contained needing no other software.
Windows and Mac versions available.
90 day money-back guarantee.

The Least You Need to Know

- A good CPA is someone who will single-mindedly watch after your company's finances, keep up with tax laws, give you an objective opinion, and give you the opportunity to focus on what you're the best at so you can build wealth faster.
- If you'll take the time to get to know your CPA and help him learn more about your business, you'll have an inexpensive partner who can help you solve problems, plan for your company's future, and build your wealth to your desired level.
- Use your CPA to help improve your relationship with your banker by systematically offering copies of your financial statements, even if they're not required.
- Wealthy business owners automate the basics of their business accounting using one of the many accounting software packages available.

Chapter 19

Your Banker Is Your Friend

In This Chapter

- Establishing good credit
- Building the perfect loan proposal
- Knowing the right questions to ask your banker
- What if your loan is denied?
- What if you can't pay your loan off?

To reach Wealth Levels 4 and 5, you almost have to have a good relationship with your banker. You're going to eventually need money to invest in your business, and bankers are the key to inexpensive money. All you have to do is pay yearly interest which is usually offered at the most competitive rate available. If you go anywhere else for a loan, you're almost guaranteed to pay a higher rate. Therefore, you must make a habit of getting to know your banker. The wealthy people I know take their banker to lunch, they play golf with them, and invite them and their spouse to dinner parties.

Two things never seem to change in the business world: Businesses need to borrow money to survive and be profitable, and banks need to lend money to survive and be profitable. If it's that simple, why are so many people turned down for loans? It's because they don't understand how to borrow money from a bank. Bankers look for very specific documentation before they can lend money. If you have the qualifications and know the documentation needed and how to present it, you should be able to borrow all the money you need.

A professor at my college taught me one thing I will never forget. He said, "Larry, there will always be more money chasing good ideas than good ideas chasing money." I consequently found out that he was right. There are many different sources of capital or money for your business venture. There are banks, venture capital firms, investment bankers, pension funds, insurance companies, and private placement firms. What you must understand is that some are more expensive than others. The least expensive is a bank loan. Banks don't usually ask for equity positions (ownership) in your company. All they want is interest paid on the loan and the principal paid back on a timely basis. Plus, the rate of interest they ask for is usually the lowest of all other sources. Therefore, a bank loan is the most efficient and cost-effective source of capital. A good relationship with a banker who understands your company and your needs is key to your wealth building success. A good relationship must include both financial and personal character. Your financial character is measured by your net worth as well as your proven ability to produce a cash-flow from your business. A good personality isn't enough to satisfy a banker. You must develop a track record of cash-flow (actual profitability from your work). A large net worth also helps, but cash-flow can be just as important. Fortunately, you can do this in your existing job before you start your business. Start keeping records of your own success and ability to produce results. Illustrate this for your banker before you start your company and your chances of landing a loan are much greater.

Establishing Good Credit

The first thing you must have before you approach a bank is good credit. Establishing good credit is vital to the wealth building process. How do you do it? Borrow money and pay it back on time. It's as simple as that! Make this a habit and never be late on a payment. The very first thing a banker will want to know is how well you've done this in the past regarding your ability to pay back loans on time. He finds out using a report called your *credit history*. This report will tell you (and your banker) all about most of the loans you've had, as well as any late payments on bills or loans. Considering how important this report is, I suggest you get a copy before you banker does.

When you call one of these credit agencies, don't get frustrated with the automated answering service. Stay on the phone until you get what you need. You can also write these agencies and request your report. Be sure to give your complete legal name and social security number.

When your credit report arrives, go over it carefully and look for anything that might be detrimental to your credit. If you see any discrepancies that might disturb your banker, sit down and type up an explanation of your side of the story. Include all the facts, names, and dates. By law, you can insert up to 100 words into your file at the credit agency. When your banker sees the discrepancy, he'll also see the explanation. This might calm his fears.

Here are the largest of the credit agencies below:

TRW
National Consumer Assistance Center
P.O. Box 949
Allen, TX 75002-0949
800-682-7654
(they offer a free report once a year)

Equifax
Credit Information Services
P.O. Box 105873
Atlanta, GA 30348
800-685-1111

Trans Union Corporation
P.O. Box 390
Springfield, PA 19064-0390
216-779-7200

How to Find the Right Banker for You

The right banker can help you reach Wealth Levels 4 and 5. Notice I said banker and not bank. I prefer someone who can make a decision. The two bankers I use currently are the president and CEO of the bank. They can make any loan decision I bring to them. That's important to me. Most large banks don't like smaller businesses. They focus on medium- and larger-size companies. Smaller loans are usually delegated to the junior lending officers where both inexperience and turn-over can be problems.

The best way to find a good banker is to get recommendations from other successful small businesses in your area. Find at least three bankers. Stop by and introduce yourself. Tell them you are looking for a banker and that you will have a proposal soon to present to them. Get to know a little about them personally. Do they seem easy to talk to? Are they interested in you and your company?

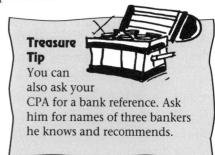

Treasure Tip
You can also ask your CPA for a bank reference. Ask him for names of three bankers he knows and recommends.

That Reminds Me...

My company was recently nominated for Arkansas' Small Business of the Year by the *Arkansas Business Magazine.* I was amazed at how many different banks called on me once the nominees were listed in the paper. What infuriates me is that they didn't call on me until after my business was five years old. When my company and average deposits were much smaller, banks didn't care much about me. I had to find a bank that could empathize with me and understand my needs as a small business owner. The larger banks never seemed able to do that for me very well. Therefore, I chose a smaller growing bank that could identify with my situation. That bank was and still is Bank of Little Rock, and if you're lucky enough to have a banking relationship like mine, you'll understand the peace of mind it can give you.

The Perfect Loan Proposal

You need money to start and maintain your business so you can expand and achieve Wealth Levels 4 and 5. Your banker needs to lend money, and all he wants is a client who can borrow money and pay it back on a timely basis. The best way to prove you can do that is by preparing a proper loan proposal. Your business plan should double as a loan proposal. Some of the segments will be more important to your banker than others. What will he be looking for? Here is a list of the five most important items:

- Your credit history.
- The collateral you have to back the loan.
- Your personal and business cash-flow.
- The amount of liquid assets you have available.
- Your own personal character.

These items can be presented several ways. It's best to include them in your loan proposal. Follow these up with several additional documents listed below and you'll have the perfect loan proposal. First it must cover your corporate history. This explains your company's mission and direction.

Second, the proposal must include a summary of the loan request which can be a simple sentence. My proposal read, "WCI is requesting a loan of $100,000 for new office equipment, furniture, and additional working capital."

Next, the proposal must include a cash-flow statement. This should be included in the financial statements of the proposal. This statement shows exactly how much cash your business generates as well as a projection of future cash-flow over the next three years.

Fourth, the proposal should list all the possible sources of collateral that can be used to back the loan. This includes furniture, equipment, property, stocks, bonds, CDs, and anything of value. The bank will want you to personally guarantee the loan which means that you are willing to pledge everything you have to pay off the loan.

Fifth, the proposal must have detailed financial statements which include at least a balance sheet and income statement. These statements should include the past three years as well as projected statements for the next three years. Your banker will pay particular attention to the effect of your business operations on your corporate equity. This figure is calculated by subtracting your company's liabilities from its assets. They will also look at how you have balanced your assets and liabilities.

Sixth, the proposal should include copies of your personal and business credit reports. Call the credit agencies listed earlier in this chapter and request both.

Seventh, the proposal should include a list of more than one source of repayment. Your banker will want to know if there is any other source of income, other than your business, that can be applied to payments if you have trouble.

Your business plan or loan proposal should also be considered a wealth plan. It is your ticket to the capital you'll need to build your business and ultimately achieve your desired wealth level. Be sure to do the best job you can and always maintain it as a working plan.

Words of the Wealthy

Collateral is something of value that is pledged against a loan in case of default. When you list collateral such as furniture, equipment, property, or accounts receivable, you should also include documents that will evidence the value of these items.

That Reminds Me...

When a bank takes care of you, don't forget them. They make money off deposits, as well as loans. Be sure to maintain a significant amount of your company's deposits in an interest-bearing checking account with that bank. You could go to a brokerage firm money market account for a higher rate, but the marginal interest rate you'll make isn't worth spoiling your relationship with your banker. You might need to borrow more money later.

Finally, the proposal must include a personal financial statement which summarizes your own personal assets, liabilities, and sources of income.

Your banker will also be looking for several other documents such as:

- Personal (and business) tax returns for the past three years.
- Articles of incorporation, bylaws, corporate resolutions, and partnership agreements.
- A detailed expense budget (a personal budget will also help).
- A detailed marketing plan including a list of your top three customers or prospective customers. If applicable, be sure to ask for your customer's permission.
- Your competition and what makes you better.
- A personal résumé on you and any partners you may have.
- Letters of recommendation (clients, previous employers, and so on).
- Proof of life insurance.
- Copies of your property titles.
- Copies of all your current bank and brokerage accounts statements.

This is a lot of work, but it will increase your chances of getting the loan you want under the terms you ask for. The less information a lender must ask for, the more credibility you'll earn. By skimping on information, the banker might think you are trying to hide a negative aspect of your business or personal history. Loans are more likely to be made on a marginal transaction if the lender believes in the customer. Make certain your proposal is completely free of spelling errors and grammatical mistakes. These just might kill your chances of getting a loan. Hire an English teacher if you have to.

That Reminds Me...

If you want additional help with your loan proposal, there is a software package that can help you called LenderPro. The cost is $295.00 and it's produced by Money Soft (800-966-7797) in Phoenix, Arizona. It is a stand-alone DOS system, and no Windows version is available yet. This self-contained program needs no additional software and comes with a 30-day money-back guarantee. It offers several amortization options, lets you create many different funding scenarios, and the written text of your plan can be exported to word processing software such as Microsoft Word.

Questions to Ask When Interviewing Bankers

The banker you select will be a vital part of your wealth building journey. Don't just settle for the first one that says "yes." Spend some time getting to know them. You're about to start a long-term relationship that could be very beneficial to the both of you.

Once you have your loan proposal ready, set appointments with at least three bankers. Before you give them the proposal, get to know them as a person. What are their interests? What do they enjoy about being a banker? Then ask the following questions:

- **How much capital does your bank have?** A national bank can only lend a customer up to 15 percent of its capital. Some states will allow their banks to loan as much as 20 percent of their capital. If the bank has only $500,000 in capital, it can only lend you $75,000. This might be enough now, but what about later? Will the bank be large enough next year for your needs?
- **What is your bank's capital ratio?** This is the ratio of capital to assets and it measures a bank's strength and its availability of capital. Make sure your bank's ratio exceeds 6 percent. A ratio lower than 6 percent might mean the bank is having some difficulties.
- **What is your non-committee loan limit?** This is the amount of money your banker can approve without having to present your loan to a committee. I don't like committees and prefer to deal with bankers who can approve my loan. If you need a great deal of money, you may have no choice. You at least want to deal with a banker who can approve a significant amount of money.
- **What is your loan-to-deposit ratio?** All banks are require to publish this ratio in the local paper every quarter. If your bank's loan-to-deposit ratio is less than 50 percent, you may be dealing with a bank that's too cautious about lending money. They would rather invest in government and municipal bonds, federal funds, and other items other than loans because those securities offer less risk. Make sure your bank has a loan ratio exceeding 50 percent. A ratio above 50 percent shows that your bank is eager to make loans. That's the kind of bank you want.

Treasure Tip

Be sure to dress professionally when you go to meet and interview your prospective banker. Be candid, honest, and yourself. They want to do business with people with good character and integrity.

Words of the Wealthy

A bank's **capital ratio** is calculated by dividing the bank's capital by its total assets. This ratio measures the bank's availability of capital, as well as it's financial strength.

- **Has your bank recently merged with a larger bank?** Avoid banks that have merged with larger or similar-size banks. The confusion, disturbance in job security, and chances of you getting a different loan officer are too great to worry about.
- **Does your bank have areas of emphasis or expertise?** Some banks specialize in consumer loans and some focus on business loans. Some banks do a lot of business with a particular industry such as real estate. Knowing this about your prospective bank might give you some insight into how well the bank might be able to serve your credit needs.
- **Can you give me a list of client references?** This might completely blow your banker's mind, but you need to know what other people think about him or her and the bank. Even if you were referred to this bank by a friend, you might want to do some of your own research. Ask for clients who also have small businesses who can relate to your needs and concerns. When you call the references, be sure to have some specific questions ready. Use the questions in Chapter 9 as a guide. If the banker refuses to call any of his clients to ask if they would mind being a reference, go to another bank. Don't waste your time with that bank.

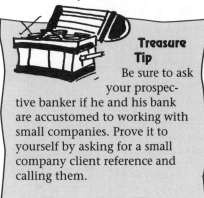

> **Treasure Tip**
>
> Be sure to ask your prospective banker if he and his bank are accustomed to working with small companies. Prove it to yourself by asking for a small company client reference and calling them.

What if Your Loan Is Denied?

The wealthy people I know didn't build their wealth being timid or shy. They were tenacious in their efforts and when they were faced with a "no," they continued to look for a "yes." If you get turned down by a banker, ask why and try to correct the problem. Then resubmit the proposal. Make sure the problem isn't bank-related. If they give you a vague answer, ask them to be more specific. If they continue to be vague, don't do business with them. They might be having some problems of their own.

Don't give up. Go to several other banks and present your proposal. After my own bank turned me down in 1994, I presented a proposal to four other banks and got four offers.

That Reminds Me...

In my fourth year in business, my banker made the mistake of telling me over the phone that he wouldn't even consider helping me structure a $100,000 bank loan to expand my business. This was a complete surprise to me. It just didn't make any sense. I had been with this bank for several years and had, in a timely manner, paid off all my loans except for my company car loan, which I was still making payments for. Well, I took it personally, which was wrong of me, but it sure motivated me to shop around at other banks. I presented my loan proposal to four other banks and all four wanted to loan me the money (structured the way I wanted). I picked Bank of Little Rock, and paid off the five-year loan within two years. But, this is not the end of the story. Three months after the first bank refused to consider my loan request, I called to draw on my $20,000 line of credit which was still at the first bank and had been in force for the previous two years. When I called, the teller said that my line of credit had been canceled. I called the same guy that turned me down for the loan and said, "Can you explain why my line credit has been canceled?" This is what he had to say: "Well, I assumed that you were going to another bank. So I canceled it." The bank canceled my line of credit without even sending me a notice. But good things come from bad, and this story does have a happy ending. I called my new banker and told him I needed a $40,000 line of credit. He said, "Come by now and we'll have the paperwork ready for you." I just love these guys and they love my company. Don't be discouraged if the bank initially tells you "no." Find one that wants your business.

What if You Can't Make Your Payments?

Wealthy people do what ever it takes to make their loan payments. However, occasionally there can be unexpected problems. Fortunately, bankers understand this. They're human too. If you see a potential problem with your cash-flow and you don't think you can make a payment, immediately sit down with your banker and explain to him the problem and that you want to pay the loan off as soon as you can. Ask him to work with you on a new payment plan. Your banker doesn't want to foreclose on your loan. It might completely blow his chances of you paying the money back. Therefore, he may be willing to do all he can to help you. Ask for an extended payment plan or a lower interest rate. Do whatever it takes to pay the loan off. Bankruptcy should not be an option. If you file for bankruptcy, it will haunt you for the rest of your life. No bank or lending institution will ever look at you the same again.

The Least You Need to Know

- A good banker can be your key to unlocking the door to Wealth Levels 4 and 5, but before you go to a banker, check out your credit by calling one of the "big three" credit agencies and requesting a copy of your credit report.
- The perfect loan proposal will tell the banker about your credit history, the collateral backing the loan, your cash-flow, amount of liquid assets, and your personal character.
- The key to finding the right banker is asking the right questions, getting the right answers, and talking to some of his other clients.
- If your loan is denied, do what other wealthy people do and don't give up—find out why, solve the problem, apply again, and consider other bankers.

Chapter 20

Hire the Best and Delegate

In This Chapter

- Before you hire, consider out-sourcing
- Manage payroll and you'll improve your margins
- Hire the best by stealing the best
- Why pay your new employee more than they expect?
- The power of a net bonus program

This chapter has the single greatest potential for catapulting your business forward into profitability. That means that this chapter also has the greatest potential of getting you to Wealth Levels 4 and 5. I know this from experience. My employees have empowered me and my business to grow faster and more profitable than almost all of the money management firms in the U.S. My profit margins currently exceed 60 percent. The goal was originally to exceed 50 percent. How did we get to 60 percent? This chapter will give you the answer. It wasn't just one strategy that got us there, it was a combination of tactics that my employees and I implemented together along the way. I could not have done it without them.

Getting Help—Don't Be So Quick to Hire

Before you run out and hire someone, ask yourself first if you can out-source the work. Out-sourcing allows you to hire the best without having to take them on your payroll. For example, unless you are a CPA, you're going to need accounting work done for your business. Instead of hiring a CPA and putting him on your payroll, you can out-source your accounting work by paying an independent CPA to do the job for you. Look at every procedure of your business and ask yourself if it can be out-sourced. Then find someone willing to do the work. You can find help from:

- Temporary services
- Employee leasing companies
- Vendors who offer help

Keeping Payroll at 25 Percent

One other thing you need to be aware of before you hire is your total payroll costs. If you can get payroll costs under control, you are well on your way to being more profitable and more wealthy. Many business owners go out and hire what they think they need well before they look at their budget for payroll. The inevitable result is a poor profit margin or a layoff. Establish a goal to keep your payroll costs at or below 25 percent. My definition of payroll costs includes salaries, payroll taxes, and insurance costs for all employees (excluding you). I've let my payroll exceed 25 percent temporarily as I hire someone new, but within six months, it returns to the 25 percent mark.

How to Find and Steal the Best Employees

Building wealth using your business is directly tied to the capacity of work your employees can handle. The amount of work they can handle is directly tied to their desire to achieve company goals. The level of desire they have will depend upon their passion for the business and their belief that if they work hard in your company, they can achieve their own personal goals.

How do you find the right employees for your business? First you have to decide exactly what you are looking for in an employee. Using great detail, describe the best employee you could hire. Write this down before you begin your search. This will help you keep on track of what kind of person you want to hire.

Second, look at your competitors and suppliers for possible employees. These people know your industry better than anyone walking in off the street. Their experience will greatly reduce the amount of training they will need. Plus, if they are really good at what they do, they'll be known by all the primary business people in your industry. This means that you can ask others (in confidence) about these people before you hire them.

Ask Key People You Know in Your Industry

If you don't know anyone specifically in your industry that you can hire, ask key people you know for referrals. Explain exactly what you are looking for. Ask them who the best candidate would be.

> **That Reminds Me...**
>
> After one year in business, I asked around in my industry and found out that the best support person in the state was unhappy with her employer. Her name is Linda and I had worked with her before. I called her and asked her to come in for an interview. She later accepted my job offer and has been working with me ever since.

Look for Those Who Are Disgruntled or Seem to Want More

If you have to, go visit other similar companies or get your friends to and ask around. Find out who might be unhappy with their current position. Look for someone who wants a bigger challenge and more responsibility.

> **That Reminds Me...**
>
> When I need a new employee, I ask a few key people to "bird-dog" for me. In fact, I myself become a bird-dog. What do I mean by a bird-dog? A bird-dog is a dog on a mission. He has one thing on his mind and nothing else. Birds, birds, birds. He can't think of anything better. He'll go without food, without water, and without sleep just to get a chance at seeing a bird. If you've ever seen these dogs in action, you know exactly what I'm talking about. Not every business owner can do this. But if you're looking for a key employee (which all of mine are), you stand a better chance of getting a good quality person by doing some sniffing around. It may take some time and so you may have to be patient. Great employees don't grow on trees. The best ones are loyal and are slow to leave their current employer.

Pay Employees a Little More Than They Expect

Wealthy business owners know the value of paying employees a little more than they expect. It's a great way of telling your new employee that they are worth the extra money. This not only builds self-confidence in the employee, it also builds loyalty and trust. Show me a company with loyal, trustworthy, and confident employees, and I'll show you a wealth-building machine. If at all possible, pay your new employee a little more than they expect. First, find how much you can afford to pay them. Then ask exactly what they need. You want to find the smallest amount of salary they need to feel comfortable coming to work for you. If they are really excited about working for you, they should, more than likely, give you a relatively low figure to begin with. Once you've established this amount and you're ready to hire them, offer them a little extra and tell them it's because they're worth it. If you've really done your homework and you're face to face with a great potential employee—it will be worth the extra salary to get the talent. The little extra could be a net bonus program.

Establish a Net Bonus Program

A "net bonus program" is an incentive pay program based upon a certain percentage of the net income from your business. It is the key to motivating your employees to help achieve your company (and therefore your wealth building) goals.

The first bonus program I installed was based upon gross income. This motivated my employees to grow, but they had no incentive to spend money efficiently. During our weekly meetings, they had little interest in working on saving money. All they could think about was growth. The day I changed the bonus program to be based upon net income, THE ENTIRE COMPANY CHANGED! My employees instantly became interested in reducing overhead expenses. It was like magic. Suddenly they thought like I did. They became interested in reducing every expense they could find. They also began to take more of an interest in planning for the company's future.

Treasure Tip

I give my employees 15% of my company's net income. This lump of money is then divided and distributed according to each employee's percentage of payroll.

It's imperative for you to understand how powerful this concept of a net bonus is for your business. I will never run a business again without it. Overnight it can change your business forever. Try it.

The easiest way to calculate net bonuses every month or quarter is to build a computer spreadsheet that can calculate it for you. Once your monthly financial statements are produced, all you'll have to do is enter the data and, PRESTO, you have everything done.

The net bonus program is designed to allow your employees to share a pre-determined percentage of your net income. Once you have decided upon the percentage and calculated the net bonus total, you then divide the bonus dollars according to each employee's percentage of payroll. Half is paid immediately and half is placed in a pool to be distributed at the end of the year. However, an employee must still be employed by the end of the year in order to receive the other half.

You should include all employees in your bonus program. However, there should be an initiation period for new employees. Mine is currently 6 months. All new employees must wait 6 months before they are placed in the bonus program. Here's how I calculate my bonuses:

	Operating income
Subtract	**Overhead expenses** (minus depreciation)
Subtract	**Loan payments** (for capital expenditures)
Subtract	**Money for cash reserves** ($2,000, for example)
	Net income
	× 15 percent
	Net bonus amount
	× 1/2
	Immediate Bonus
	× **Percentage of payroll** = employee's bonus

You Have to Delegate

Most wealthy people will tell you that delegating is initially very difficult to get accustomed to. However, if you can do it successfully, you dramatically increase your chances of achieving Wealth Levels 4 and 5. It took me several years to understand this concept. It wasn't a natural transition for me. During the first few years of my business, I had to do just about everything myself. Slowly I recognized the need for help, and began looking at all the options. I could hire someone without experience for very little money, but I would have to train them. This would take time. Therefore, I decided to spend more money and get someone with experience—someone who could walk right in and go to work. I hired the best person in the state and began delegating all my administrative work to her. This lady turned my business around. The day I hired the best employee in the state and began to delegate work to her is the day my company's growth took a turn upwards.

Treasure Tip

Do all you can to make your company an exciting and fun place to work. The results will amaze you. Your employees will be more efficient, effective, and much more loyal.

The lesson that I learned is that you can't do it alone, you need help. In the early years of starting a business, you are a manager of activities. Soon you have to hire help, and you become a manager of activities and people. Eventually you become a manager of people. If you want to increase your business to any significant size, you must become a manager of people. If this is the natural evolution of a business, wouldn't it be smart in the early years to focus your efforts on hiring the best employees? I say it's absolutely imperative.

That Reminds Me...

One day I decided to start a newsletter for my clients. I asked my newest employee, Angie, if she would take the project, and she gladly accepted. She had absolutely no experience and very little guidance from me. I explained the concept, bought her software and training, and then got the heck out of the way. The result was incredible. Now she is producing two newsletters at the same time. These are her babies and she's darn proud of them—so am I. When you delegate a task, step back and let your employee figure it out.

Match Responsibilities with Personality

When you hire, make sure the responsibilities you want taken care of are properly matched with the personality of the prospective employee. Ask your prospective employee what they really enjoy doing. Ask them about their strengths and weaknesses. Find out what they do best and make sure that it matches what you are looking for. If the person you need to hire is going to be in sales, find someone with excellent people skills. If you need an administrative person, make sure they enjoy working with numbers. This is an ongoing process too. You have to stay abreast of your employees' personalities as they develop over time. Personalities do change sometimes, so be sure to meet individually with each employee on a regular basis.

Meet with Your Employees Individually

If you really want to build wealth through the growth of your business, you need to know each of your employees' personal goals and aspirations. If you care enough to help them achieve these goals, they'll be much more loyal and dedicated to your vision. Help them and they'll help you. I don't believe in the traditional employee review meeting. Instead, I get to know the employee's own personal goals and I help them accomplish those goals through the success of my company. If I can show my employee how she can accomplish her personal goal by accomplishing the company's goal, we have both won. Plus, there's no need for me to be a motivator. If my employee sees how her personal goal can be accomplished through the success of the company, then she'll naturally be motivated to produce. It's a very simple concept.

Conduct Regular Team Meetings

To be a successful and profitable business that can be sold later, you must hold weekly, monthly, and yearly meetings. Team meetings are so vital to the success of a business. They hold together the people and the responsibilities of an organization. They develop and maintain a team spirit that is necessary for success. Weekly meetings should be for monitoring the progress of goals set each month. They shouldn't be any longer than one hour in length. The primary purpose of monthly meetings is for discussing the results of each goal in progress and setting new goals. Monthly meetings should be an all day event. Yearly meetings should be at least two days in length and should be held outside the office. The primary purpose of a yearly meeting is to set goals for the upcoming year.

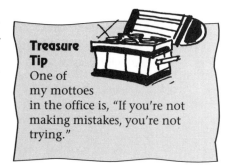

> **Wealth Warning**
>
> My last boss literally "met" us to death. Almost every day there was a meeting. What made it worse is that he would lecture all of us for the mistakes of a few. We didn't deserve to be treated like that. I learned both the value of a weekly meeting, as well as the value of one-on-one employee counseling sessions.

The basic weekly and monthly meeting agendas should at least include:

- Old business. Items from last week that need attention.
- Goal review. Review the status and results of current goals.
- New Business. New goals and any other items to discuss.
- Calendar planning. Go over everyone's calendar.

The great thing about meetings in my firm is the "old business" section. This is a great way to keep everyone (including me) accountable for the projects that should be in process. If they are in process too long, they should be eliminated, delegated, or tabled to later dates.

> **Treasure Tip**
>
> One of my mottoes in the office is, "If you're not making mistakes, you're not trying."

You must also encourage an open and flexible meeting where anything can be discussed. If your employees are intimidated or afraid to give their opinions, you may have problems for years before you ever see them. Your employees should be your greatest asset. Most employers don't realize their employees' full potential.

Develop Your Vision and Let Your Employees Help

The key to long-term business success and the wealth building process is getting employees involved in developing your vision, and then letting them run with it. Your role should be to manage these people and support them. If you have a big vision, chances are you're not going to be able to do it all yourself.

Consider an ESOP Plan

An ESOP plan is an employee stock ownership plan. It is used to give employees of private and publicly traded companies the opportunity to buy stock in a company over time. The employees become owners, which makes them feel more a part of the company. The owner gets motivated employees and an opportunity to sell his stock and raise cash. ESOP plans have made many business owners very wealthy, and it could be your ticket to Wealth Levels 4 and 5.

All ESOP's require a legal document setting up the plan and trustee. A certain percentage of each employee's salary is expensed as a profit sharing plan deduction and put into the plan to buy company stock.

Before you do anything, take some time to decide exactly what you want to accomplish with your ESOP. This should be your first step. Communicate these goals to your attorney before he begins designing the plan. There may be another way to accomplish your objectives without starting an ESOP.

Second, sit down with your employees and discuss what an ESOP can do for them. Get an attorney to help explain it if you have to.

Third, the ESOP plan must be written and designed properly by an attorney who specializes in these plans. Make sure the attorney is independent of any bank or institution. You want him to be as unbiased in this deal as possible. If he works for the bank, who's best interest will he serve first?

Fourth, begin the plan and let it work for you. Your attorney can help you as things change.

The Least You Need to Know

- Before you run out and hire that perfect employee, examine the responsibilities of the job and find out if you can out-source the work.
- If you'll pay your new employees a little more than they expect, you'll be rewarded with happy, loyal employees, a much more profitable company, and a faster ride to Wealth Levels 4 and 5.
- Pay all your employees a bonus based upon a percentage of net profits and watch your company and net worth grow like a weed.
- If you really expect to grow your business significantly and reach Wealth Levels 4 and 5, you must become more of a manager of people than a manager of tasks.
- If you really want to build your business and your net worth, hire the best, match their work with their personality, give them responsibility, and get the heck out of the way.

Chapter 21

Maximizing Profits and Selling Your Business

In This Chapter

- Leaping completely over the competition
- Determining the value of your business
- Finding a buyer
- Negotiating the sale of your business
- Taking your company public

As you know from Chapter 3, you have achieved Wealth Level 4 if the market value of your business would produce (after capital gains taxes) enough proceeds to build a portfolio sufficient to support and substantially increase your desired lifestyle, while at the same time keeping up with inflation. Regardless of whether or not you plan to sell your business in the future, if you plan to achieve Wealth Level 4 using your own business, you need to understand the theory of preparing your company for a sale.

One of the benefits of owning your own business is the opportunity to build wealth at a much faster pace relative to the traditional method of monthly investments in the stock market. Since the equity value of your business is tied to its growth and profitability, the key to building wealth is maximizing earnings growth. This not only makes you money, it also makes your business worth more to a buyer. What I've learned is that what makes your business worth more to a buyer also makes you money in the process. Therefore, you should run your company as if you were going to sell it sometime in the near future. Whether you can sell your business or not, you can at least save part of your earnings. If you actually sell your business in the future, your efforts will be further rewarded at the time of the sale.

This chapter will teach you how to build a company that will not only make you a lot of money, but will also make a buyer salivate.

23 Business Strategies that Will Make You Rich

Are you ready to learn how to get to Wealth Levels 4 and 5? These are all common sense measures to help you increase profits, build your equity value, and make your company more attractive to buyers. Every business is different, which means that a few of these might not apply to your situation. Therefore, use what you can and leave the rest.

1. **Maximize your profit margin.** Take steps to improve your earnings enough to produce a profit margin that exceeds industry standards. Your trade organization should have some data on this. This can be done two ways: cutting your overhead expenses and maximizing sales or gross income. Many business owners try to minimize taxes so much that they inevitably forget about profits. If you plan to sell your business, you need to focus on maximizing profits because that's what the new owner is looking for. Eliminate anything that hides profits.

2. **Get audited financial statements.** Have your financial statements audited by a reputable CPA firm. The first thing a potential buyer will want from you is your company's financial statement. Accurate financial statements will build trust between you and your potential buyer. Plus, the buyer will want to have your statements audited anyway. Having them done in advance will save you a lot of time.

3. **Maximize sales and earnings growth.** Focus on maximizing your company's sales and earnings growth. Your goal should be to achieve a growth rate that exceeds industry standards. Call your trade organization and ask about the average sales and earnings growth rates in your industry. You might also ask who the most successful firms are in your industry. Call them and ask if you can come visit in order to share ideas.

4. **Show the potential for more growth.** Build a case that illustrates for the new buyer more potential for growth in sales and market share. If your company dominates the market with a 60% market share, the buyer will be worried about the prospects for further growth. Show him how your market may be growing. Illustrate for him how he can achieve a 70% market share. Make it easy for him to visualize success.

5. **Design written systems and procedures.** If you and your employees will take the time to design and maintain written systems and procedures, your company will not only run more smoothly and efficiently, your prospects for a sale will greatly improve. Empathize with a potential buyer and imagine yourself trying to make a buying decision between two businesses. If everything else was held constant, except that one had a written procedures manual for all operations and all employee positions in the company, which one would you choose? You'd choose the company that can operate the best with the least supervision—the one with written systems and procedures that anyone can follow. That's every businessperson's dream.

6. **Clean house.** Do you find yourself cleaning your house prior to company coming over? Well, you need to do the same thing when prospective buyers start to visit. Implement a procedure to keep your facility as neat and tidy as possible. You might even want to consider painting or other improvements that might be more attractive to a buyer. If this was your house, what would you do?

7. **Smiling, happy people.** If you want to really impress your prospective buyer, show him a group of happy, enthusiastic, team-oriented employees. If you haven't taken the steps to create this, I suggest you do it now. You can't produce this overnight, but you can at least get started.

8. **Keep it confidential.** You may not want to tell your employees about your interest in selling. It could create unwanted confusion and fear. Regardless of truth, if your employees think they might lose their job as a result of a sale, they will immediately begin to look elsewhere.

9. **Always take time to plan.** So few people take time out to plan. They get so caught up in their work that they never have time to plan. It's like the lumberjack who was so busy sawing that he didn't have time to sharpen the saw. Every six months, my friend Ted and I escape to the wilderness and spend a day planning. What I enjoy the most is his enthusiasm in the planning process. This makes it easier and a lot more fun. I'll share more on this with you in Chapter 26.

10. **Find the best at your business.** If you want to leap completely over your competition and experience exponential growth, find the best people in your business today and model after them. Some people are reluctant to help others, especially if you are in their own town. Therefore, focus on those who are out of your geographic area. Ask them if you can visit with them about their business.

Treasure Tip

One thing my father taught me by example is that a clean and organized place of business is more attractive to the customer and more enjoyable for the employee. It also cuts down on injuries and the resulting insurance costs. Thanks, Dad.

11. **Do what you love to do and delegate everything else.** I covered this in Chapters 17 and 22, but it's important enough to repeat.

12. **Always have a big vision.** In order to build a better business, you have to have a vision of what you want to build. This vision must be big enough to drive you and challenge you. I have found that if my vision is too small, it eventually bores me. However, if it's big and wonderful, I become naturally motivated. The only way you'll know if your vision is big enough is to try to achieve it first. Remember to expect set-backs and to use the tools in Chapter 18 to get you back on track.

That Reminds Me...

I remember when I was young, I built a tree-house with my friend Brandon. We would spend weeks building what we thought was the best tree house in the world, and in our little world, it was the best! We'd play with great pride in that tree-house. It was our escape. However, within a week, we got bored. We thought of all the things we'd do differently, and all the things that needed improvement. We knew we wanted a bigger, better house so we built another. We got bored again and built another. It took me many years to understand the moral of that adventure. I had learned that you have to have a dream big enough to challenge you all your life. Otherwise, you'll end up building one tree-house after another.

13. **Focus on what you're good at.** What are you better at than most people? What do others say you're good at? If you'll identify your strengths and use them, you might find yourself with a natural competitive advantage that will speed you on to success. If you're really good at something now, just imagine how competitive you'd be if you focused on improving that skill even more. Use your natural strengths to build your business and beat your competition.

14. **Eliminate the fear of failure.** Fear of failure will kill your business. You should always ask yourself, "What is the worst thing that can happen?" Next, you should ask yourself, "Can I handle the worst thing?" If the answer is yes, then don't worry about it any more. Make plans to handle the worst thing, and then eliminate the fear.

15. **You must work hard.** The average executive work week is about 60 hours. However, if you have an exciting vision and a plan to achieve it, you might find yourself wanting to work more than 60 hours.

16. **Avoid negative people.** If you want to ruin your vision, spend time with problem-oriented, negative, and jealous people. If you want to build a better business, focus your social efforts on associating yourself with positive people who are also success-oriented. Successful business owners associate themselves with others who appreciate win-win relationships. They celebrate each others' victories and are eager to help in the defeats.

    The same is true with business relationships. If you know that a potential or existing client is going to be a problem in the future, you might want to give them to your competitor. Just explain that you really feel that their objectives will be better served by the other company.

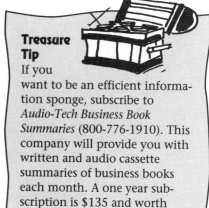

> **Treasure Tip**
> Trade shows and conventions held for your industry are by far one of the greatest learning tools available to you. Few people understand their value. I asked an advisor friend of mine if he was attending the annual financial advisors convention sponsored by Charles Schwab & Co. He said, "No. I never really get anything out of those conventions." I said, 'That's because you don't ask enough questions.'

17. **Be an information sponge.** In today's world of computers, the Internet, and fast-paced business transactions, you have to keep track of many changes. If you want to learn new ways to improve your business, you must become a Curious George and ask a lot of questions. You also need to be able to read a lot of information in a short amount of time. What should you focus your attention upon? The following list gives the most common fast-paced changes that will affect your business:

    - Improved computer systems that improve your efficiency
    - Internet software that can connect you to your customer
    - Changes in your industry and the economy
    - Changes in the needs of the customer
    - Changes in your competition

> **Treasure Tip**
> If you want to be an efficient information sponge, subscribe to *Audio-Tech Business Book Summaries* (800-776-1910). This company will provide you with written and audio cassette summaries of business books each month. A one year subscription is $135 and worth every penny.

18. **Keep a good attitude.** If you want to build a better business, you must develop an air of confidence, enthusiasm, and humility. For example, if you try to make a sale with a fearful

or hungry attitude, the prospective buyer will more than likely run away. You have to be confident in yourself, your product, and your business. You also have to be optimistic and see the opportunity in every problem you encounter.

19. **Focus on helping others.** Customer service is simply the art of helping others and exceeding their expectations. The most successful companies in the world don't try to just meet their customer's needs, they try to exceed them. This should be part of your company's core policies. One way to start this process is to examine your marketing efforts. If you exceed the expectations of a prospective buyer, you increase the odds of them becoming a client. For example, after the first 12 months of starting my business, I changed my marketing focus from selling to teaching. The rewards have been outstanding. During the following three years, my company grew more than 100 percent each year. Why? Because I changed my marketing focus on helping others learn how to invest. The more I helped other people learn, the more my business grew. If every company understood this one single principle, the world would be a better place to live.

> **Treasure Tip**
>
> Selling is a lot like dating. If you need the client bad, he'll run away. If you don't need the client, he'll never leave.

20. **Develop your genius.** Genius is not knowledge. My definition of genius is someone who can single-mindedly focus on one thing at a time. This may sound easy to you, but with all the hats you're going to have to wear as a business owner, "it ain't easy!" Make it easy on yourself and don't try to do more than one thing at a time. If you have to leave the office to think, do it!

21. **You must be a decision maker.** First, ask yourself this question: "Am I a decision maker?" If your answer is yes, then proceed. If your answer is no, ask yourself this question again until your answer is yes. To be a good decision maker, you must understand two things. First is the principle of the worse case scenario. As I said earlier in this chapter, if you can handle it, then don't worry about it. Second, list all the pros and cons to the decision. Weigh each alternative and select the best alternative. Accept the fact that you'll be wrong some of the time.

22. **Make sure you need it before you buy it.** Within six months of starting my own business, I spent over $10,000 on software that I never used.

> **Treasure Tip**
>
> I learned a valuable lesson in customer service from the man who takes care of my laundry. Raymond is, by far, the most customer service oriented person I know. What's his secret? When I asked him, he replied, "Basically, what I do all day is try not to say 'no' to any of my customers." This says it all.

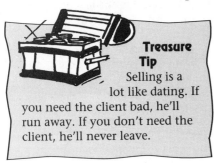

I honestly thought I needed it, but when I narrowed my focus from financial planning to money management, the software became obsolete. This was an expensive lesson in planning. That money could have been spent on so many other things. It still drives me crazy to know that I spent that much money on something that wasn't needed during a time when every penny counted. Learn from my mistake. Before you buy anything—especially a big ticket item—think about it for a while and make sure you need it.

23. **Establish some barrier to entry.** Do whatever it takes to set up as many barriers to entry as you can. A barrier to entry is simply something that deters or prevents other people from competing against you. The best barriers are licenses, patents, copyrights, and professional degrees. If none of these apply to your business, then consider other tactics such as:
    - Advertising and dominate your market
    - Be willing to do what others won't do
    - Establish yourself in the local media as the expert
    - Establish an outrageous customer service program

Treasure Tip
Any software package worth buying will offer you a trial period. If the software offers no trial period, I would suggest you shop around for one that does.

Why Sell?

Everyone is different and every business owner has his own reasons for selling. Your reason might be to build a liquid portfolio that would provide more than enough income for you to live—Wealth Level 4. The most common reasons business owners sell their business (or a part of it) include the following:

- Retirement
- Desire to diversify into other businesses
- Need for additional capital to continue growth
- Strategic alliance with larger company allows economies of scale and new markets

What's Your Business Worth?

In order for you to know when you've reached Wealth Levels 4 or 5, you need to know how your business is valued. Putting a price on a closely held business is a difficult process. To put it bluntly, the value of a business is equal to the most amount of money anyone is willing to pay for it. It's not like selling a house where you have comparable sales transactions within the same neighborhood. In contrast, sale prices of closely held companies aren't usually public information, and that makes the valuation process quite difficult. Therefore, you often have to calculate an estimate of fair market value based on very vague criteria. The fair market value is only an estimate. In the end, the real value is whatever price the buyer and seller agree upon at the time of the sale.

Some business owners jump to the conclusion that their company is worth 16 times their earnings, just like some companies traded on the New York Stock Exchange. They fail to recognize that publicly traded companies have several advantages over most closely held companies:

- Easier access to capital
- Ability to use stock for acquisitions
- Highly scrutinized financial reporting to the SEC
- Diversified group of management and directors
- The company's success doesn't rely on one person

The most common methods of valuation involve mathematical models which take into effect the company's assets, past and future earnings, industry outlook, strength of management, and uniqueness of the product/service. The three most common valuation methods are described next.

The Asset Method

The easiest valuation method is the asset method. The asset method simply sums up the fair market value of the company's underlying assets minus the liabilities. This approach is considered best when valuing a company with significant tangible assets such as real estate and commodities. This would not be a good valuation method for a service business with very little in tangible assets.

The Market Comparison Method

The most common method of valuation is the market comparison method which is quite similar to the methods used today in valuing real estate. Using this method, the company's financial performance and operations are compared to other similar companies recently involved in a sale transaction. It is imperative that the companies chosen for comparison are in the same business and similar in size. Factors are used to compare each business with yours in order to come up with a price that's fair to both parties. These factors are ratios which divide the price of the company's stock with other financial numbers. The most common factor is the P/E ratio or price to pre-tax earnings ratio. If you knew the average P/E ratio of the last 5 companies in your industry that were sold recently, you could easily multiply that average factor to your own pre-tax earnings to produce a good estimated fair market price. You can do the same thing with these other common factors, if you have the following information about other companies that have recently been sold:

- Price/pre-tax earnings
- Price/cash-flow
- Price/book value

Unfortunately, since privately held business transactions are not disclosed to the public, the financial information you need to make these comparable measurements is difficult, if not impossible, to find. However, you may find that your industry's trade organization keeps up with these factors. Maybe they can give you a rule of thumb. The alternative is to do the research yourself by calling the new owners of companies that have been recently purchased. Explain to the new owner that you don't necessarily need to know how much he paid for the business, you just want to get some relative measurements such as the ratios listed above. You might even promise to share your ratios after you sell your company at a later date. Some business owners will cooperate, and others will not.

The Discount Method

The third way to value a company is called the discount method or income capitalization method. This method is based upon the theory of estimating the present worth of the future financial benefits your company can offer the new owner. More specifically, this method calculates the present value of a company's expected future earnings over a certain period of time using a discount or present value factor. The calculation is complicated, which is another reason why you may want to get some help from a business broker or intermediary.

You'll also find that every industry has its own unique pricing methods. These are specific valuation measurements that others in your industry have used in past transactions. For example, the beer and soft drink industries both typically use the number of cases sold in a year to come up with an estimated value. They call this the price per case method. If a distributorship sold 500,000 cases last year and the price per case factor is $1.25, the distributorship is worth approximately $625,000.

One final note on valuing your business. You can spend time valuing your own business if you like that sort of thing. However, a good CPA would be happy to do it for you.

Who Else Can Help with Your Company's Valuation?

You might ask the owners of businesses in your industry if they know of anyone who specializes in doing valuations of companies in your industry. If you have trouble finding someone, contact these folks:

Management Advisory Services
A Division Of MOSS ADAMS, LLP
1001 Fourth Avenue, Suite 2700
Seattle, WA 98154-1199
206-442-2600
206-233-9214 fax

Corporate Finance Association Of Northern California
Henry S. James, President
344 Village Square
Orinda, CA 94563
510-254-9126
510-254-2160 fax

Finding a Buyer

Before you can sell your business and get to Wealth Level 4 or 5, you must find a buyer for your business. Buyers can be hard to find if you don't know who the players are in the market. Even if you do know the players, will you know how to conduct the sale? Selling a business involves complex valuation methods, tax considerations, and strategic negotiations. Can you do all that alone?

- **There are people who can help you.** Depending upon the size of your business, there are basically three types of people who can help you find a buyer and walk you through the sales process. They will also help you negotiate the sale. If you own a small business with less than $1 million in sales, you can hire a business broker. You can find business brokers listed in the Yellow Pages of most major cities.

  If your business has $2 to $50 million in sales, you're considered a middle market business, in which case you would want to hire what is known as an intermediary. They are similar to business brokers, but are accustomed to dealing with much larger businesses and more sophisticated negotiations. Intermediaries are hard to find unless you live in a major metropolitan city. If your business grows to over $50 million in sales, you may want to consider hiring an investment banking company. These companies are easy to find in the phone book.

Be sure to do your research before you hire one of these people. At the very least, ask for references and call them with questions. If you know of a company in your industry that's been sold recently, ask the seller and buyer who helped them. Most trade organizations also keep track of intermediaries that specialize in their industry.

- **Maximize your company's exposure to buyers.** Make sure your company is in all the local chamber of commerce listings. Confirm the way they categorize your company, who they list as president, and all other pertinent information. This includes the membership list, as well as other directories that might apply, such as the book of local manufacturers.

  Ask your state industrial development office for their guide to businesses in your state. Are you listed? Is the information up to date? Think of all the different services your company offers and make sure you are properly listed in the phone book under these services.

- **Talk to local CPAs, attorneys, and bankers.** These people know others who might be looking for a business to buy.
- **Offer a reward.** You might want to offer a reward for the person who can bring you a referral that results in a sale.
- **Don't list your business in the local paper.** You may not want everyone to know you're selling, plus you'll have all kinds of people calling you, most of which will not be qualified. If you do list locally, be anonymous and let your business broker or intermediary help you.

Building a Business Profile

A business profile is similar to a business plan. It will be used by your prospective buyers as they begin their research on your company. This profile could make you a very rich man if you design it carefully. Given the right amount of profitability, it may be your ticket to Wealth Level 5. Be sure to be accurate and honest. An outline of a typical business profile follows:

- I. Introduction
  - A. Summary of operations
  - B. Financial summary
  - C. History of company
  - D. Ownership
  - E. Reasons for sale
  - F. Company strengths and opportunities
- II. Description of Business
  - A. General business description
  - B. Description of market and current market share
  - C. Future growth potential
  - D. Sales and marketing
  - E. Competition
  - F. Management and employees
  - G. Current customers
  - H. Suppliers and contracts
- III. Business Facilities
  - A. Location and facilities
  - B. Equipment
- IV. List of Exhibits
  - A. Audited financial statements
  - B. Marketing material and brochures
  - C. Listing of major equipment and furniture
  - D. Résumés and job descriptions of all key employees
  - E. Results of recent client survey
  - F. Business advisors and references

Making the Sale

Most of the clients I know who have achieved Wealth Levels 4 and 5 have all sold their business. They knew what their company was worth, they negotiated with the buyer to agree upon a win/win deal, and they had help all along the way.

What Do You Want from the Sale?

The following list of questions should help you decide exactly what you want out of the sale.

- Would you be willing to finance the sale?
- Do you want to continue to work with the company after it's sold?
- If you were required to work for another year or two as part of the negotiation, would you be willing to? How long?
- If you did work, what hours would you want to keep? Do you need to continue your health insurance? What responsibilities would you want to focus on?
- How will you structure the deal to achieve your financial goals?
- Do you have key employees or your children in your business that want to continue working? Will the new owners keep them?
- What would your employees do if they knew you were thinking about selling? Should you keep it confidential?

Once you know what you want out of the transaction, prioritize each item by it's level of importance to you. This will make the negotiation much easier because you'll know what you can and cannot compromise. Be sure to let your attorney know these items and make sure he keeps the win/win concept in mind. Many attorneys will fight tooth and nail without compromising anything. Don't let this happen. You must be willing to compromise some things.

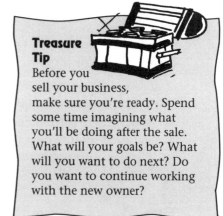

Treasure Tip

Before you sell your business, make sure you're ready. Spend some time imagining what you'll be doing after the sale. What will your goals be? What will you want to do next? Do you want to continue working with the new owner?

How to Negotiate the Right Way

The negotiation process takes time and therefore a lot of patience. You and the buyer must both be willing to work hard to make the transaction go smoothly. Here are several tips that will make the process a little easier and less time consuming:

- Know exactly what you are willing to compromise and what you're not.
- As long as you know your goals, be flexible as to their accomplishment.
- Don't insist on winning every argument.

- Empathize with the buyer and his needs.
- Don't get too excited if you get a better deal than you expected.
- Never hesitate to walk away from a sale that doesn't meet your goals.
- Never threaten to walk away unless you are serious about it.
- Listen for the buyer's goals.
- Listen and find out what exactly the buyer is willing to compromise.
- Be honest and strive for win/win.

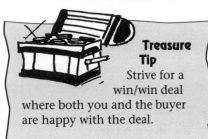

> **Treasure Tip**
> Strive for a win/win deal where both you and the buyer are happy with the deal.

How to Make the Sale Go Smoothly

Make sure you understand, in advance, the tax liabilities of selling your company. Hire a tax lawyer who can help you structure the sale to minimize taxes.

Don't procrastinate or be unprofessional in the transaction. Be patient and understand that this is a difficult process. However, don't allow your buyer to stall for no reason.

The personality of the buyer is very important, especially if you plan to continue working with the company. If you have more than one attractive offer, be sure to give a lot of consideration to the nature of the person or people you'll be working with. Spend some social time with the buyer and get to know him personally. This can improve the level of trust and rapport necessary for a good transaction.

> **Treasure Tip**
> Be sure to do your research on your buyer. Make sure you know who you're dealing with. Do they have adequate capital? Are they capable of running the company? Make the research process for the buyer easy. Try to do the homework for him in advance. Be honest and don't try to hide anything that can surprise your buyer later.

Allow the new buyer to get to know your employees on a social level. If your employees are happy with the new owner, things will run much more smoothly for both you and the buyer.

Make sure the buyer has enough money after the sale for working capital and emergencies. You might get your business back if he runs out of money. If the buyer says he plans to make up for the lack of cash through net earnings from the business, make sure your company's profitable enough to accomplish this. You also want to make sure you get enough money up front to cover two things: Any commission you might have to pay to your broker or intermediary, and any expenses you might encounter if you happen to get the business back.

Make sure your company is profitable enough to cover the debt payments for the buyer. If your buyer can't pay the debt on the business, he'll have to give it back to you.

Taking Your Company Public—The Initial Public Offering

If your heart is set on achieving Wealth Level 5, you must understand how to take your company public. When you make an initial public offering (IPO), you sell a certain percentage of your company's stock to the public for money. You usually sell only a minimal amount of stock so that you can still maintain control. The underwriter helps the company decide upon the price of the new shares and the timing of the IPO.

Taking your company public gives you the opportunity to cash in on your company's success without having to give up control or sell your majority interest of the shares. The benefits of taking your company public include:

- You only sell a part of your company
- You can still be the largest shareholder and maintain some control
- The value of your company is much higher as a public company
- Your stock is much more liquid
- Publicly held stock can be used as collateral easier

Words of the Wealthy
An **underwriter** is a brokerage firm that handles the process of offering a company's stock to the public through an **initial public offering**.

All these benefits come with a price:

- You have to give up some future profits
- You will have to fully disclose financial information on your company
- Your company will be highly regulated by the SEC
- You must answer to shareholders
- You must answer to your board of directors

Other Books That Can Help

If you decide to start you own business, be sure to check out *The Complete Idiot's Guide to Starting Your Own Business*. It is filled with great tips and all the ideas you need to get started. Your library and local bookstore might also have other titles that will help.

The Least You Need to Know

- Maximizing the profit margin of your business will not only help you get to Wealth Levels 4 and 5, it will also make your business more attractive to a buyer.
- The best way to grow exponentially, completely dominate your competition, and achieve Wealth Levels 4 and 5 is to find the most successful businesses in your industry and model after them.
- Don't try to sell your business without a business broker or intermediary.
- Before you begin to negotiate the sale, take time to reflect upon what you expect from the sale and what it will take to reach Wealth Level 4 or 5.

Part 4
Rich People Have Rich Habits

One thing I've noticed about most, if not all, wealthy people I know is that they have certain habits that help them maintain their wealth for themselves as well as their heirs. I've covered many of these habits in the earlier parts of the book, but this part of the book will cover a few more you should be aware of as you approach Wealth Levels 3, 4, and 5.

First, wealthy people pay close attention to the amount of taxes they pay. Second, they live their lives with certain rules or paradigms that seem to prolong their wealth. And third, they use planning methods that allow them to achieve extraordinary goals. The last three chapters in this book will teach you these habits so you can maintain wealth for yourself and generations to come.

Chapter 22

Reducing Your Tax Bite

In This Chapter

- The only tax shelters left
- Silly mistakes people make that cost them big
- Estate planning made simple
- Why you will need a tax attorney

The importance of minimizing taxes is directly related to the size of your wealth and the amount of taxes you pay. My accountant estimated the amount of taxes I would have to pay by April of next year, and I nearly had a heart attack. Suddenly I'm motivated to do everything I can to fight taxes. However, I know from experience that certain tools and strategies work and others do not. This chapter focuses on the habits and strategies that do help, as well as the habits that don't. Unfortunately, there are not a lot of tax shelters or loopholes left anymore. However, this chapter does cover several strategies you can still use.

What about your heirs? If you died today, would your assets be distributed to the right people? Who would be your executor? This chapter will also help you understand the basics of estate planning as well as get you started on your own plan.

The Last of the Great Tax Shelters

Back in the late 1970s, limited partnerships were the hottest tax shelters around. They lured billions of dollars from investors who were looking for tax breaks. What the majority of these investors got instead was a big loss. They thought tax savings was more important than making money.

Things are different now and the real tax shelters for the most part no longer exist. What remains now are a few tools that allow you tax-free income, such as municipal bonds. Other tools will allow you to defer taxes until retirement, and these are the last of the great tax shelters. I've mentioned them before, but here is a complete list along with the key benefits they offer:

- **IRAs** This account is one of the most common things I see wealthy people use to build their wealth. The main attraction here is the benefit of having an investment account that can grow tax deferred for many years. You can only deposit up to $2,000 annually, but over time this can compound fast. Not until you are 70 1/2 do you have to begin taking withdrawals based upon your life expectancy.
- **SEPs** This is just like an IRA, but it's designed for small business owners who want to put more than $2,000 in their IRA. This account is often combined with an IRA and is sometimes referred to as a SEP/IRA. You can put up to 15 percent of your salary or $30,000 annually, whichever is less. The real benefit of this plan is that there are no end of the year tax forms to file and there's no need for an attorney to write up a plan document.
- **Keogh plans** These plans have made many physicians very rich, but you don't have to be a physician to start one. You just need a business. These plans are somewhat complicated. However, they will allow you to defer paying taxes on as much as 25 percent of your salary, which in turn can be placed in this account and invested just like an IRA or SEP. This is a SEP on steroids! I say that because this plan allows you to deposit so much more each year into the account. Unfortunately, there are end of the year tax forms to file on this plan as well as a legal document to maintain that can be somewhat expensive.
- **Profit sharing plans** This plan is actually part of a Keogh plan and can be set up on its own. You can only deposit up to 15 percent of your income, (just like the SEP), but you do have the ability to establish a vesting schedule. This schedule will allow you to phase in your employees into the plan over time. For example, after one year, your employees may only be 20 percent vested, which means that if they left your company, they could only take with them 20 percent of their share of the profit sharing plan. This acts as a golden handcuff that often makes employees think before they leave the company.

- **Money purchase plans** These are also a part of the Keogh plan and can be set up on their own. The key difference between this plan and a profit sharing plan is that a money purchase plan requires that you the employer must establish a set percentage of your payroll to be deposited into this account. There is no flexibility here. You can deposit as much as 25 percent of your salary, but you have to stick to that percentage. The profit sharing plan has more flexibility, but the maximum contribution is much lower (15 percent). Everything else is about the same.
- **Defined benefit plans** If you are over the age of 40 and you are the oldest person in your company (or the only employee), this plan might be right for you. It is unique from all the other plans above because the deposits you make into the account are based upon your life expectancy and a target (defined) amount of money toward which you are aiming for when you retire. The deposits each year can be much higher than the set limits of a Keogh, SEP, or any other plan. Just like the other plans, the deposits are made pretax and the account grows tax deferred.
- **Annuities** These are not my favorite tax shelters, but they do offer tax deferred growth of your investment. There are fixed annuities and variable annuities. I explained these in more detail in Chapter 7. The problem with fixed annuities is that they come with big commission penalties if you withdraw your money within the first several years. The problem with variable annuities is that they offer so few investment alternatives within the annuity plan. Therefore, I don't recommend them very often. The only variable annuity I would ever consider would be a true no-load annuity like those offered by Vanguard or Charles Schwab & Co.
- **Life insurance policies** I'm very hesitant to list these as a tax shelter because they should never be considered for investment purposes. However, they are excellent for estate planning, which I will discuss in more detail later in this chapter.

Words of the Wealthy

A **qualified plan** is an account into which pre-tax dollar contributions are made with the intent of using them later during retirement. The primary benefit is that all assets within the plan grow tax deferred until taken out at a later date. These accounts include the IRA, SEP, profit sharing, money purchase, Keogh, and defined contribution plans.

Wealth Warning

Don't let an insurance salesmen talk you into using a life insurance policy for the purpose of accumulating cash value during your lifetime for investment and retirement income purposes. It's way too expensive and far too complex for these purposes.

Let me stress one very important observation. Just because an investment is tax free or tax deferred doesn't mean that it's a good investment. Qualified plans are great, but I don't suggest annuities or life insurance policies for the sole benefit of tax deferred growth. Refer back to Chapter 7 before you use annuities or life insurance products for investment purposes.

Starting a business and expensing your hobby might seem like a great tax shelter. However, the IRS says you have to have a profit motive. How do they determine this? The *Federal Tax Handbook* says that you have to show a profit for any three or more out of five consecutive years. There is one exception: If you breed, show, or race horses, you only have to be profitable two out of seven years.

The Most Common Tax-Related Mistakes People Make

One of the most common habits I see among wealthy people is their knowledge of taxes and their tenacity to eliminate tax-related mistakes. They hate mistakes, especially when it means paying more taxes than they should. They do everything in their power to pay the least amount of taxes. A large part of this effort is eliminating the silly mistakes most people make.

Priority Number One: Save Taxes

For those people who make building wealth a priority, the most common tax-related mistake is the belief that saving taxes is more important than making money. Believe it or not, this happens every day. Don't let this happen to you. Always do your due diligence before you attempt to save taxes. Remember your first goal is to build wealth. Saving taxes must be, at best, your second goal.

Silly Mathematical Errors

Treasure Tip
When you do your own tax work or financial statement projections, remember the carpenters rule: "measure twice, cut once." That is, double check your work!

One of the best ways to reduce your tax is to reduce mistakes. In fact, after talking to a number of CPAs, they all said that the most common mistake was simple mathematical errors. These mathematical errors can continue to affect your numbers, especially if you've designed your own spreadsheets for estimating your taxes and financial statement projections. I know this from the silly mistakes I've made in the mathematical formulas I use while doing my financial statement projections. Once the mistake is made, it can continue to be a problem forever until it's detected.

Poor Record Keeping

Failing to keep good records of expenses will cost you a lot of money, but it is easy to correct. If you can't correct it, hire someone who will. Set up a system of records and maintain it well. Keep track of all contributions to charity, cost basis of investments, confirmations of buys and sells from your brokerage firm, and all check registers. Otherwise, you are going to overlook deductions, lose important records, and pay your CPA and the IRS more money than you should.

Wealth Warning
A classic example of poor record keeping is the mutual fund buyer who purchased a mutual fund years ago but has no statements or records of all the dividends that have been reinvested. Every reinvestment of dividends creates a new cost basis for the purchased shares.

Trying to Do It All Yourself When You Know You Need Help

I see this all the time—people trying to do their own taxes and financial statements just to save a dime. Why not hire a specialist who can do all this for you? Here's a list of reasons why:

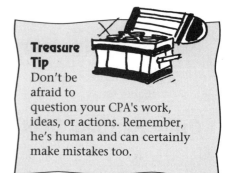

- A CPA is a specialist who knows the tax code
- One person dedicated to this will do a better job
- Other people may be more objective than you
- Hiring help should eliminate any possibility of procrastination
- The cost is nothing compared to the potential mistakes and sleepless nights of worry

Treasure Tip
Don't be afraid to question your CPA's work, ideas, or actions. Remember, he's human and can certainly make mistakes too.

Overlooking Deductions

The following is a list of some of the most overlooked deductions:

- Fees for tax preparation services and IRS audits
- Amortization of taxable bond premiums
- Appreciation on property donated to charities
- Business gifts of $25 or less
- Cellular telephones and charges

- Cleaning and laundering services when traveling
- Commissions on sales of property
- Contact lenses
- Depreciation of home computers
- Fees for a safe-deposit box to hold investments

Withholding Too Much or Too Little

If your tax refund is large, you are withholding too much money, and consequently, the IRS is getting a tax-free loan from you. Don't let this happen too long. You'll lose out on the power of compounding over time that's so important to building wealth. However, be careful not to withhold too little money. Have your CPA calculate your estimated quarterly taxes for you each year, and adjust your withholding or quarterly tax payment accordingly. A penalty for underpaying your taxes would be a total waste of money.

Not Taking Advantage of a Qualified Retirement Plan

As I said earlier in this chapter, a qualified retirement plan is one of the best tax shelters available today.

Using Personal Debt Instead of Mortgage Debt

This is such an easy mistake to correct. If you are able to itemize expenses each year on your personal tax reporting form, you can use your mortgage interest as an itemized deduction. Therefore, you should focus on using a home equity loan for any personal debt you have. For example, if you have a credit card with a consistent balance of $5,000 or more, call your bank and arrange for a home equity loan, and use the loan to pay off that credit card. You'll more than likely get a lower interest rate, plus you'll get to deduct your interest.

Investing in Municipal Bonds to Save Taxes While in a Low Tax Bracket

Municipal bonds are IOUs issued by city, state, and local municipalities. The interest they pay is not taxable at the federal level. Therefore, they don't have to pay the bond holder as much interest as other taxable bonds to be attractive. Sometimes I see investors in the lowest tax bracket buy these bonds. This is an easy mistake to make if you don't know your tax bracket or understand how municipal bonds work. It's even easier to make this mistake if you fall victim to a slick bond salesman. Just make sure you're in a high enough tax bracket to make the tax-free income worth investing in.

Before you buy a municipal bond, take the time to estimate your income and tax bracket if your income has increased this year, or simply look back at your tax forms from the prior year. If you are in the 15% bracket, do not buy a municipal bond.

> **Wealth Warning**
> Don't fall victim to a slick municipal bond salesman over the phone. I know bond salesmen that can make a bond sound so delicious that you'll have to pry yourself off the phone to keep from buying it. Do your homework on the salesperson and yourself before you buy one.

You Can't Take It with You

It is important to recognize the fact that at your untimely death, you can't take any of your wealth along with you. Therefore, it is imperative that you plan for the distribution of your wealth well in advance of your death. This brings us to one of the most important habits of the rich—estate planning.

What Exactly Is Estate Planning?

Estate planning involves the accumulation and disposition of property (or the estate) for the owner and his family or other heirs. The term "planning" implies the existence of goals. The goals in the case of estate planning can include one or more of the following:

- To provide security for the direct surviving family
- To make sure your assets go where you want them to go
- To minimize the financial cost in the transfer of assets, especially estate taxes
- To simplify the transfer of assets at your death
- To minimize family conflict, hardship, and emotional stress
- Provide for the valuation and transfer of a closely held business

Estate planning is also very useful in preventing the worse case scenarios such as:

- Direct family members left with financial insecurity
- Improper distribution of assets to beneficiaries
- Property transferred to minors who aren't old enough to manage it
- High estate taxes with only illiquid assets available to pay

> **Words of the Wealthy**
> **Estate planning** is simply the art and study of preserving wealth for family and future generations to come. It involves planning tools and techniques that cannot only reduce estate taxes, but also make things a lot more simple after your death.

- Unnecessarily high administrative expenses
- Family bitterness and jealousy

The Tools of Estate Planning

The will is the most important tool used in estate planning. It is used primarily to maintain wealth for the next generation. It can:

- Designate the primary and secondary beneficiaries
- Establish trusts through which assets are transferred
- Identify how estate taxes will be paid
- Appoint guardians for children
- Appoint executors, trustees, and fiduciaries as well as how they are to carry out their respective duties

The unified credit against gift and estate taxes is a rule that says you can give your family up to $600,000 after your death without the recipients having to pay estate or gift taxes. Estate taxes will be levied on any amount above this. The federal estate tax rates range from 37 percent to 55 percent.

Trusts are also important tools. They are written documents that appoint a trustee and provide beneficiaries the benefit of property ownership without the responsibility of managing that property. They are used in addition to wills to take full advantage of the tax laws regarding estate planning. The typical trust sets up an account in the name of the trust into which assets are placed for the benefit of the owner or her heirs. There are "inter vivos," trusts that are created by the estate owner before death and testamentary trusts that are created in the estate owner's will and go into effect at death.

Wealth Warning
Life insurance commissions are usually equal to at least the first year's premium or at least 7% if you pay a lump sum premium. Insurance is important and not all life agents are bad, you just need to be aware of the huge influence the commission creates. Shop around before you buy.

Gifts are common estate planning tools that wealthy people habitually utilize to reduce their potential estate tax burden. You can transfer or gift up to $10,000 per person per year without the recipient having to pay gift or estate taxes. Since only $600,000 in assets can be transferred tax free after your death, you can use $10,000 gifts before your death to help transfer additional assets out of an estate prior to death. These gifts can be larger than $10,000 but you either have to pay taxes on the amount over $10,000 or let it be considered part of the $600,000 tax free transfer.

Life insurance can also be important for two reasons. First, if you don't have an estate to leave your family, life insurance can provide them with one. This in turn would help ensure their financial security after your death. Second, life insurance can be used to pay the estate taxes at your death.

Retirement plans are also a tool for estate planning. All qualified plans require a designated primary and secondary beneficiary. At the account holder's death, the proceeds are paid directly to the primary beneficiary or the secondary in the case where the account holder and primary beneficiary die at the same time. Since the proceeds go directly to the beneficiary, they can sometimes provide instant liquidity for the estate, which may be needed for various reasons.

Getting Started

You must first realize that estate planning is not a one-time thing. After you get the basics set up, you must make the maintainance of your estate plan a habit. The first step to estate planning is deciding what you want to happen after your death, where you want your assets to go, and how your heirs will be able to pay any potential estate taxes that might result. Almost all tax attorneys will provide you with an estate planning questionnaire that will make the planning process much smoother.

The second step involves hiring a tax attorney to help you design the plan as well as the right tools you'll need to make it all happen. How can you find the best attorney? Ask other successful business friends who they recommend. You might also ask your CPA for a referral. Talk to several attorneys before you select one. Ask for client references and call them.

The third step is getting the plan in place and maintaining that plan. This involves yearly check-ups with your attorney to make any changes that are necessary.

Remember, I am not a tax attorney nor a CPA, and no book can take the place of either. Therefore, be sure you check with your CPA and tax attorney before you use any of the tax or estate planning ideas in this book.

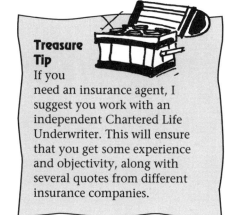

Treasure Tip
If you need an insurance agent, I suggest you work with an independent Chartered Life Underwriter. This will ensure that you get some experience and objectivity, along with several quotes from different insurance companies.

The Least You Need to Know

- Wealthy people realize that just because an investment product offers tax free or tax deferred income doesn't make it suitable for you or worth investing in.
- The best place to find the right CPA for you is by referral from another business owner whose business is growing and experiencing the same problems you will be.
- Wealthy people make it a habit to eliminate all personal debt and they use mortgage debt only when necessary.
- Wealthy people take advantage of all the estate planning tools available by hiring experienced tax attorneys.

Chapter 23

The Wealth Paradigms, and Why People Fail to Get Rich

In This Chapter

- Why people don't get rich
- The definition of a paradigm
- Why paradigms are so important
- The paradigm of past performance
- The paradigm of philanthropy

Your mind is your biggest asset when it comes to building wealth. Unfortunately, it can also be your biggest liability. Most wealthy people understand this concept and use it to their advantage. They understand the mind sets or mental habits necessary for building wealth, which I've discussed in detail throughout this book.

What you need to examine now are your own mind sets or paradigms. First, you have to understand the definition of paradigms. Second, you need to know how they work and how they can affect you in your everyday life. Once you understand them, you can use all the habits and strategies in this book to build your own wealth paradigms.

11 Reasons Why People Fail to Get Rich

There are hundreds of reasons why people fail to build wealth. Take a look at the following list, and if any of them sound familiar, do all you can immediately to correct the problem and change the way you think.

- They work hard but not smart.
- They're not willing to delegate.
- They accept self-imposed limitations.
- They don't live within their means so they don't have enough to save, and are too proud to scale back their lifestyle.
- They're waiting for an inheritance.
- They're not willing to take risk.
- They don't do enough homework to protect themselves from scavengers.
- They don't channel their efforts in the direction of their passion.
- They lack single-mindedness of thought.
- They let pride get in the way.
- They expect and accept entitlements (like welfare).

Realistically, this list is endless. However, each of the items has something in common. Everyone of them involves a mental belief or mind-set that ultimately prevents the person from building any significant wealth. These are paradigms. If you understand what paradigms are and how they work, maybe you can improve your chances of building your own wealth.

The Study of Paradigms

In my attempt to fully understand the human mind and the tendency to develop mind-sets, I was led to the study of paradigms. This single subject has been one of primary catalysts for my success in business and my achievement of Wealth Level 4. Without the knowledge of paradigms and how they affected my own life, I don't think I would have ever achieved what I have in the last five years. I'm not exaggerating one bit. My business would have more than likely failed, and I would not have had the opportunity to write this book. Paradigms are incredibly powerful. If you're not aware of your own set of paradigms and how they control your life, you're destined to fail. Take my advice, learn all you can about your own paradigms immediately. You'll never make it to Wealth Levels 4 or 5 without this knowledge.

The greatest contemporary book written on paradigms is by Joel Arthur Barker and is titled *Future Edge*. It will certainly forever change the way you look at your world—and for the better.

A paradigm is a set of rules that people perceive as their reality. This same set of rules tells you what can and cannot happen. It also defines success and failure. It's like playing cards. Someone years ago decided upon the rules of the game, and therefore, that's how to play the game. For some unknown reason, no one really ever questions the rules. They just play the game.

Take a minute to let me illustrate the power of paradigms using an example. Look at the nine dot diagram shown below, and draw one like it on a piece of paper.

The objective is to connect all nine dots using four straight lines, and without picking up your pen. Take your pen and begin on one dot. You can only draw four straight lines, and remember, you cannot take your pen off the paper. Each line must be continuous from the last. If you really want to understand how the human mind thinks, you'll try this exercise. After you try the exercise, flip ahead to find one way to solve the puzzle.

Words of the Wealthy

The word **paradigm** (pronounced pair-a-dime) originates from the Greek word "Paradeigma" which means model or pattern.

Treasure Tip

A paradigm is simply a mind-set or way of perceiving the world. It's the smile of a mother to a baby, it's the forest to the deer, it's the water to a fish, and it's the New York Stock Exchange to the broker on the floor as he screams out a trade.

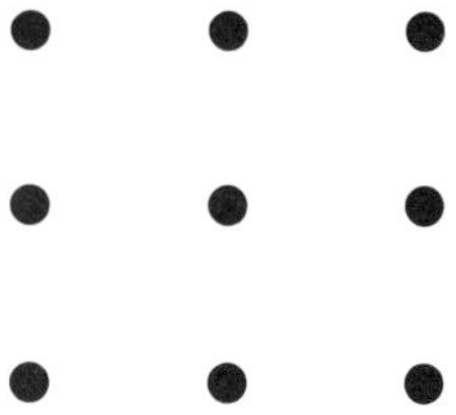

Nine dot diagram.

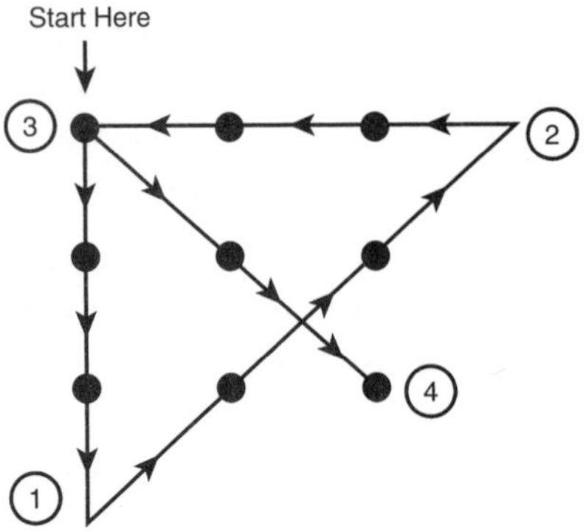

One answer to the nine dot exercise.

This exercise is more than just a game or puzzle. It's a lesson in life, at least it was for me. Take a look at the completed puzzle. Ask yourself this question: What had to happen for the puzzle to be solved?

After sharing this with thousands of people in my workshops, the most common reply I get is, "You had to get out of the box," or "you had to go out of the boundaries." My reply is simply, "What box? What boundaries? I drew nine dots."

Did you see a box or boundaries when you first saw the nine dot diagram? If you drew a box in your mind and limited yourself to its boundaries, you could never have solved the puzzle. If you did not draw a box in your mind and were open minded enough not to limit yourself, how many times did you try to solve the puzzle?

There are two things to learn from this exercise. First, your ability to achieve wealth is directly influenced by your ability to identify and control your own personal paradigms. The only way you will be able to do this is through honest reflection and self-examination. Constantly ask yourself these three questions:

- Why did I react the way I just did?
- What happened in the past to cause me to react that way?
- Are there any of my beliefs (paradigms) that I need to reexamine?

This is very important because to the degree to which you can open your mind and see outside your box (your imagined boundaries or paradigms), you'll be able to achieve all the wealth you dream of.

Treasure Tip

One thing that will hold you back from building serious wealth in your life is a self-imposed limitation. They are usually easy to set-up, but often difficult to notice and eliminate.

Second, think about how many times you tried to solve the puzzle. Why was this important? Your ability to achieve wealth is directly influenced by your own level of tenacity or "stick-to-it-ness." Your path toward wealth will more than likely involve some obstacles, and if you don't have the passion to stay with the process, you may not make your goal.

> **That Reminds Me...**
>
> I saw a T-shirt recently that had a rodeo scene of a cowboy riding a bull. It said, "Guts, cuts, and sore butts." Seems like the same thing I encountered starting my own business to pursue my path to wealth.

How many times will you try? How much faith do you have in your ability? Will you give up and surrender, or will you continue until you achieve your goal? Your creativity, faith, and tenacity are directly related to the level of wealth you are capable of achieving.

When Galileo proved Copernicus's theory correct that the Earth revolved around the sun, he was exiled for years. Why? Simply because the world was not ready for this new idea. Besides that, all the books on the subject would have to be changed. What irony. This guy was exiled for a theory that happened to be correct.

As you develop your plans to build wealth, are you ready to test your willingness to accept new ideas? Are you ready to look at conventional wisdom that you have used for years and accept the fact that it may no longer work? Will you let conventional wisdom intimidate you?

The Wealth Paradigms

For over 10 years, I've studied investors who have built their wealth using wealth paradigms. In fact, this entire book is based upon these paradigms. Each of these paradigms has been taught in the context of habits, investment selection tactics, and laws. There's no point in repeating them all, but it is important to understand how they work. Therefore, I've selected three paradigms that have helped me build the foundation of my investment strategies which you'll recognize from Part 2.

Most of the wealth paradigms I've found usually fly directly in the face of conventional wisdom. The ones I'm about to discuss are certainly no exceptions. Therefore, it is important to understand not only the wealth paradigms, but also the conventional wisdom it goes against, which I call the "anti-wealth" paradigms. In each of the descriptions below, I begin with the anti-wealth paradigm and finish with the wealth paradigm. You'll notice that most of these involve the concept of investing, but each one can be applied to other situations in life.

Past Performance vs. Hockey Puck

What criteria do you use when selecting a mutual fund? Most investors use a one to ten year track record. And that's not surprising, considering the fact that almost all the books ever printed on the subject of mutual funds state past performance as the key criteria for selection. Go to any extensive magazine rack within the U.S. and chances are you will find one if not two magazines addressing the issue of, "Top Performing Funds," or "The Best Mutual Funds." All of these funds address one primary issue—past performance and its use in selecting a mutual fund. What makes this concept so ironic is the disclaimer you see with each of these ads and articles: "Past performance is no indication of future returns."

A friend of mine once said to me, "Hey, why not use past performance? If you wanted to predict the top passers in the NFL this year, I'd be willing bet that you would find that eight of the top ten were in the top 15 during the previous season." He might be right about the NFL, but the mutual fund world doesn't work that way. I've studied this stuff for years and it's been proven in many different studies that the top performers last year (or the past 5, 10, 15 years) are seldom the big performers the next year (or the next 5, 10, 15 years). If what they say is correct and past performance can be used to predict next year's winners, we could put together a quantitative model and build a winning portfolio consistently over time. Unfortunately, the stock market and mutual fund market don't work like the NFL. If that were true, I'd pick the very best players each year and beat everyone else. It's simply not that easy. If you have ever read any of the magazines in your local grocery store, you'd certainly think it was—but it's not. Just about every book ever printed on mutual funds says the same thing my friend did, but I'm telling you it just doesn't work. If it were that easy, everyone would own the very best funds every year.

That Reminds Me...

If that's not enough to catch your attention, consider this: How far would you get in your car (in a forward direction) if you had to look in your rearview mirror 95% of the time? If markets repeated themselves, past performance would give you an indication of future returns. Unfortunately, the market changes exponentially on a daily basis. Therefore, no matter how well a fund did last year, it is a new year now and everyone (including the fund manager) is faced with completely different circumstances—completely different markets.

Barker said in his book *Discovering the Future,* "Your past guarantees nothing." He explains that it doesn't matter how good you are at the old paradigm. When the new paradigm begins, everyone starts all over at zero. Barker's statement above holds true when investing. The first and most common investment paradigm is what I call the Past Performance Paradigm. This is one of the most devastating and misunderstood of all investment related paradigms.

When I see a list of last year's best performing funds, I think, "Wow! What a waste of paper!" It reminds me of when I watch a football game and the play-by-play announcer starts talking about last year's game, who won, all the statistics, and uses the information to comment on the possible outcome of the current night's game. How completely crazy is this? You have totally new teams, maybe even a new coach, new plays, a new quarterback, and probably a whole new field!

The proper paradigm to use is what I call the hockey puck paradigm which I described earlier in the book using the story of Wayne Gretzky. He said he skates to where he thinks the hockey puck is going to be while everyone else skates to where the hockey puck is (or used to be). The best way to select any investment, whether it be a mutual fund, stock, bond, real estate, or a business is to determine where the market is going, and invest in that direction.

> **Words of the Wealthy**
> The **past performance paradigm** is the mind-set and belief that the past performance of an investment should be the primary justification for purchase.

Fear vs. Contrarian

Another one of the most interesting paradigms concerning investment psychology is the reaction most investors have to sudden heavy market declines. One of my clients panicked when Gorbachev was kidnapped and the market dropped suddenly. He wanted to sell everything, and I could not talk him out of it. His paradigms prevented him from seeing any other alternative. Consequently we sold at the lowest prices that day. Of course, the market suddenly reversed and most funds went back up in price quickly before he changed his mind. His mind set was, "get out before we lose everything." He fell victim to the fear paradigm.

> **Words of the Wealthy**
> The **fear paradigm** is the mind-set and belief that when everyone is afraid of an investment, it should be avoided. The opposite is the **contrarian paradigm,** which is based on the belief that if everyone hates an investment, it should definitely be considered.

The opposite of the fear paradigm is the contrarian paradigm. A contrarian is someone who invests when everyone is selling. Sudden heavy losses in the market are common and will occur randomly with great intensity. A contrarian views this as an opportunity to purchase investments at lower prices. If you refer to a chart of the stock market over its history, you will notice that all bear markets are followed eventually by a bull market. The contrarian completely understands this. For example, how could anyone be more afraid of owning one of the tobacco companies today? The contrarians who own the stock today are betting that their company could spit off the tobacco related business and unleash a perfectly good company uninhibited by the litigation. It might be a stretch, but it could happen.

Greed vs. Philanthropic

Victims of the greed paradigm focus single-mindedly on building their wealth without any plans for sharing with others or contributing to charity. This is a terrible trap that will inevitably result in loneliness and horrible self-esteem.

The most successful and happiest wealthy people I know contribute regularly to their favorite charities. They find that they ultimately get back more than they give. It may be direct or it may be indirect, but personally I do get back much more than I give away to charities. I call this my philanthropic paradigm. It's not that you should expect anything back, and I think that's important to understand. You must give unconditionally. If you do, you'll be rewarded many times. Call it divine intervention or synchronicity, but it does work. You reap what you sow. Everything goes full circle in the balance of life, and charitable giving is no exception.

I urge you to give this paradigm a chance in your life. Once you experience it, share it with others. Be a role model for giving in your community. Encourage your friends and business associates to contribute to their favorite charities and to become role models for philanthropy. Your contribution doesn't have to be monetary. You could simply offer hands-on volunteer work.

That Reminds Me...

One of the most philanthropic people I know told me recently that his parents had given to numerous charities anonymously. They had also funded college educations for local children who couldn't afford tuition. They did almost all of their giving on a private basis. This might seem generous, but my friend said the privacy was unfortunate. He wishes now that his parents had been more public with their giving. They could have been excellent role models for the community throughout the year.

One Final Note on Paradigms

There are too many paradigms to cover. Now that you understand how they work, it will be much easier to develop your own set. Throughout your journey toward building wealth, the most important thing to remember is that some paradigms will help you and some will hurt you. The key is to continue reexamining the paradigms you pick up. Identify them, isolate them, and make sure they are based upon beliefs that coincide with truth and reality—not just the past.

The Least You Need to Know

- The reason why people don't get rich is because of their negative mental paradigms related to wealth, finances, and self-imposed limitations.
- Once you understand paradigms and how they can affect every aspect of your life, you'll then be able to achieve anything you can think of, including Wealth Levels 4 and 5.
- As you build your wealth, you must adopt a philanthropic paradigm to ensure your contribution to society and your value to your community.

Chapter 24

Planning Secrets that Will Build Wealth Faster

In This Chapter

- The most powerful planning tool
- The best time management systems
- Brainstorming, mind-mapping, and project planning
- Yearly, monthly, weekly, and daily planning
- How to make better decisions

If you want to build great wealth, you must learn how to set goals and achieve them. All wealthy people plan regularly. Every great accomplishment of mine has been the direct result of planning skills, which are simple to learn and develop. After using over 11 different time- and life-management systems, I've developed what I consider to be the best planning system available. Use the ideas in this chapter to design your own system that works best for you.

I've learned that whatever you plan for is achievable to the exact degree to which you believe you can achieve it. Therefore, it is imperative that you believe in yourself and your ability to realize the goals you have. The planning secrets in this chapter will help you do just that. You'll learn both the tools and the strategies necessary to acquire great wealth.

The Power of Your Mind

Before we discuss the actual planning process, you must first understand and appreciate the power of your mind. It is the most important wealth building tool you have. For example, did you know that your mind doesn't know the difference between reality and imagination? That makes your ability to imagine quite a powerful tool. It allows you to actually live (or practice) every experience in advance. This is called mental imagery.

Mental imagery is the most important tool in the planning process. You can use mental imagery to go through the motions before you actually attempt your task. This will give you the opportunity to capture every step so that you can plan for it and improve it prior to actually executing the plan. You'll be able to know in advance exactly what to expect. You'll know the resources necessary, what needs to be delegated, the possible obstacles to overcome, and the key people you'll need helping you.

Try this exercise. Have someone read the next paragraph to you while you close your eyes. For this exercise to work, you must keep your eyes closed. Ask the helper to carefully read the paragraph aloud at a fairly slow and gentle pace.

> *Imagine that you have a nice fresh bright yellow lemon in your hands. Feel the rough, almost oily texture. Bring it up to your nose and smell it. (pause a few seconds) Smell the wonderful lemony scent. It smells clean and fresh. Now take the lemon and slice it in half. Bring one half up to you nose and smell it once again. (pause a few seconds) Now take a deep breath and BITE IT! (pause a few seconds). Is your mouth watering?*

Maybe I'm crazy about lemons, but my mouth was watering like crazy. I wanted a lemon so badly, I almost had to go out and get one. It proved to me the power of my imagination.

That Reminds Me...

The world's greatest golfers probably understand the concept of mental imagery the best. Before they drive their ball off the tee or take any other shot, they go through every little motion in their mind as if they were actually making the shot. Most of them do this more than once. The mental practice helps them perfect the shot before they even swing the club in reality. You can do this too in your own life. It doesn't matter whether you mow yards or do brain surgery, mental imagery can help improve your performance.

Time and Life Planning Tools

I've used over 11 different time- and life-planning systems. I've concluded that they all have their own strengths and weaknesses. Everybody is different, and what works for me might or might not work for you. Here are the three best systems:

- **Priority Management, 800-221-9031, Bellevue, WA.** This system involves a half day workshop and at least a one hour personal consultation from one of the company's 300 representatives throughout the world. The cost of all this and the planner is $500. I personally recommend this system. Parts of it are based on Dan Stamp's book *The Invisible Assembly Line* published by AMACOM, New York, NY.
- **Seven Habits Organizer, 800-331-7716, Provo, Utah.** This system is based on Stephen Covey's book *The Seven Habits Of Highly Effective People.* It comes in three different sizes and includes a Quick Start guide and an audio tape to teach you the system. The cost is between $65 and $90, depending on which size you prefer.
- **Franklin Day Planner 800-869-1776, Salt Lake City, Utah.** This system is based on information contained in Benjamin Franklin's autobiography. He carried a book in which he listed 13 values and goals and incorporated them into his day. His system of self improvement was used to design the Franklin Day Planner. The system costs between $36 and $50 depending on the size you prefer and includes a catalog through which you can order training tapes or register for training seminars.

Before you spend money on a system, do a little research. Call each of the three and request information. No matter how good a system is, don't hesitate to customize or improve the system for your needs.

The planning steps within the rest of this chapter are my own personal favorites. They are best implemented using one of the systems listed above. You can certainly design your own system; however, it would take away from the valuable planning time you'll need to accomplish your own goals. My point is that these systems do cost money, but they are worth every dime.

Yearly Planning

Yearly planning is a key wealth-building habit. This section will describe the most important elements of the yearly planning session. Use these to design your own session.

Mission Statement Work

Have you ever asked yourself this question: Who am I? Take a minute and think. What are the most important values in your life? What do you value the most in life? Look back at your answers to the three questions in Chapter 5. Your answers will help you start your list. I've listed my value categories below. Yours will be different, but maybe the categories will be similar.

- Spiritual
- Physical well being
- Family
- Friends
- Financial security
- Knowledge improvement
- Fun and recreation
- Career

For each of your value areas, write a mission statement that explains exactly what is important to you, as well as your primary goal regarding that area of your life. Below the mission statement, begin listing your dreams and goals within that particular area. Keep this list handy so you can add more dreams and goals later. It should be considered a working list that will be added to regularly. Anytime you think of something you want to accomplish, write it down and add it to the list. Be sure to check off each goal as you accomplish it.

Conventional Brainstorming

So few people understand how to brainstorm properly and even fewer appreciate the power that can come from it. To be successful at brainstorming, you need just a few guidelines. If you take the time to follow the guidelines for brainstorming that follow, you will immediately increase your chances of achieving your desired wealth level. The objective of a brainstorming session is to produce the largest number of ideas possible. You're looking for quantity first, and quality second. Here's how it works.

First, start with an open-ended question. For example, your question might be, "How can I reduce my monthly expenses?" Perhaps you want to address a problem or paradigm that's holding you back in your wealth-building activities. Put it in the form of a question—"How can I eliminate this mind-set and think more objectively?" Your goal is to write down as many answers to the direct question as you can possibly think of within an hour. Second, write down the first things that come to your mind without concern for grammar or spelling. Just write whatever you think about—no matter how ridiculous or crazy the answer seems. (If you brainstorm in a team setting, make sure no one criticizes any answers.) Third, sit in solitude with no possible interruptions from other people or the phone. Fourth, do this outdoors or be as close to nature as you can. Sit by a house plant if you have to. If you can't get close to nature because it's dark and cold outside and there are no house plants, try to find a quiet place or put on some soothing classical music. Your goal is to create a peaceful atmosphere free from distraction that will open your imagination. Fifth, don't stop until you have at least 20 answers.

Go back to the section titled, "What Business Will You Start?" in Chapter 17. The three questions listed are great brainstorming questions to work on. They should also be part of your yearly planning sessions.

Mind-Mapping

My favorite way to brainstorm is called mind-mapping. It was taught to me by my business consultant, Roger Lane, who teaches the Priority Management Course. In fact, every chapter in this book was written initially using a mind-map. I'll explain how they work using the mind-map I drew to brainstorm the topics for this chapter.

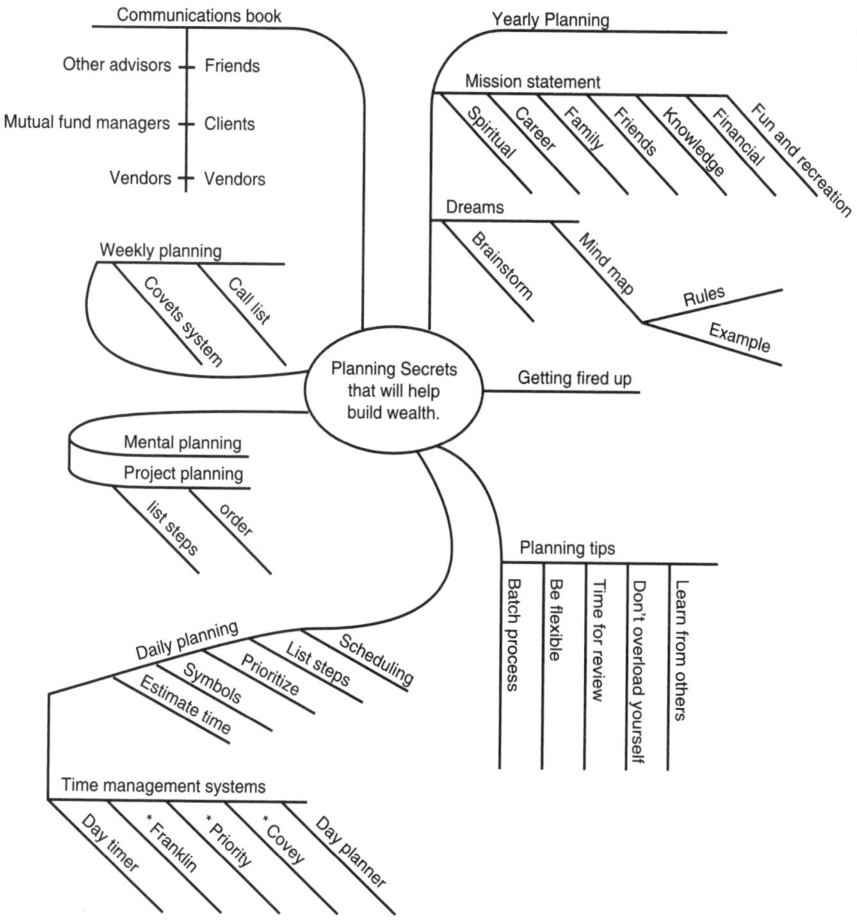

A mind-map example.

First, in the center of a blank piece of paper, I wrote the name of the chapter and circled it. In your case, you would write down the idea or yearly goal you want to brainstorm about. Second, from that circle, I drew a line out to the upper left-hand corner and wrote down the first thing that came to my mind which was my "communications book." Below this I wrote down the categories within that book. I continued to write down all the ideas that came to mind without any concern for order. You would do the same when creating your own map, getting related thoughts about the question down on paper as they occur to you.

Once you've completed your mind-map, use it to organize and plan your goal—which in my case was to write this chapter. Take your mind-map and identify the main topics or tasks. Then list all the steps necessary to accomplish each task in chronological order. The end result should be an organized list of tasks and an organized plan that can actually be used to accomplish a goal. I wrote every chapter in this book using mind-maps. Almost every great goal I've achieved in the last several years began with a mind-map.

Why is mind-mapping better than conventional brainstorming? According to the research I've studied (as well as my own experiences), the human brain doesn't necessarily work chronologically. It produces thoughts randomly instead of logically. The people who understand this and allow their minds to create ideas in this fashion are much more effective planners. Because mind-mapping gives the brain the opportunity to express ideas naturally, it is the tool of choice for planning and brainstorming.

Monthly Planning Sessions

Your personal monthly planning sessions should be conducted mostly in solitude. I often bring a friend just to bounce ideas off of, but most of the time I try to sit in solitude. These sessions allow me to think freely without interruption. This section points out the primary elements of my monthly planning session.

Prioritize Goals

From your categorized list of dreams and goals, decide which goals you want to work on now and which ones you want to save until later. Continue this process until you've prioritized the entire list. Don't be surprised if your priorities change occasionally. Select the most important goal and proceed to project planning. For example, let's assume that your goal is to achieve Wealth Level 3 in 10 years.

Project Planning

Once you decide on a goal, your goal or dream has now become a project for you to plan. The first step is to state your objective and expected results as specifically as possible. Write it down—you want to achieve Wealth Level 3 in 10 years. Add any more specifics that come to mind. Second, use a mind-map to list all the steps necessary. Write your goal in the middle of the page and begin writing down anything that comes to mind. One part of your mind-map might be to set up budget. Another might be to go through the steps in Chapter 4 and calculate your Target Savings Goal. Part of this mind-map should include the resources, equipment, and facilities that will be needed. It should also include the key people who can help. Be sure to include possible obstacles, as well as solution ideas. Once the mind-map is completed, the tasks should be prioritized, and a project plan should be written.

This project plan is primarily a prioritized list of all the necessary tasks that need to be completed. Each task should be put in chronological order and include:

- Steps necessary for completion
- Estimates of time each task will require for completion
- Estimated starting date
- Deadline for completion

The project plan should also include several lists such as:

- Key contacts and phone numbers
- Resources, equipment, and facilities needed
- Possible obstacles and how each one can be resolved
- What tasks can be out-sourced
- What tasks can be done in house
- Estimated costs

Once you have all the steps and resources listed, use your calendar to identify when you plan to accomplish the tasks. Select the days you plan to focus on each specific task.

The Project Notebook

One way to keep up with all your projects is to build a project notebook which is a three-ring binder with dividers for each project. This tool will help keep your life, as well as your planning sessions, better organized. Use dividers to separate key elements of your project. In the case of achieving Wealth Level 3, you might set up the following dividers: investment account, retirement plan, budgeting, and business ideas. You might want to include your mind-map for future reference.

> **That Reminds Me...**
>
> My project notebook is a large three-ring binder with dividers for each project. Under each divider is my project plan along with all the supporting documents. If a project begins to take up too much space, I make a separate project notebook specifically for that project. This book, for example, became a separate project notebook.

Reorganization

Each month you may want to take some time to reorganize your tasks if necessary. Things do change and you must be flexible. I guarantee that you're going to constantly come up with new ideas that will require you to change your path. Therefore, you must review your plan once a month. Review your wealth-building plan at least once a month and keep it in order so that you can keep a close eye on your progress.

Weekly Planning

Weekly planning is not as important to the wealth-building process as daily planning, but it is still a great habit. Some people like to plan their week in advance. Others like to plan one day at a time. If you like the idea of weekly planning, Stephen Covey's system has a weekly planning sheet that's very handy to use. It allows you to organize your tasks according to your list of values. The key to any plan is prioritization. First, you should spend most of your time prioritizing the tasks needed to accomplish your monthly goals. Second, you should spend a little time planning the tasks you've selected for this week. What days will be dedicated to these tasks?

I still make a weekly call list that I use each week. For years, I would list people to call for the day, only to recreate more than half of the list the very next day because they were unavailable and never called me back. Finally I wised up and began making a weekly list. I keep track of my daily call progress using symbols like "LM" which stands for "left message," or "WCB" for "will call back."

Daily Planning

Daily planning is vital to the wealth-building process. The more you can accomplish in one day, the faster you can build your wealth. The best planned days produce the most results. One of the most powerful planning strategies in the world is planning for tomorrow one day in advance. Why is this so powerful? It's primarily because your mind is given ample time to imagine accomplishing all that you need to accomplish. Subconsciously, your mind has time to work through all the tasks, as well as identify all the potential conflicts or problems. This enables you to awaken the next day knowing exactly what you are going to accomplish that day. You not only know what you are going to do, you also know exactly how you're going to do it. The steps to planning your day are simple:

1. Look through your goals for the month (or week) and list the necessary steps you want to accomplish that day. Record any appointments listed in your monthly calendar.
2. Prioritize the list of steps.
3. Identify which steps must be accomplished that day using the letter "A" or number "1."
4. Identify the steps that can wait until tomorrow using the letter "B" or number "2."
5. Estimate the time it takes to accomplish each of these tasks and schedule time to work on them.

Planning Tips

- Stick to your plan, but be flexible. Things do change unexpectedly, and you might have to find a better way to achieve the wealth level you desire.
- Batch process your work and control your interruptions. Batch processing just means that you are going to single-mindedly focus on one project at a time for a given time period. You can control your interruptions by closing your office door or going to a private place with no phone. Wealthy people understand the power of their own office door.
- Everywhere you go, keep paper and pen ready. You might want to carry a mini-cassette recorder. It sure makes it easy to record thoughts, especially when driving.
- Don't forget to learn from others and their mistakes. You don't build wealth by reinventing the wheel. Save some effort, time, and money by finding others who have done what you are wanting to do. Copy and improve their successful actions, habits, etc.
- The secret to great wealth is not to get overloaded. Do one thing at a time. Don't try to accomplish too many goals at one time. Select the most important one for now and focus on it. Then go to the next one.
- Take time to review your progress toward building your wealth. Find new ways to accomplish your goals faster. Find someone who will hold you accountable for your

goals. Accountability can be very important to the accomplishment of your goals. You can be accountable to yourself, but you might also want to get a friend to be an accountability coach. They may also be a great source of ideas.

How to Get Fired Up

If you really want to get fired up about a particular goal or project, take a piece of paper and list all of your greatest accomplishments in life including the year you accomplished them. Spend as much time as it takes to fill at least one page. These accomplishments can include anything that was important to you at that time. You could even include the day you learned how to tie your own shoe! I remember the first time I ever drove a car. Boy, was I excited and proud. I'm an avid water skier and remember vividly the first time I made it through the six buoys of a water ski slalom course. After that, I felt I could accomplish anything, including Wealth Level 5!

Any time you need some inspiration, just pull out this list. Pick one of your accomplishments that you're really proud of, and think back to that time. Close your eyes and re-live the excitement and feeling of accomplishment. Now imagine yourself today accomplishing your current goal or project. Whether it's Wealth Level 1 or 5, imagine feeling the same way as you achieve that next wealth level. Keep that feeling with you and draw power from it.

How to Make Better Decisions

Building wealth requires an enormous amount of decision making ability. If you approach every major decision with the same decision making procedure, you'll find that decisions become a lot easier to make. Here are the steps I take when making a critical decision:

- Describe the primary goal. What am I really trying to accomplish?
- Identify all the issues related to this goal
- Gather all the information necessary
- List all the alternatives to choose from. For example, doing nothing may be an alternative
- List the pros and cons of each alternative
- Identify the alternative that best achieves your goal in the least amount of time with the least amount of cost
- Use the answers to prioritize the alternatives and select the best alternative

If your decision involves another decision made in the past, you might want to consider using the same strategy I mentioned earlier in the book regarding sell decisions. It's called zero-based thinking. Ask yourself this question, "Knowing what you know now, would you have made the same decision in the past?" If the answer is no, you may want to reconsider your current situation.

Communications Book

One of the most powerful tools in my wealth-building arsenal is my communications book. I learned this idea from consultant, Roger Lane, and the Priority Management System he taught me. In this book I have categorized and listed all the names, addresses, and phone numbers of all the people I know and work with. Here are the categories listed in my book:

- Friends and family
- Clients
- Vendors
- Other Advisors
- Mutual Fund Managers
- Business Advisors

Each of these people are also listed in a database so that I can sort, list, and send mail to them whenever I need to. The printed copy serves as a back-up for the database, and the database copy serves as a back-up for the printed copy.

Everyday, I seem to add another person to the list. Therefore, it is important that you keep your communications book near your workplace or home. Mine is over three inches thick so I can't very well carry it everywhere I go. If yours is small, you might want to incorporate it in with your daily planner.

The Least You Need to Know

- The most powerful planning tool toward building wealth or anything else is the mind because it doesn't know the difference between imagination and reality, which means you can use mental imagery to practice accomplishing your goals in advance.
- The first step in the planning process is the identification of your values, which will represent the core of your entire planning process.

- In order to plan efficiently and effectively for the accomplishment of your next wealth level, you must learn how to mind-map and brainstorm properly.
- If you want to really achieve the highest wealth levels possible, build a project notebook and communications notebook that can be taken with you on planning sessions outside your office and home.

Words of the Wealthy—the Whole List

12b1 Fees 12b1 is a securities regulation that allows mutual funds to charge a fee in addition to the management fee for such things as "marketing expenses, distribution expenses, or sales expenses." These expenses, in essence, disguise a commission. Be sure to avoid **12b1 fees** in excess of .25percent.

Asset Property with a market value that can be sold for cash is an asset. This can include stocks, bonds, real estate, and privately held stock. Liquid assets can be sold quickly while illiquid assets, such as real estate or a small business, usually take some time to sell.

Capital Ratio A bank's capital ratio is calculated by dividing the bank's capital by its total assets. This ratio measures the bank's availability of capital and financial strength.

Certified Financial Planner (CFP) Someone who has completed comprehensive courses and passed the CFP exams administered by a company in Denver, Colorado called the College for Financial Planning. CFP's can be brokers, insurance agents, salespeople, or fee-only advisors.

Collateral Something of value that is pledged against a loan in case of default. When you list collateral such as furniture, equipment, property, or accounts receivable, you should also include documents that will evidence the value of these items.

Contrarian A contrarian investor is one who invests contrary to everyone else, buying when the market is correcting and selling when the market reaches new highs. Contrarians welcome bad news because they know investors will over-react and as a result, certain stock prices will fall lower than they should.

Estate Planning This is simply the art and study of preserving wealth for family and future generations to come. It involves planning tools and techniques that can not only reduce estate taxes, but also make things a lot simpler after your death.

Fear Paradigm The mind-set and belief that when everyone is afraid of an investment, it should be avoided. The opposite is the contrarian paradigm, which is based on the belief that if everyone hates an investment, it should definitely be considered.

Fee-Only Advisor A money manager or financial planner who receives a fee for service, which is usually based on a percentage of assets under management, or time. Fee-only advisors do not receive any commissions for recommended investments.

Fiduciary An advisor who has been authorized to buy and sell securities on behalf of the client. This authorization is given in the form of a limited power of attorney signed by the client. An advisor has fiduciary responsibility when he is responsible for buying and selling securities for the client.

Fixed Annuity A contract with a life insurance company whereby you give a sum of money, and based on your age, life expectancy, and current interest rates, you'll eventually receive monthly payments for as long as you live. You decide when you want to receive payments, and until then, the money grows tax-deferred.

Full Service Brokerage Firm A firm that offers its clients securities as well as advice. The firm is compensated by commissions, which are paid at the time transactions are made. A discount brokerage firm offers the same selection of securities, but because they do not offer advice, their commissions are usually lower.

Fundamental Analysis The study of the basic facts that determine a security's value. A fundamental analysis of a mutual fund includes the study of the securities within the fund, the manager, the philosophy, expenses, and average p/e ratio.

Gross Domestic Product (GDP) The total value of goods and services produced by a country during a year. The GDP's rate of growth is much more popular in the news than the actual total GDP number. When plotted on a graph, this growth rate illustrates the economic cycle.

Growth A growth-oriented manager is one who searches for stocks with high earnings growth. Investors are willing to pay relatively higher prices for these stocks for the chance that they may rise even higher later.

Haggle The word haggle came from the Old English term "heawan," which meant to beat or cut. Haggling is the process of negotiating the lowest price possible in a purchase transaction. The U.S. is one of the few countries where haggling is not a normal process of everyday shopping.

Harvesting An unconventional way of deriving income from a portfolio that includes not only dividends and interest, but also capital gains.

Hodad Describes people who are generally fake or phony. Hodads may look and smell like they're rich, but if you take a close look, they owe lots of money and lease everything they have.

Inflation Most people think that inflation is the simple rise in prices. The technical definition is an increase in the volume of money and credit relative to available goods, which results in a substantial and continuing rise in the general price level. The rate of inflation is measured by the month to month percentage change of the consumer price index (CPI).

Junk Bond Also known as a high yield bond, a junk bond represents an IOU issued by a company whose ability to repay its interest and principal in a timely manner depends on the economy and the company's ability to sell its products or services. Standard & Poors as well as Moody's Investment services offer corporate bond ratings. A junk bond is any bond with a rating below BBB or Baa.

Letter of Engagement A document prepared by a CPA that outlines in detail what he or she will do for you. The letter should also illustrate how the CPA will be compensated and at what rate.

Liquid Assets Includes those assets that can be instantly converted into cash and illiquid assets are just the opposite, they are not easily converted into cash.

Micro-delegation Simply the delegation of micro-view business responsibilities to other professionals. This strategy enables you to focus on the big picture for your business. It also allows you to delegate the details to other people who are often better at them than you.

Money Manager Another name for a fee-only investment advisor.

Multi-level portfolio management A term I use to describe the use of many different mutual funds in a portfolio. These funds add additional layers of diversification and together produce a certain synergy unachievable by any one investor alone.

Net Asset Value The net asset value of a fund is the actual true value of each share of a mutual fund. This is calculated by dividing the total value of the fund by the number of shares outstanding.

No-load Funds No-load funds are mutual funds that can be purchased, sold, and owned without any commission charges. The only charges involved are management fees. Shares are sold at the net asset value price, and no salesperson is paid to sell the shares.

No Transaction Fee (NTF) The NTF program, started by Charles Schwab & Co., allows investors the ability to buy hundreds of different no-load funds within the same account without paying any transaction fees. The program is so popular that even full-service brokerage firms are beginning to follow in their footsteps.

Out Source A new term that simply means to pay someone outside your firm to do a job for you. It's an alternative to directly putting someone on your payroll.

Over-The-Counter Market A secondary market where securities are traded by phone and computer. The NASDAQ market is the largest and most popular over-the-counter market.

Paradigm The word paradigm originates from the Greek word "paradeigma," which means model or pattern.

Past Performance Paradigm The past performance paradigm is the belief that the past performance of an investment should be the primary justification for purchase.

P/E Ratio The price of a stock divided by the yearly earnings per share. It compares the price of a stock relative to its earnings, which is important to know when you compare one stock to another. It is also important in determining if a stock is under- or over-priced relative to other stocks.

Privately Held Company A privately held company's shares are not publicly traded. Privately held stock is issued to a small number of shareholders, and the value or price of the stock is usually determined by comparisons with other similar companies using factors such as earnings and gross income.

Pro-forma Financial Statements Pro-forma financial statements are used to project the estimated financial results of a new company. They consist of an income statement, balance sheet, and cash-flow statement.

Qualified Plans 401k(s) and SEPs are the only type of qualified plans that will allow employees to deposit part of their own salary into the plan. The deposit is made pre-tax and the account grows tax deferred. Each employee has their own individual account in which they can select from a number of different investment alternatives.

Quantitative Analysis Financial quantitative analysis involves the study of numerical information for the basis of decision making. Under the idea of quantitative theory, everything is expressed in measurable form and therefore also predictable. Investors who use this theory believe that by studying specific market data, they can accurately predict the market's movements.

Relative Strength A graphic illustration of the percentage (or fractional) difference between the price of a security and an index (or any other security). If the security and index rise and fall equally at the same time, the graph would be a straight line.

Return on Investment (ROI) A company's return on investment can be calculated by dividing the net income by the amount of capital invested in the company. There are two ways to increase ROI: reduce expenses or increase sales.

Secondary Market A secondary market is any market where previously issued securities are traded. The New York Stock Exchange (NYSE) is the most well-known example. Here investors can buy and sell stocks from each other through the designated traders on the floor of the exchange.

Soft-Dollars The term soft-dollars refers to an indirect way many advisors are paid a commission for using the services of a particular brokerage firm or mutual fund. The brokerage firm or mutual fund company usually provides the advisor with research, software, or quotation machines that are normally part of the advisor's overhead expenses. Therefore, soft-dollar payments tend to be the equivalent of commissions.

Stock When you buy shares of stock directly or though a mutual fund, you become part owner of a company. These shares can build your wealth by paying you dividends and by rising in price.

Target Savings Goal (TSG) Refers to the amount of money required each year to build a portfolio large enough to support your preferred standard of living at retirement.

Technical Analysis Using charts to read the price history and other statistical patterns of stocks or mutual funds is known as technical analysis. Many investors and most professionals use these charts to make investment decisions. A technical analyst is also known as a "chartist."

Total Return Total return, also known as portfolio performance, refers to the percentage return of a portfolio, which includes dividends, interest, and capital gains.

Underwriter An underwriter is a brokerage firm that handles the process of offering a company's stock to the public through an initial public offering.

Value A value-oriented manager is one who searches for undervalued stocks that are priced below what the manager actually thinks they're worth. The goal of the value manager is to sell at a profit once the market realizes the stock's true value.

Variable Annuity A variable annuity works the same way a fixed annuity does except its value and pat-out amount varies in value according to the performance of a portfolio of mutual funds from which the contract holder can select. Typically these policies offer a stock fund, a bond fund, and a money market fund.

Wealth Wealth is defined by *Webster's Dictionary* as an, "abundance of valuable material possessions or resources," and the word wealthy is defined as, "extremely affluent." But the definition of affluent sounds even better, "having a generously sufficient and typically increasing supply of material possessions." However, your own definition is however you want to define it.

Index

Symbols

A

C

G

H

I

J-K

L

M

N

O

P

Q

R

S

T

U

V

W

X-Y-Z

Personal Finance

The Complete Idiot's Guide to Buying Insurance and Annuities
ISBN: 0-02-861113-6 ▪ $16.95

The Complete Idiot's Guide to Managing Your Money
ISBN: 1-56761-530-9 ▪ $16.95

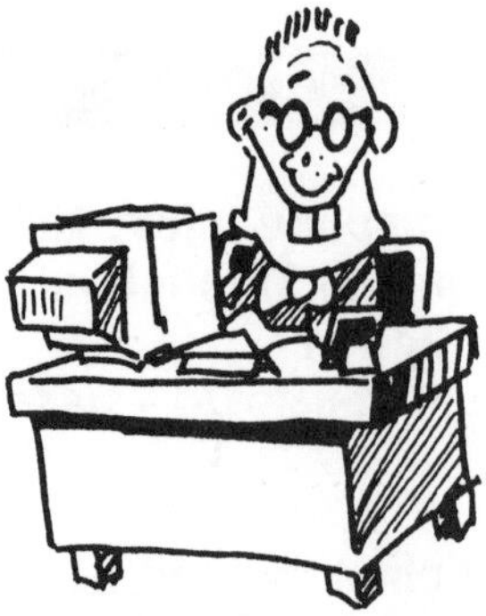

Complete Idiot's Guide to Buying and Selling a Home
ISBN: 1-56761-510-4 ▪ $16.95

The Complete Idiot's Guide to Doing Your Extra Income Taxes 1996
ISBN: 1-56761-586-4 ▪ $14.99

The Complete Idiot's Guide to Making Money with Mutual Funds
ISBN: 1-56761-637-2 ▪ $16.95

The Complete Idiot's Guide to Getting Rich
ISBN: 1-56761-509-0 ▪ $16.95

You can handle it!

Look for The Complete Idiot's Guides at your favorite bookstore, or call 1-800-428-5331 for more information.

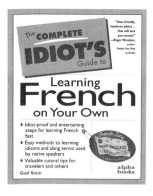

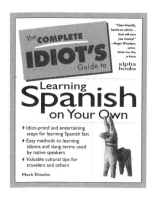

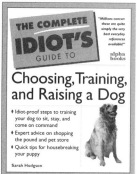

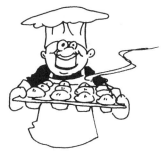

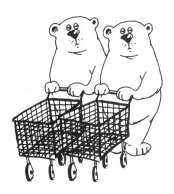

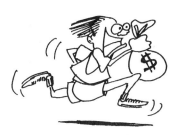

Lifestyle

The Complete Idiot's Guide to Trouble-Free Car Care
ISBN: 0-02-861041-5 ▪ $16.95

The Complete Idiot's Guide to the Perfect Wedding
ISBN: 1-56761-532-5 ▪ $16.99

The Complete Idiot's Guide to Getting and Keeping Your Perfect Body
ISBN: 0-286105122 ▪ $16.99

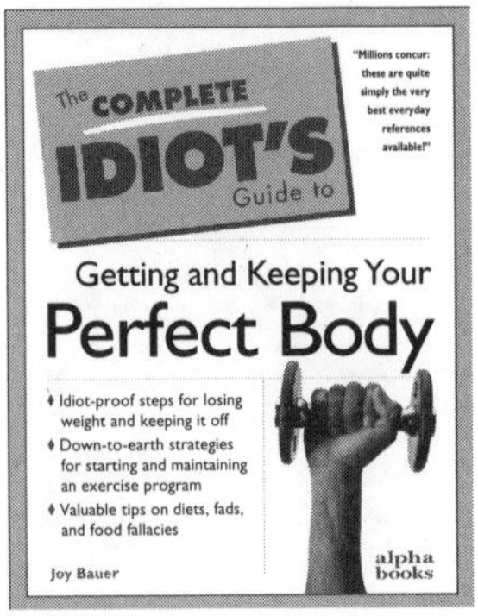

The Complete Idiot's Guide to First Aid Basics
ISBN: 0-02-861099-7 ▪ $16.95

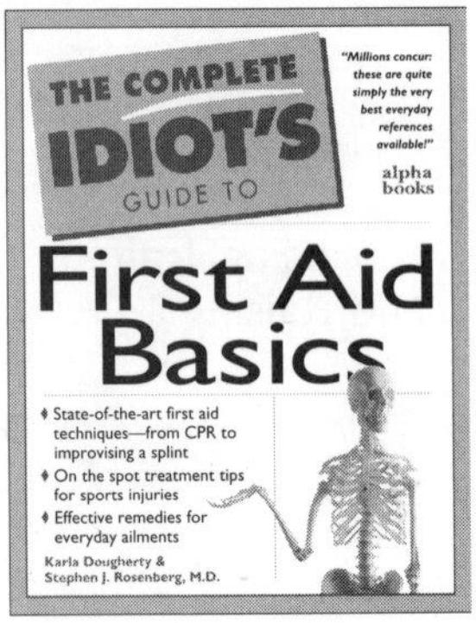

The Complete Idiot's Guide to the Perfect Vacation
ISBN: 1-56761-531-7 ▪ $14.99

The Complete Idiot's Guide to Trouble-Free Home Repair
ISBN: 0-02-861042-3 ▪ $16.95

The Complete Idiot's Guide to Getting into College
ISBN: 1-56761-508-2 ▪ $14.95

You can handle it!